The LAST PRINCESS

The Devoted Life of Queen Victoria's Youngest Daughter

MATTHEW DENNISON

Weidenfeld & Nicolson
LONDON

First published in Great Britain in 2007
by Weidenfeld & Nicolson

1 3 5 7 9 10 8 6 4 2

© 2007 Matthew Dennison

A CIP catalogue record for this book
is available from the British Library.

ISBN-13: 978 0 297 84794 6
ISBN-10: 0 297 84794 5

Typeset by Input Data Services Ltd, Frome

Printed and bound by Butler and Tanner Ltd,
Frome and London

Weidenfeld & Nicolson

The Orion Publishing Group Ltd
Orion House
5 Upper Saint Martin's Lane
London, WC2H 9EA

www.orionbooks.co.uk

the ROYAL OAK

VICTORIA REGINA 1837-1887

A Jubilee Genealogical Tree, showing the Descendants of Her Majesty Queen Victoria.

The LAST
PRINCESS

To the much-loved memory of
Shelagh Robertson,
this book's first reader

CONTENTS

LIST OF ILLUSTRATIONS

Osborne House on the wedding day, from the *Illustrated London News,* 1 August 1885. (Illustrated London News Photo Library)

AUTHOR'S NOTE

I gratefully acknowledge the permission of Her Majesty Queen Elizabeth II to publish material from The Royal Archives, and thank Pamela Clark and Jill Kelsey for their assistance at Windsor Castle. I am grateful to Professor Dr Eckhart G Franz, Grand Ducal Archives, Darmstadt; Virginia Murray, John Murray Archives; Adrian Allen, University Archivist, University of Liverpool; and the staff of the following libraries, records offices and archives: University of Birmingham Library (Special Collections); The British Library; Churchill Archives Centre, Churchill College, Cambridge; Glasgow University Archive Services; Leeds University Library (Special Collections); Lincolnshire Record Office; Nuffield College Library, Oxford; Rochdale Libraries; Staffordshire Record Office; Isle of Wight Record Office.

I am also grateful to Hannah Cumber, The Royal Institute of Public Health; Clare Fleck, Knebworth House; Neil Evans, The National Portrait Gallery, London; Frances Dunkels, The Royal Collection; Len Ley, Craig-y-Nos Castle; Mitzi Mina, Sotheby's London; Peta Liddle, The Ravenswood; Luci Gosling, Illustrated London News Picture Library; and Brett Croft, Condé Nast Library; to Geoffrey Munn, Charlotte Zeepvat, Countess Mountbatten of Burma, and especially to Hugo Vickers and Yvonne Ward. And, of course, to Albin Milkurti, who late at night retrieved the lost manuscript from a tube train heading north.

I am grateful to the following friends for kindness and hospitality during the research and writing of this book: Ivo and Pandora Curwen, Georgina Fletcher, Rosalind Gray and, especially, Jim and Fern Dickson.

I am grateful to my editor, Ion Trewin, and Anna Hervé and Bea Hemming who helped him, and to my agent, Georgina Capel; to my wonderful parents, my parents-in-law, and, most of all to my beloved Gráinne, who not only provided tireless support but, in tactful constructive criticism, made this a much better book.

The Children of Queen Victoria and Prince Albert
·•·

VICTORIA m ALBERT
Queen of Great Britain | of Saxe-Coburg-Gotha
(1819–1901) | (1819–61)

VICTORIA	ALICE	HELENA	ARTHUR	**BEATRICE**
Princess Royal	(1843–78)	(1846–1923)	(1850–1942)	(1857–1944)
(1840–1901)	m	m	m	m
m	LOUIS IV	CHRISTIAN	LOUISE	HENRY ('LIKO')
FREDERICK III	of Hesse-	of Schleswig-	of Prussia	of Battenberg
of Germany	Darmstadt	Holstein	(1860–1917)	(1858–96)
(1831–88)	(1837–92)	(1831–1917)		

ALBERT
EDWARD
(EDWARD VII)
(1841–1910)
m
ALEXANDRA
of Denmark
(1844–1925)

ALFRED
Duke of
Edinburgh &
Saxe-Coburg-
Gotha
(1844–1900)
m
MARIE
of Russia
(1853–1920)

LOUISE
(1848–1939)
m
MARQUESS
of Lorne
(1845–1914)

LEOPOLD
(1853–84)
m
HELEN
of Waldeck-
Pyrmont
(1861–1922)

eight
children
including
WILLIAM II

five
children
including
GEORGE V

seven
children
including
ALIX
Tsarina
of Russia

five
children

four
children

three
children

two
children

ALEXANDER	VICTORIA	LEOPOLD	MAURICE
Marquess of	EUGENIE	(1889–1922)	(1891–1914)
Carisbrooke	(1887–1969)		
(1886–1960)	m		
m	ALFONSO XIII		
Lady Irene	of Spain		
Denison	(1886–1941)		
(1890–1956)			
	seven children		
one child			

House of Erbach-Schönberg

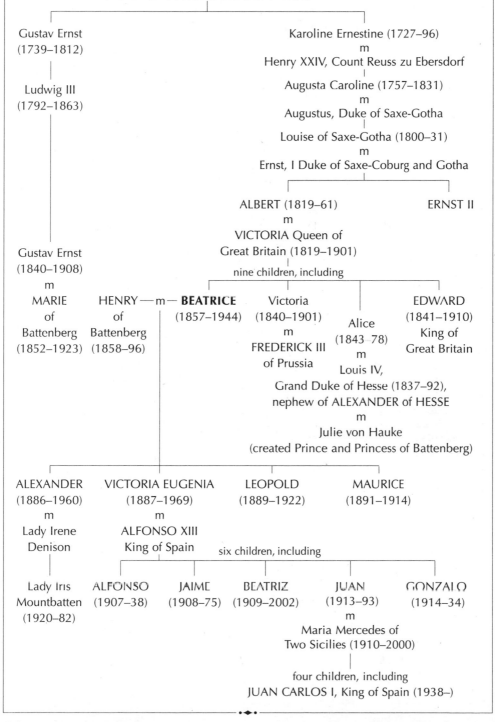

Georg August
of ERBACH-SCHONBERG (1691–1758)

Gustav Ernst
(1739–1812)

Karoline Ernestine (1727–96)
m
Henry XXIV, Count Reuss zu Ebersdorf

Ludwig III
(1792–1863)

Augusta Caroline (1757–1831)
m
Augustus, Duke of Saxe-Gotha

Louise of Saxe-Gotha (1800–31)
m
Ernst, I Duke of Saxe-Coburg and Gotha

ALBERT (1819–61)
m
VICTORIA Queen of
Great Britain (1819–1901)

ERNST II

Gustav Ernst
(1840–1908)
m
MARIE
of
Battenberg
(1852–1923)

nine children, including

HENRY — m — BEATRICE
of   (1857–1944)
Battenberg
(1858–96)

Victoria
(1840–1901)
m
FREDERICK III
of Prussia

Alice
(1843–78)
m
Louis IV,

EDWARD
(1841–1910)
King of
Great Britain

Grand Duke of Hesse (1837–92),
nephew of ALEXANDER of HESSE
m
Julie von Hauke
(created Prince and Princess of Battenberg)

ALEXANDER
(1886–1960)
m
Lady Irene
Denison

VICTORIA EUGENIA
(1887–1969)
m
ALFONSO XIII
King of Spain

LEOPOLD
(1889–1922)

MAURICE
(1891–1914)

six children, including

Lady Iris
Mountbatten
(1920–82)

ALFONSO
(1907–38)

JAIME
(1908–75)

BEATRIZ
(1909–2002)

JUAN
(1913–93)
m

GONZALO
(1914–34)

Maria Mercedes of
Two Sicilies (1910–2000)

four children, including
JUAN CARLOS I, King of Spain (1938–)

House of Saxe-Coburg-Saalfeld

(showing the relationship of Beatrice to her maternal great-grandmother,
Duchess Augusta of Saxe-Coburg-Saalfeld, diarist of *In Napoleonic Days*)

•◆•

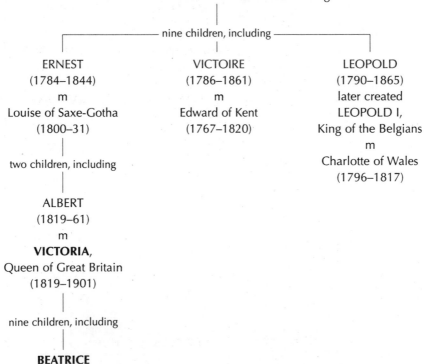

Ernest Frederick
(1724–1800)

m

Sophia Antonia
of Brunswick-Wolfenbüttel
(1724–1802)

seven children, including

Francis Frederick
(1750–1806)

m

AUGUSTA CAROLINE
Reuss zu Ebersdorf
(1757–1831)
daughter of Henry XXIV Reuss zu Ebersdorf
and Karoline Ernestine of Erbach-Schönberg

nine children, including

ERNEST	VICTOIRE	LEOPOLD
(1784–1844)	(1786–1861)	(1790–1865)
m	m	later created
Louise of Saxe-Gotha	Edward of Kent	LEOPOLD I,
(1800–31)	(1767–1820)	King of the Belgians
		m
two children, including		Charlotte of Wales
		(1796–1817)

ALBERT
(1819–61)

m

VICTORIA,
Queen of Great Britain
(1819–1901)

nine children, including

BEATRICE
(1857–1944)

•◆•

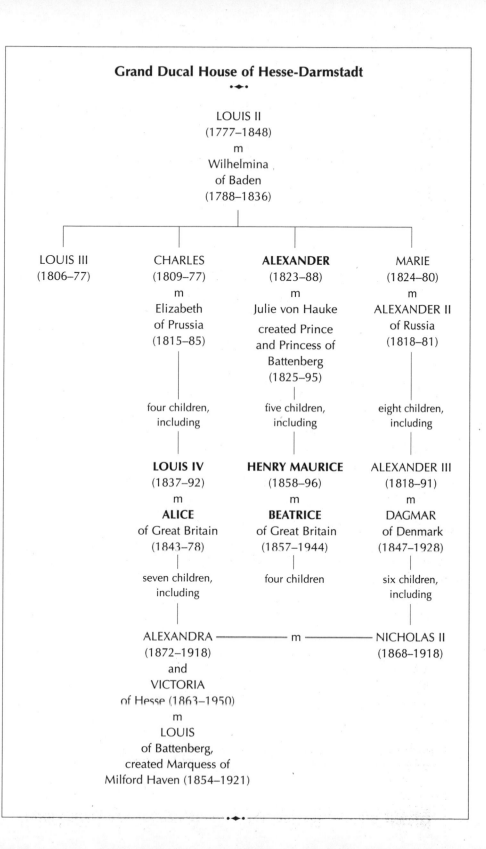

Grand Ducal House of Hesse-Darmstadt
•◆•

LOUIS II
(1777–1848)
m
Wilhelmina
of Baden
(1788–1836)

LOUIS III (1806–77)	CHARLES (1809–77) m Elizabeth of Prussia (1815–85)	**ALEXANDER** (1823–88) m Julie von Hauke created Prince and Princess of Battenberg (1825–95)	MARIE (1824–80) m ALEXANDER II of Russia (1818–81)
	four children, including	five children, including	eight children, including
	LOUIS IV (1837–92) m **ALICE** of Great Britain (1843–78)	**HENRY MAURICE** (1858–96) m **BEATRICE** of Great Britain (1857–1944)	ALEXANDER III (1818–91) m DAGMAR of Denmark (1847–1928)
	seven children, including	four children	six children, including

ALEXANDRA ———————— m ———————— NICHOLAS II
(1872–1918)   (1868–1918)
and
VICTORIA
of Hesse (1863–1950)
m
LOUIS
of Battenberg,
created Marquess of
Milford Haven (1854–1921)

•◆•

'*I have a dear devoted child who has always been a dear, unselfish companion to me*'

Queen Victoria to Alfred Tennyson,
August 14, 1883

•◆•

ONE

'It is a fine child'

•◆•

*I*t should not have happened, and never would have done had medical counsel prevailed. In February of the previous year, 1856, Sir James Clark – appointed Queen Victoria's physician on the first day of her reign – had confided to his diary, 'I feel at times uneasy. Regarding the Queen's mind, unless she is kept quiet ... the time will come when she will be in danger.'[1]

It was Easter Monday, 1857. The Queen had been married to Prince Albert for eighteen years. She had given birth to eight children, ranging in age from seventeen to four. She was six weeks away from her thirty-eighth birthday, and twelve years short of the age at which her grandfather George III had collapsed on to the shoulder of one of his seven surviving sons and exclaimed, 'I wish to God I may die, for I am going to be mad.'[2] The Queen was a woman of intense emotions and violent passions. She also inclined to feelings of deep unhappiness and unsettlement both during pregnancy and after the birth of her children, later confiding to a married daughter the result of many pregnancies in quick succession: 'One becomes so worn out and one's nerves so miserable.'[3] Sir James had made known to Prince Albert his fears about the Queen's mental well-being: further post-natal disquiet, he believed, could provide the weight that tipped the scales. The only safeguard was for the Queen to have no more children. What's more, as the doctor also reported, his patient shared his fears: 'The Queen felt sure that if she had another child she would sink under it.'[4]

Sir James's appeal ought to have proved persuasive. For Prince Albert the spectre of Queen Victoria's Hanoverian inheritance – the family's chequered and all too recent history of madness and badness – loomed ever large. Yet on 13 April, fourteen months after Sir James's expression of anxiety and a fortnight later than her doctors had predicted, Queen Victoria went into labour for the ninth and last time.

In the delivery room at Buckingham Palace, the Queen wore the shift she had worn at each of her eight previous confinements, being superstitious and sentimental about such things. Behind her now was the unhappiness of this last pregnancy: the indulgence of grief she had unleashed over the death in November from paralytic seizures of her troublesome half-brother Charles of Leiningen; her habitual irritation at the restrictions imposed by her condition – in this case, including being prevented from 'showing off on the ice' with Prince Albert on the skating pond at Windsor in December;[5] and the deep sense of degradation she had told the Prince her inflated physical condition caused her. Long forgotten were her reservations, once so forcibly expressed to her uncle Leopold of Belgium, about becoming 'mamma d'une nombreuse famille'. The Queen may not have felt, as she had seventeen years earlier, giving birth to her first child, the Princess Royal, 'so strong and active',[6] but she drew comfort from the presence at her bedside, as on that occasion, of her much-beloved husband, the accoucheur Dr Charles Locock, and Mrs Lilly, midwife and monthly nurse, who had attended the Queen at every delivery. In a room close by, helpless now despite his expressed misgivings, Sir James Clark was joined by Dr Robert Ferguson; in due course both would be co-signatories with Charles Locock of the official bulletin announcing the birth. Members of the Royal Household gathered alongside the Lord Chancellor, Lord Cranworth, the Prime Minister, Lord Palmerston, and the Bishop of London. Prayers were offered in English and in German. Also present was the physician to the Crown Prince of Prussia, Dr Wegner. On 25 January of the following year the Crown Prince would marry the Queen's eldest daughter. An heir would be expected of the union. 'While German oculists and even surgeons are cleverer than ours, – there is not a doubt that in the particular line of childbirth and women's illnesses the English are the best in the World, more skilful and much more delicate,' the Queen would write later.[7] For the Princess Royal's future comfort and safety Dr Wegner must observe and note how such things were managed in England.

Management on this occasion was slow. 'The labour was lingering,' recorded Dr John Snow in his casebook. It was also, up to a point, pioneering. Snow was a GP who acted intermittently as an obstetrician. He discovered the mode of spread of epidemic cholera and, significantly for Queen Victoria, became an early advocate of anaesthesia, publishing 'On the Inhalation of the Vapour of Ether in Surgical Operations' less than a year after the first recorded British use of an anaesthetic. In 1853, three months after easing with anaesthesia the extraction of a tooth for one of the Queen's ladies-in-waiting, Snow had administered chloroform to Queen Victoria at the birth of Prince Leopold – to be precise, fifty-three minutes' worth of what the Queen described as 'that blessed Chloroform ... soothing, quieting and delightful beyond measure'.[8] The result, Snow noted with satisfaction, was that 'the Queen appeared very cheerful and well, expressing herself much gratified with the effect of the chloroform'.[9] So gratified, in fact, that she did not consider enduring her final confinement without it.

Snow's task was a controversial one. His use of chloroform in 1853 had been roundly denounced by the leading medical journal *The Lancet*: '... Her Majesty during her last labour was placed under the influence of chloroform, an agent which has unquestionably caused instantaneous death in a considerable number of cases ... In no case could it be justifiable to administer chloroform in perfectly ordinary labour.'[10] Not only the medical profession but the public, too, feared for the Queen's safety; and some disapproved on religious grounds of her championing apparently painless childbirth. Snow's presence in the delivery room represented for the rising doctor both an honour and a burden. During the birth of Prince Leopold, Dr Locock had complained that the use of chloroform, whatever its palliative effect, prolonged the intervals between contractions and retarded labour. Given the Queen's enthusiasm, and its wholehearted seconding by Prince Albert, Locock's reservations counted for little. More worrying for Snow was that exactly a week before his summons to the palace he had experienced his first anaesthesia death.

Happily, neither the Queen nor her two-weeks-tardy child died. Early on Monday afternoon the familiar pains began. They continued, without sign of progress, into the evening. Doctors Locock and Snow were in attendance when, at around two o'clock the following morning, came the onset of labour proper. Throughout the early hours the Queen's contractions proceeded – but still with no indication of imminent birth. The Queen's suffering was considerable and it was Prince Albert, sitting beside his wife, who offered the first relief, 'a very little chloroform on a handkerchief, about 9 and 10 o'clock'.[11] At the same time Dr Locock gave a dose of powdered ergot, eager, as during Leopold's birth, to keep things moving along; he would offer a second dose at noon with greater success. Despite her suffering Snow adhered to his usual practice and withheld administering chloroform in earnest until the onset of the second stage of labour. He then folded a handkerchief into a cone, poured on to it ten minims of chloroform and, with each contraction, placed the cone over the Queen's face – the 'open-drop' technique of anaesthetic application that Snow had by this stage of his career largely forsaken, even suggesting it might be dangerous. (In the Queen's case, however, this was the method he had used four years previously: its familiarity may have been intended to reassure her.)

The Queen was tired. She had not slept. Already it was nearly twenty-four hours since she had experienced first preliminary pains. The final weeks of her pregnancy had not relaxed her: feeling harried by political concerns, in March she had instructed Sir James Clark to inform the Prime Minister that she was in no condition to endure a change of ministry; at the same time, her anxiety about the inadequacy as heir of her eldest son Bertie, Prince of Wales, continued to grow. Listlessly she had moved between her bed and a sofa, carried by Prince Albert or, during his absences, a footman called Lockwood. Now she asked for more chloroform, complaining that it did not take away the pain.

Her complaints were probably justified: the dose the Queen

was receiving from Snow was only two-thirds of the strength he had administered during Leopold's birth. But Snow, sobered by his experience of the previous week, did not increase the measure. Between contractions the Queen dozed, slipping in and out of consciousness. When at last, nearing one o'clock, Dr Locock saw the baby's head resting on the perineum and asked the Queen 'to make a bearing-down effort', she replied that she could not. Snow withheld chloroform for three or four contractions, the Queen rallied, 'and the royal patient made an effort which expelled the head, a little chloroform being given just as the head passed'.[12] There was, Dr Snow went on to report, 'an interval of several minutes before the child was entirely born; it, however, cried in the meantime. The placenta was expelled about ten minutes afterwards.'[13] The time was quarter to two – as Prince Albert wrote to a correspondent the following day, some thirteen hours after labour began.

A fortnight later, Queen Victoria confided to her Journal, 'I was amply rewarded and forgot all I had gone through when I heard dearest Albert say "It is a fine child, and a girl!"'[14] For the fifth and final time, the Queen had given birth to a daughter – Victoria and Albert's 'Baby', as she was to remain for all her mother's life, their last and for the Queen the ultimate child, the last princess.

Prince Albert's letter to the Princess Royal's soon-to-be mother-in-law, Princess Augusta of Prussia, was written from the Queen's bedside on 15 April: 'Mother and baby are well. Baby practices her scales like a good *prima donna* before a performance and has a good voice! Victoria counts the hours and minutes like a prisoner. The children want to know what their sister is to be called, and dispute which names will sound best.'[15]

Laconically, Dr Snow had recorded the Queen's immediate physical reaction to the princess's birth and his administering of anaesthetic: 'The Queen's recovery was very favourable.'[16] The Queen's own comment was characteristically more emphatic, its discernibly triumphant tone indicative of the degree of anxiety she had suffered during this ninth pregnancy: 'I have felt better and stronger this time than I have ever done before.'[17] In her relief at having once more endured unscathed the hated business of childbirth, the Queen allowed herself a moment of hoodwinking congratulation.

But on some matters the doctors were not to be overruled and the Queen remained in bed – convalescing 'like a prisoner' – while Prince Albert returned to the business of state, the Queen's correspondence private and official, and the eight older royal children. On the same day as he wrote to Princess Augusta, the Prince received from the Queen's octogenarian aunt, Princess Mary, Duchess of Gloucester, a letter thanking him for the invalid's sofa he had earlier sent her, and '[thanking] God that dear Victoria is going on well'.[18] The Duchess – the last of the daughters of George III – was slipping inexorably towards death. While the Queen rested at Buckingham Palace, her husband and several of their children visited this survivor of a previous royal generation. 'The Prince Consort and the junior members of the Royal Family have been out daily,' reported the *Illustrated London News*, 'generally calling at Gloucester House to enquire after the illustrious and venerable Princess whose dissolution is hourly expected'.[19] It would be nearly two weeks before that 'dissolution' occurred. In the meantime, the Queen herself had visited the tall house to the west of Hyde Park, accompanied by her second daughter Princess Alice; and the royal children, disputing what their newest sister was to be called, had been given a clue to one of the infant's names.

To the last princess, though she slept in a silk-lined cradle, its canopy like the frame of a four-poster bed, with fringed silk hangings caught up by swags and knots of striped silk cord (she was photographed gazing from this cradle, a tiny baby, by Caldesi), attached none of the historical or dynastic significance of her eldest siblings. Soon the Princess Royal would marry the heir to the throne of Prussia, cementing Anglo-German amity; Bertie, the princess's eldest brother and the only heir apparent ever born to a reigning British queen, would one day succeed his mother as Edward VII. But the last princess, ninth in line to the throne, with eight older siblings, could never expect to reign at home, and with four older sisters would hardly be wanted for a grand match abroad. Her birth gave private pleasure; despite its announcement by salutes of guns in Green Park and at the Tower of London, its public import was limited.

This was not, however, to be the line the Queen adopted concerning her youngest child. At the christening of the Prince of Wales, at St George's Chapel, Windsor in January 1842, the Queen had presided over a banquet and firework display; the christening cake had measured eight feet in diameter; the celebrations had been appropriately princely in expense and extent. For her youngest daughter, the Queen had devised an occasion she afterwards described as 'very brilliant and nice'.[20] In the private chapel of Buckingham Palace, on 16 June, the last princess received from the Archbishop of Canterbury, assisted in his task by a further six clergymen including the Bishop of London, who had been present at the princess's birth, the names Beatrice Mary Victoria Feodore. An anthem specially written for the occasion – 'Princess Beatrice's Anthem' – was sung, the start of a lifelong association with music. The baby wore the Honiton lace christening gown the Queen had commissioned for the Princess Royal's baptism in 1841 and which had been worn in turn by all of the Queen's babies; Beatrice's forehead was anointed with holy water from the font designed by her father Prince Albert, an elaborate, floriferous design made in silver gilt by London silversmiths E. J. & W. Barnard. The Queen was led into the chapel not by her husband but by the Archduke Maximilian of Austria, then on a visit to England. Lunch followed in the palace ballroom. The Queen sat between her daughter's fiancé, the Crown Prince of Prussia, and the same Archduke – later, with tragic consequences, Emperor of Mexico – who made on her a markedly positive impression. 'I cannot say how much we like the Archduke,' she wrote afterwards to her uncle Leopold, soon to be Maximilian's father-in-law. 'He is so charming, so clever, natural, kind and amiable, so *English* in his feelings and likings.'[21] Such a liking did the Queen conceive for her Austrian guest at Beatrice's christening that, following his death in 1868, she commissioned

Albert Graefle to copy for her Maximilian's portrait by Winterhalter.

Though a lifelong favourite of the Queen's, the Crown Prince did not inspire such a eulogy on this occasion, overshadowed by his imperial counterpart. Fritz of Prussia and the Princess Royal were two of baby Beatrice's three sponsors (the third was her maternal grandmother, the Duchess of Kent); the Queen would later remind the Princess Royal, then married and living in Germany as Crown Princess, that she had forgotten to send Beatrice a christening present.

The Duchess of Gloucester was dead but not forgotten, her name included among those of the great-niece she never met who, like her, would become the last survivor of a large family. Queen Victoria's elder half-sister Feodore was remembered, too ('Feodore', the Queen once announced, 'is a dear name which I love to see repeated'[22]) – as were the Queen herself, her mother and her first-born daughter, all three Victorias. 'Beatrice' was the only surprise among the infant's names, associated with England's Plantagenet monarchs and perhaps, for the thoughtful, artistic Prince Albert, with the poetry of Dante, the romance of Dante and his Beatrice being a popular subject among contemporary artists both at home and abroad. Nine days after Beatrice's christening the Queen created Prince Albert Prince Consort by letters patent, thereby plucking from the royal couple's side a thorn of long standing concerning the Prince's rank and title. For her part, the Queen received for her pains 'a lovely lilac silk peignoir, trimmed with guipure lace',[23] a present from the Empress Eugénie of France, the very thing with which to celebrate the end – for the final time – of her 'degraded' physical condition. If the Prince felt vindicated by his wife's official affirmation of her reliance upon him in her public as well as her private life, the Queen felt only happiness. No nervous indisposition followed her daughter's birth. On the contrary, she was embarking on what she would afterwards recall with pride and pleasure as an epoch of 'progress'.[24]

The Queen removed to her seaside retreat of Osborne to recover fully, but was back in London in June, faithful to her self-imposed rule that the lying-in period not exceed six weeks. That month she and Dr John Snow encountered one another under more decorous circumstances, at a palace levee for leading men of the day. The following year, aged only forty-five, Snow died. Neither doctor nor anaesthetic was forgotten by the Queen, who in 1859 wrote to a friend to congratulate her on the birth of her first daughter: 'The Queen is very glad to hear that Minnie is going on so well & had the inestimable blessing of chloroform wh[ich] no one can ever be sufficiently grateful for.'[25]

Almost two decades after the birth of her first child, Queen Victoria's '*nombreuse famille*' was complete. Its dissolution was imminent. On 29 June the palace announced the engagement of the Princess Royal to Frederick William, Crown Prince of Prussia. Beatrice's eldest sister would be married within less than a year of the last princess's birth.

TWO

'The most amusing baby
we have had'

•—•—•

$\mathcal{I}$t was not a family to enter lightly. The Queen disliked babies, abhorred breastfeeding (a practice then growing in popularity among upper-class women) and, herself the only child of a widowed mother, with few girlhood friends of her own age, felt ill at ease with children, her own included. 'I have grown up all alone,' she would remember when Beatrice was two; 'accustomed to the society of adults (and never with younger people).'[1] Added to this, in her role of mother, as in every role she embraced, she was indissolubly Queen too, writing to one grown-up daughter in years to come that she expected 'that *confidence* and *consideration* which are due to me both as a mother and as the Sovereign'.[2] For Queen Victoria, although a constitutional monarch, central to the role of Queen was an instinct for government. The year after Beatrice's birth Lord Clarendon quoted the opinion of a Prussian courtier: 'The Queen is really insane about her maternal authority.'[3] None of the Queen's children ever fully escaped her vigilance and her sphere of control. Even marriage offered limited respite, as the Prince of Wales discovered: 'Much talk in London about the extraordinary way in which the Queen undertakes to direct the Prince and Princess of Wales in every detail of their lives ... A daily and minute report of what passes at Marlborough House [the Waleses' London home] is sent to [her],' Lord Stanley reported. It was June 1863; the Prince of Wales was rising twenty-two.[4]

'It is indeed a pity that you find no consolation in the company of your children,' Prince Albert wrote to his wife, in one of those careful, measured missives that were his chosen channel of correction when an outburst of the Queen's temper threatened to overwhelm them both. 'The root of the trouble lies in the mistaken notion that the function of a mother is to be always correcting, scolding, ordering them about and organizing their activities. It is not possible to be on happy friendly terms with people you have just been scolding.'[5]

The Queen was not uninterested in children. She once puzzled over a lady-in-waiting's letter to discover whether or not the baby under discussion had yet been weaned,[6] and was delighted to hear that a great-grandson had been weaned early 'as it is such a big Child I hear';[7] and she was able to take pride in her babies as physical specimens: 'The Queen pleased with Her grandchildren but convinced that Her own [children] were prettier,' Lady Augusta Bruce wrote to her sister in July 1860 of the Queen's encounter with her two eldest grandchildren, eighteen-month-old Prince William of Prussia and his baby sister Charlotte. It was simply that for the Queen children did not provide companionship; they had, she felt, 'to be kept in order and therefore must not become too intimate'.[8] She did not recognize that constant checks and an insistence on order in themselves precluded intimacy, and was at a loss to alter her approach. Only for Beatrice would exceptions be made and the princess become, too young, intimate, friend, confidante and object of devotion. But by then circumstances had irrevocably changed.

'You are very wrong in thinking that I am not fond of children,' the Queen wrote to the Crown Princess, 'I admire pretty ones immensely.'[9] From birth Beatrice was gifted with an unarguable head start in her mother's eyes: she was an attractive baby with a healthy appetite and robust constitution, 'a pretty, plump, flourishing child ... with fine large blue eyes, pretty little mouth and very fine skin'.[10] To this she added liveliness and the winning disposition that, throughout infancy, would earn her licences inconceivable to her elder siblings. She is 'a darling little baby', the Queen wrote with maternal pride to Princess Augusta of Prussia, 'so fat, with a skin like satin, great blue eyes and the tiniest little mouth you can imagine; and besides she is so lively and good-tempered'.[11] Her eldest sister agreed: 'Quite the prettiest of us all, she is like a little fairy.'[12]

Such prettiness could not pass unrecorded. On 28 October, the Queen visited Upton Park, near Slough, home to the artist E. M. Ward and his wife Henrietta. She admired Mrs Ward's sketches of the Wards' children. On the following day private secretary Charles Grey wrote on the Queen's behalf to request from Mrs Ward 'a similar sketch of the youngest Princess'.[13] The resulting small image is not endearing: the large-eyed baby lies with a doll at her feet in front of an open window, contending only partially successfully for the viewer's attention with a stiff curtain and the plump cushion against which she rests her head. Evidently the Queen was pleased, however: the painting hung in her dressing room at Windsor Castle, and Mrs Ward's skills were shortly exploited again for a picture of the seven-month-old princess in the arms of Mary Ann Thurston, the young widow who, in 1844, had embarked on a tenure of more than two decades as much-loved nurse to the royal children.

The following year sculptress Mary Thornycroft was commissioned to carve a marble image of Princess Beatrice reclining in a nautilus shell. This was among the Queen's Christmas presents from the Prince Consort. It completed the series of statues of the Queen's children Mrs Thornycroft had undertaken since the 1840s, and stood with them in the drawing room at Osborne, one of several markers of that house's explicit role as family home rather than official residence. In the same year, with Beatrice approaching her first birthday, the Queen began to fret that Winterhalter, who had so successfully and so exhaustively charted her burgeoning dynasty, would be prevented by absence abroad from recording this last lovely addition to her brood: 'la petite Princesse Beatrice qui est si jolie', as she wrote to the errant portraitist.[14] But Winterhalter did not desert the Queen. On her fortieth birthday, in 1859, the Prince Consort was able to present his wife with a circular portrait of the golden-haired princess wearing a string of fat beads and a mauve dress. Never one to trust to chance, at the same time the Queen had commissioned from Winterhalter another picture of her own, an engagingly mischievous image of Beatrice in a pink dress wearing an Arab headdress and holding an exotically costumed doll. Since this image was a sketch rather than a finished portrait, Winterhalter received only £20 for his pains, half the sum the Prince Consort had paid him, but the Queen was sufficiently pleased to hang it in her bedroom at Buckingham Palace. For Albert's birthday the same year she repaid like with like, presenting him with a full-length portrait of Beatrice by John Calcott Horsley. A lesser practitioner than his German counterpart, Horsley, whose public opposition to painting the nude earned him the nickname 'Clothes' Horsley, was an appropriately 'moral' choice to paint the infant princess.

The much-painted Beatrice was fifteen months old when her nearest brother Prince Leopold wrote to his father: 'Baby makes such a noise, and when I am sitting opposite to Baby on the left side of the carriage, she kicks me and she goes on saying oogly oogly.'[15] Within weeks Leopold wrote again: Beatrice was still kicking but by then had started to walk. Fairy-like in appearance she may have been, but her instincts were those of a very human child. The Crown Princess was absent from her first birthday party but sent presents in the form of a rose-shaped brooch set with coloured stones and a toy lamb. Both were placed on the table of presents arranged for the infant, at the centre of which was a large 'B' made of flowers. 'Her table of birthday gifts has given her the greatest pleasure,' the Prince Consort wrote to his daughter, 'especially the lamb.'[16]

From the first Beatrice was bright, precocious and able to charm. The Prince Consort described her to his mentor Baron Stockmar as 'an extremely attractive, pretty, intelligent child – indeed the most amusing baby we have had',[17] a view with which all who encountered her concurred. The Queen even went so far as to take pleasure in Beatrice's bathtime, a daily event in which she had seldom joined (in several cases she had *never* involved herself with bathtime), for Vicky, now eighteen and married, Bertie, seventeen, Alice, fifteen, Alfred ('Affie'), fourteen, Helena ('Lenchen'), twelve, Louise, ten, Arthur, eight, or Leopold, five.

For both her parents Beatrice was different from her siblings. Despite the fear she had expressed to Sir James Clark in 1856, the Queen accepted only reluctantly that there must never be a tenth baby in the royal nurseries. Torrent-like, she expended on Beatrice all the maternal affection of which her nature was capable. For the Prince Consort, Beatrice's timely arrival went some way to filling what he described as the void in his heart caused by the removal to Berlin of the Princess Royal, the child who most closely resembled him. Repeatedly his letters to his married daughter related Beatrice's winsome antics and her comical sayings, a narrative free from censure, ardent only in affection. Once, the Queen had praised her husband's skill as a father, singling out his ability to combine kindness with firm management. Where Beatrice was concerned, kindness prevailed. 'I was very naughty last night. I would not speak to Papa, but it doesn't signify much,' boasted the three-year-old princess – a statement it is hard to imagine her eldest brother Bertie ever uttering.[18]

Beatrice brought about a transformation in the Prince Consort. Mary Bulteel, a maid of honour from 1853 to 1861, remembered the Prince as 'without a spark of spontaneity ... As for his sense of fun ... I never could discover it ... His ... jokes were heavy and lumbering';[19] while in a letter to her father written five weeks before Beatrice's birth, fellow maid of honour Eleanor Stanley indicated how seldom the Prince behaved in an openly affectionate way towards his children: 'I came in for a charming ride yesterday ... the Prince, like an affectionate father, taking charge of his eldest son and daughter in front, which it is rather a grievance among the younger branches of the family that he can very seldom be induced to do.'[20] But in 1860 Prince Arthur's governor, Major Elphinstone, observed the Prince with his youngest daughter: 'He commenced to play with the little Princess; took her on his knee, and I was much struck with the affectionate manner in which he played with the child.'[21] Early in the morning, before her mother was yet dressed and about, Beatrice visited the Prince in his dressing room. She watched him while he shaved, or fed his little caged bird, one of a long line of successors to that favourite German bullfinch that, after its death, was stuffed and given to the royal children for their natural history museum at Osborne's Swiss Cottage. One of these birds had been trained to say '*Guten Morgen*'. The Prince sang nursery rhymes to his daughter, in German and in English. He dandled her on his knee while he played the organ or piano, as he had her brothers and sisters before her – only Beatrice, by four years the youngest, did not have to share her father. The Prince was tired in mind and body, overworked and conscientious beyond the capacity of his middling constitution. He relished these precious minutes with his pretty youngest daughter, deriving simple happiness and even a measure of renewed strength from her straightforward pleasure in his company. The Queen noted Beatrice's effect on the Prince, and would remember it later.

These were the golden days, when a child's unfeigned joy could provide a fillip for her father's failing spirits. Soon, when sudden death had riven the Royal Family, only the disadvantages of being the youngest of nine children would be apparent, chief among them the extreme brevity for Beatrice of this enchanted childhood. For now hers was an enviable position.

In December 1846, *éminence grise* Baron Stockmar had drawn up a memorandum for the education of the three eldest royal children. It included a strict timetable that accounted for the whole of a child's waking day, apportioning hour-long sessions to English, French and German governesses. Confidently, it stated: 'It is intended that these classes and these persons are to do for all the children now extant and possibly to come''' – as indeed, in some measure, they did. Except that by the time Beatrice was old enough for her education to be entrusted to governesses the urgency of cramming tiny, unformed minds with princely accomplishments and virtues – what the Queen referred to as late as 1858 as the 'good education of our Children'[23] – was no longer the guiding principle of the royal parents. The Queen's warnings to the Crown Princess over the education of the latter's first child, made while Beatrice was still a toddler – 'Too much constant watching leads to the very dangers hereafter which one wishes to avoid'[24] – echo the advice Melbourne had given the Queen twenty years earlier, which she had then summarily ignored: 'Be not over solicitous about education. It may be able to do much, but it does not do so much as is expected from it.

It may mould and direct the character, but it rarely changes it.'[25] So Beatrice's days, though simple in externals – she slept in an iron bedstead and experienced the 'quite poor living, only a bit of roast meat and perhaps a plain pudding'[26] that was the lot of all nine children – lacked the Spartan emotional character of the nursery and schoolroom experiences of her siblings, warmed by her parents' interest and less often overshadowed by Teutonic exactings beyond the capacity of any but the most brilliant child. Possibly, in this late-flowering leniency, the Queen was subconsciously guided by that mistrust of 'clever' women that Mary Bulteel, after fifty years at court, would recognize as one of her chief characteristics, and that partly accounted for the Queen's jealousy of the Prince Consort's relationship with the Crown Princess, when she felt no pangs at his obvious doting on his tiny youngest daughter.

Unsurprisingly, Beatrice responded to her parents' partiality – 'She adores her Mama, kisses Her hand, is very grateful for the affection shewn her by her parents'[27] – and missed them when royal duty or the sporting calendar took them away from her. Beatrice was at Osborne without her parents for the Prince Consort's birthday in August 1860. With the help of her governess, the royal children's 'Lady Superintendent' Lady Caroline Barrington, known as Lady 'Car', she composed a letter to the absent Prince conveying her birthday wishes and entreating, 'I hope dear Mama will soon come back again from Balmoral, to dear baby, I will love her and kiss her, and dear Papa too.'[28] In her Journal for 18 September, Queen Victoria recorded the welcome Beatrice extended to the royal couple on their return, the Princess waiting 'at the door with a nosegay, so delighted to see us again'.[29] This pretty reception may have been stage-managed by a clever courtier: chief among the Prince Consort's birthday presents from the Queen had been another portrait of Beatrice, this time by Scottish artist John Phillip (after his death acclaimed by the Queen as 'our greatest painter'[30]), the three-year-old sitter wearing a party dress and extending towards the viewer a stiff bouquet of flowers.

In their treatment of Beatrice her parents may have recognized that, in this particular family, to be born in 1857 was too late, that to be ninth and last child was to have missed out on so much. In 1859 Lady Car had arranged a musical performance to mark the Queen and Prince Consort's nineteenth wedding anniversary. She herself accompanied Princesses Helena and Louise on the piano, while Prince Arthur played a drum and five-year-old Prince Leopold a triangle. When the Prince Consort died in 1861, Beatrice had not yet reached an age for triangle-playing in public; her father would never hear his most musically gifted child at the piano or organ, instruments at which she excelled.

For most people, the quintessence of the childhood of Queen Victoria's family is the Swiss Cottage at Osborne House. But the children had laid the cottage's foundation stone in 1853 and officially accepted the house as their own on the Queen's birthday the next year. By the time William Leighton Leitch, watercolourist and tutor in painting to the Queen and her daughters, painted the cottage in 1855, its garden was already laid out with the series of plots, each containing fourteen beds, in which the royal children gardened using miniature tools and wheelbarrows painted with their names. In time, Beatrice too would have a plot of her own, but by then the family was halved, the Princess Royal, Prince of Wales and Princess Alice married, and Prince Alfred away at sea. The children who remained continued to enjoy the house – 'I spent yesterday afternoon at the Swiss Cottage with the Babes,' Lady Augusta Bruce wrote on 15 August 1859, 'Prince Leopold in his little carriage with his arm round Baby, every moment bending down to *hug her*.'[31] After her marriage, they baked cakes and pies for the new Crown Princess in Germany at the miniature range in the cottage kitchen, and sent them to her weekly by Queen's Messenger.

But time was running out for the little log-built house. Beatrice would never entertain her parents to dinner there in the yellow dining room with its bobbin-turned chairs, would never be taken swimming by her father off Osborne's sheltered beach, would never knowingly take part in the summer birthday parties when the Swiss Cottage was decked with flags. She would never chase her brothers and sisters along the nursery corridors of

Buckingham Palace on a makeshift pony fitted with a horse's head and tail; never accompany her parents over hill and moor at the family's new castle of Balmoral, or even venture abroad with them, as the Princess Royal and Prince of Wales had done in 1855, accompanying the Queen and Prince Albert to Paris for their dazzling state visit to Napoleon III and the Empress Eugénie; would not be old enough to appreciate the lavish Germanized Christmases the royal family celebrated with genuinely regal magnificence. Although the Prince Consort, as in summers past, may have constructed for Beatrice a house of building blocks taller than he was, he never rehearsed her in an excerpt from Racine's *Athalie*, *Les Deux Petits Savoyards* or a *tableau vivant* inspired by the pastoral poems of Thomson, never chased butterflies with her or flew a kite with her – all activities that were part of the fabric of Beatrice's siblings' holiday lives. The princess's life had overlapped with that of her great-aunt the Duchess of Gloucester for only a fortnight; there would not be for Beatrice the Berlin woolwork stool the Duchess had embroidered for eight older great-nieces and nephews. Beatrice would scarcely know her grandmother, the Duchess of Kent, a benign, indulgent presence now that she and Queen Victoria had put behind them past differences; she died when Beatrice was only three (forty years later, the Queen would claim, improbably, 'I am glad to say that Beatrice even remembers her quite well'.[32] Nor was she a protégé of Lady Lyttelton, who had retired in 1851 as Superintendent of the Queen's Children in charge of the royal nurseries; rather, Beatrice's world was coloured by the outlook of her successor, Lady Car.

At the Swiss Cottage, Emily Tennyson recorded, Beatrice played with the toy shop that remains on show to visitors today, and served tea to the Queen, busying herself among the 'little tea caddies and tea and sugar and all sorts of good things'.[33] In the house built for a large family of children, hers were lonely hours of play. From the outset, the experiences of the last princess differed significantly from those of her predecessors. A victim of timing and circumstance, she paid a high price for the relaxing of parental attitudes towards discipline and learning.

Aged only two, Beatrice could know none of this, nor suspect the cataclysmic changes that threatened just around the corner. She was the cynosure of every eye. 'She is delicious,' Lady Augusta Bruce effused, ' – jabbers so fast and so plain, is full of wit and fun, and graceful as a fairy – meddles with everything, makes her remarks on all – quite exquisite.'[34] She was pert, confident and outspoken. Louisa Bowater, encountering the royal children in October 1861, described how they 'played about and amused themselves by trying to make the dear little Princess Beatrice, who is evidently the pet of the family, say French words.'[35] Happily the centre of attention, Beatrice invariably obliged.

'She is a most amusing little dot, all the more so for being generally a little naughty,' wrote one of the Queen's ladies when Beatrice was three,[36] and one result of her parents' indulgence, their tolerance of that naughtiness that so appealed to bystanders, was that Beatrice's relationship with them betrayed none of the awe and fear that so flavoured the family life of Victoria and Albert's older children. Admonishments stimulated not tears but cheery rejoinders. When the Prince Consort told her she was troublesome, Beatrice replied, 'No, Baby's not, she's a little girl,' while the Queen's mealtime correction, 'Baby mustn't have that, it's not good for Baby,' was greeted with, 'But she likes it, my dear,' in a voice imitating the Queen's own, as she helped herself to the forbidden dish.[37] At lunch she angered the Queen by wiping her fingers on her black velvet dress in place of a napkin. 'It'll never be seen at night,' the outraged three-year-old offered in exculpation. The Queen was not to be so easily won over, and summoned Mrs Thurston to remove the princess. 'It was only for Her [the Queen] that I came downstairs,' Beatrice told her captor. 'Such base ingratitude.'[38] On a different occasion she exacted revenge by tying the Queen to her chair by her apron strings as she wrote. The Queen did not notice her daughter's handiwork until too late; afterwards a maid had to be called to release her.

The Queen and Prince Consort had tried to devote time to all their children; in Beatrice's case, their time together gave pleasure to the extent that mother and father involved their youngest daughter in occasions from which, in other instances, extreme youth would have excluded her. In July 1860 the Royal Family was at Osborne House for the summer, as had become their custom. The Queen went out on the Solent for tea with her ladies on board her yacht the *Fairy*. Tea time coincided with supper time for Princess Beatrice, who, with her nurse, was among the party. 'Between whiles [she] enlivened us with little pieces of poetry,' remembered maid of honour Eleanor Stanley. '"Twinkle, twinkle", "Little Miss Muffet", "Humpty-Dumpty" and several others, speaking remarkably plainly and nicely, but showing a considerable degree of character in her choice of the poems and her claiming of the rewards (biscuits) for repeating them.'[39] The Queen's response to her daughter's performance is not recorded, but it is safe to assume that there were no reprimands for greed or concerns over the frivolous nature of her chosen 'poetry', as might previously have been the case.

Yet all the while the clouds of sorrow were massing. In an earlier age, the comet that the whole Royal Family, 'from the Queen down to Princess Beatrice',[40] watched from Osborne's Lower Terrace that same month would have been interpreted as a portent. That year the Crown Princess gave birth to a second child, a daughter Charlotte, making Beatrice an aunt twice over although she was only three (Charlotte's brother, Prince William of Prussia, was born in 1859). Writing to his daughter, the Prince Consort suggested the baby model herself on her aunt Beatrice, who excused herself from uncongenial tasks on the grounds that she had no time, she must write letters to her niece. The following Christmas the Prince Consort was dead and Beatrice, the model for her niece, had lost one of her own principal role models. The ramifications of that single happening would endure throughout Beatrice's life, shaping not only her childhood but her very personality, overlaying with black bombazine bright beginnings that had promised so much and given such pleasure to parents and child alike.

THREE

'Paroxysms of despair'

·◆·

The painting the Queen commissioned from Scottish painter
Joseph Noel Paton in February 1863 was from conception
entitled appropriately *In Memoriam*. Its name expressed its
purpose, as well as recalling Tennyson's poem of the same title,
which so comforted the widowed Queen.

Despite numerous sittings and a visit by the Queen to Noel
Paton at home, the painting was never completed. Unfinished, its
composition is nevertheless clear. The Queen and six of her
children are grouped around a bust of the Prince Consort by
William Theed (another memorial commission on the Queen's
part); but it is the Queen, rather than the Prince's marble effigy,
who forms the focus of the painting. Downcast, the eyes of
Princesses Alice and Helena rest upon her. The Queen in turn
gazes at Princess Beatrice, one hand resting on her head. All
dressed in black, Beatrice kneels at her mother's side. Only she
looks towards her father. Her expression is rapt.

Grief-stricken widow and reverent daughter form a tableau
they had enacted repeatedly since the Prince's death on 14
December 1861. The dual image would enter the popular icon-
ography of the mourning monarchy and establish on canvas and
camera the Queen's dependence in her sorrow on her golden-
haired youngest daughter. Outside the embrace of their intimacy
stand Alice, Helena, Louise, Arthur and Leopold, sketchy figures.
Though it was Princess Alice whose support of the devastated
Queen won plaudits in the immediate aftermath of her father's
death, Beatrice would prove the Queen's long-term prop and
stay. How fondly the Queen gazes upon her. But how firm is the
hand that holds her where she kneels. In Beatrice's expression is

no hint of protest, only a suggestion of seriousness beyond her years. Even in a half-drawn picture, the role allotted by mother to daughter is clear. It would remain thus throughout the Queen's widowhood, forty black-bordered summers and winters of discontent.

The death of the Prince, it is claimed, set in motion a sequence of events macabre even by the standards of nineteenth-century mourning. The focus of that macabreness was Princess Beatrice, the doll-like child once singled out for her father's devotion, now a picture of submission at her mother's knee. The psychological effect on the infant princess would be profound and long-lasting. Consigned to memory were her pertness, her cheeky rejoinders and boundless energy; her role henceforth would be a passive one of listening and comforting. Even if much that is claimed is not true, the fact that such rumours have ever existed to gain credence is significant.

To a child like Beatrice, still only four years old and not yet out of the nursery, it must have seemed to happen so quickly. Christmas 1860 had been among the Royal Family's happiest, celebrated at Windsor Castle, where crisp winter sunshine gilded the freezing frost, the weather suited the season and the spirits of all present soared cheerful and bright. On Christmas Day Beatrice joined the family lunch at the end of the meal, she and Leopold admitted for dessert. A skittish Prince Consort swung his flaxen baby in a large napkin. Very young children do not look forward or back, do not indulge in analysis or introspection. If she had, Beatrice would have anticipated with pleasure the New Year towards which, with such happy gusto, her father swung her. What she expected was for everything to continue as before – the laughter and fun, the naughtiness and high good humour. What awaited her was what the Queen described, even before the Prince Consort's death, as 'this sad year',[1] the extent and intensity of its sorrow beyond the comprehension of a child living in the eternal present, from moment to moment.

Beatrice had not known that 1861 was supposed to be a special year. On 10 February the Queen and Prince Consort celebrated their twenty-first wedding anniversary, a meaningless milestone for the youngest child of that marriage but one that gave both husband and wife pause for positive reflection. To her uncle in Belgium the Queen wrote, 'How very few can say with me that their husband at the end of twenty-one years, is not only full of the friendship, kindness and affection which a truly happy marriage brings with it, but of the same tender love as in the very first days of our marriage';[2] while to Baron Stockmar Albert described their love more grandiloquently but less cosily as a plant or tree, 'green and fresh, and [throwing] out vigorous roots, from which I can, with gratitude to God, acknowledge that much good will be engendered to the world.'[3] Husband and wife undoubtedly suited one another. In marriage and a happy family both found atonement for childhoods scarred by unhappiness. The Prince Consort never embraced the British aristocracy; the Queen was his foremost friend. Determinedly family-focused later in life, the Queen began her marriage with few relatives of her own age whom she accounted friends: 'I have none or only those who are useless,' as she would later tell the Crown Princess.[4] Albert was her husband but, as she was to him, he was also her confidant and only intimate contemporary. If they loved wholeheartedly, they also did so needily. Writing to his friend the Duchess of Manchester hours before the Prince Consort died, Foreign Secretary Lord Clarendon assessed the Queen's dependence on her husband: 'No other woman has the same ... motive for being absolutely guided by the superior mind of her husband. This habit, or rather necessity, together with her intense love for him, which has increased rather than become weaker with years, has so engrafted her on him that to lose him will be like parting with her heart and soul.'[5]

When the time came, the Queen would agree with Clarendon. It was a moment she had not conceived of and for which she was ill prepared. The progress of the royal marriage represented the progress of the Queen's submergence of herself in the Prince. At his death died too that part of herself she had schooled in his disciplines of self-abnegation and control. She must learn to be herself all over again. The process would be long and – because she resisted it, clinging determinedly to the Prince's shade as to a living presence – painful. For the Queen it was like sailing a boat that had lost its rudder: too weak to learn another way to steer, she imagined instead that a piece of the hull had been torn from the vessel and expended her diminished energies in struggling to remain afloat. She had '[done] nothing, thought of nothing, without her beloved and gracious husband, who was her support, her constant companion, her guide, who helped her in *everything* great and small'. Now she '[stood] alone in her trying and difficult position, struggling to do her duty', she wrote to Lord Derby.[6] She referred to herself, as habitually, in the third person, deriving infinitesimal comfort from the distance lent by the syntactical conceit, at a time when she could still not bring herself to enter in her Journal any first-person account of the dreadful night. It was surely more than anyone could bear.

Of all those close to the court only the Queen and Princess Beatrice, it seemed, had been surprised when, at quarter to eleven on the evening of 14 December of 'this sad year', the Prince Consort died of typhoid fever. Fearing for her mental health, the Queen's doctors had shielded her from their worst suspicions, even declining to name the Prince's illness, concealing all foreboding behind the euphemism 'gastric fever'. The Queen for her part had clung to the certainty that the Prince must rally. Princess Alice, the eldest of the couple's daughters still at home – cast in the role of nurse by the Queen's unsuitability for such a role (through temperament as much as inexperience) – wrote to her fiancé Prince Louis of Hesse, 'Poor Mama is very unhappy about it – but not worried.'[7] Remembering afterwards, a member of the household was clear about the line the Queen adopted: 'She could not bear to listen, and shut her eyes to the danger.'[8] Forty years later, it was the policy Beatrice would adopt in relation to the dying Queen.

'Her grief is extreme, and she feels acutely the loss of one whom she cherished and tended with affectionate and dutiful devotion,' the Prince Consort had written following the death of the Queen's mother on 16 March. 'In body she is well, though terribly nervous, and the children are a disturbance to her. She remains almost totally alone.'[9] The words have a prophetic ring to them. Now the circumstances were the same, only the suffering was intensified, the aloneness total at last. The Queen could not bear the presence of any of her children save Alice, who had nursed her father and now did the same for her mother, and Beatrice, who in his illness had diverted the Prince and must now divert the Queen. Even the sound of the Prince of Wales's voice pained his mother.

After her grandmother's death, Beatrice had been puzzled at the lack of merriment that accompanied her fourth birthday celebrations the next month, but comforted her mother by repeatedly referring to her grandmother, 'how she is in heaven, but she hopes she will return. She is a most darling, engaging child.'[10] Seven months later her task was again to provide comfort, but now the Queen's need was incalculably greater, and Beatrice's medicine took the form not of childish prattle about her father in heaven but simple distraction. When the family gathered to take their leave of the dying Prince, Beatrice remained in bed, considered too young for such a scene. She slept soundly, not suspecting that tonight her father would die. 'Dear little Beatrice had not seen him for many days previous to his death,' Mrs Thurston, Beatrice's nurse, afterwards wrote to her daughter Elizabeth Bryan.[11] Once, on 6 December, the Queen had taken her to the Prince, in the hope that her unaffected high spirits would rouse his sinking heart. 'He was most dear and affectionate when I went in with little Beatrice whom he kissed. He quite laughed at some of her new French verses which I made her repeat. Then he held her little hand in his for some time and she stood looking at him.'[12] The child had sensed that all was not well. Instead of taking the lead, she stared in silence at the enervated figure of her father, not even boastful of the new earrings she wore, having recently and bravely had her ears pierced. The Queen did not repeat the experiment. When the Prince died, Thurston told her daughter, it was astonishing that Beatrice did not speak more of him. The child was unnerved by the epic scale of her mother's grief and the immediate and complete alteration in the life she had known. The Queen did not attend the Prince's funeral at St George's Chapel, Windsor, but shortly set off with her four daughters for Osborne, that sun-kissed family holiday house away from Windsor with its death chamber and memories of twenty happy Christmases. Before they went, the Queen instructed Alice, Helena, Louise and Beatrice to cut off a lock of their hair for placing beside their father in his coffin.

Queen Victoria demanded circumspection from those who served her: 'The discretion is extreme here,' Mary Bulteel had written in 1853;[13] 'it makes the Queen furious if she thinks anything is written about what goes on here.'[14] But such a cataclysm as the death of the Prince Consort, and the Queen's response to it, could not pass unmentioned. Eyewitness accounts proliferate.

Given the absence of privacy in royal residences of the nineteenth century, these accounts are strangely at variance. Eleanor Stanley was not in waiting in December 1861 but pieced together a version of what happened from information given to her by those who were present. She describes the period immediately after the Prince's death: 'The Queen went up to the nursery first, kissed little Princess Beatrice, and came down again, alone to her dressing room, in which she had slept for about a fortnight then.'[15] This account largely agrees with that of 'an old servant', Mrs Macdonald, quoted by E. E. P Tisdall in 1961: 'It was an awful time – an awful time. I shall never forget it. After the Prince was dead, the Queen ran through the ante-room where I was waiting. She seemed wild. She went straight up to the nursery and took Baby Beatrice out of bed, but she did not wake her ... Orders were given at once for the removal of the Court to Osborne.'[16] What Mrs Macdonald did not say is what the Queen did with the baby she was at pains not to wake.

It was David Duff, writing in 1958, who offered an explanation for this point: 'It was to Beatrice that the Queen ran on the evening of her husband's death, taking her to her own bed and wrapping her in the nightclothes of the man whom she would always mourn.'[17] This ghoulish and richly symbolic turn of events so impressed Duff that he returned to it again in the same book: 'Taking Beatrice from the cot, [the Queen] hurried to her own bed and there lay sleepless, clasping to her a child, wrapped in the nightclothes of a man who would wear them no more.'[18]

David Duff drew on a number of private recollections, including accounts of Beatrice given to him by two of her children. Perhaps this information came from them, learnt from their mother. But they were not present at Windsor on that cheerless December night, and Beatrice herself could only reliably have remembered those moments had her mother confided them to her at a later date, or had she read the Queen's own account of events before herself destroying it as part of her long task of editing and rewriting the Queen's Journal after her death. All 'observers' agree that, whatever course of action the Queen pursued relative to Beatrice, Beatrice herself was not awake to observe it and commit it to memory. What's more, she was only four and a half years old. For the historian she was as effectively excluded from the scene as Eleanor Stanley, absent from the castle, and Mrs Macdonald, left behind in an ante-room, not privy to the secrets of the royal nursery or the Queen's dressing room. The Queen's own account, as it survives, emphasizes her personal agony, not the consolation she received from others, since she was, and would remain, inconsolable: 'I stood up kissing his dear heavenly forehead and called out in a bitter agonizing cry: "Oh! my dear darling!" and then dropped on my knees in mute distracted despair, unable to utter a word or shed a tear! ... Then I laid down on the sofa in the Red Room.'[19]

The story of Beatrice wrapped in her father's nightclothes by a Queen too stunned by grief to analyse her actions has become an accepted part of the legend of Queen Victoria's extraordinary mourning. Certainly, the morning after the Prince's death, the Queen, forbidden by her doctors to kiss her dead husband's features or embrace him, kissed instead his clothes. She slept thereafter in the bed they had shared, with his coat over her, according to the Crown Princess, 'and his dear red dressing gown beside her and some of his clothes in the bed!'[20] 'Sweet little Beatrice comes to lie in my bed every morning which is a great comfort. I long so to cling to and clasp a living being,' the Queen wrote on 18 December to her eldest daughter.[21] If the Queen resisted wrapping Beatrice in her husband's nightshirt as the bells tolled their desolate clarion, there is enough here to suggest how the assertion came about – by a process of Chinese whispers or the elision of discrete details into a single happening.

There is also the fact that nothing in the Queen's subsequent conduct renders such behaviour implausible. Queen Victoria shielded none of her children from the elemental force of her grief. Louise at thirteen, Arthur at eleven, Leopold at eight and Beatrice at four were all old enough for full exposure to their mother's agony, though none could have conceived what it meant for a wife to lose a husband, particularly this wife this husband, whom she loved with a mixture of idolatrous adoration and jealous passion. The Queen's 'poor heart', she wrote to Lord Palmerston six months later, 'is pierced and bleeding'.[22] This pitiable spectacle must henceforth be her children's constant study. A month after the Prince died the Queen's eldest grandson celebrated his third birthday; as a present, the Queen sent him a bronze copy of a bust of his lately deceased grandfather by Marochetti, author of the Prince's sarcophagus effigy. Thirty years later she would express concern that a seven-year-old great-granddaughter did not fully appreciate the death of her grandfather: 'Can poor dear little Alice take it all in? I trust she will never forget her dear GrandPapa.'[23] No one was too young to remember and lament. On the contrary, the innocence of the very young was in itself comforting, 'for there is something refreshing, in the midst of misery and anguish like mine even, in an innocent little child. Our baby [Beatrice] has that in her which is so soothing ...'[24] Beatrice had slept the night her father died. That very sleep gave proof of her innocence, her lack of understanding of events unfolding around her. She had gone to bed her parents' baby and, in the morning, when only one parent remained, must continue in that role, referred to by the Queen as 'Baby' long beyond the close of her nursery years. The torchlight of the Queen's grief had fallen upon her. It would never lift.

In the spring of 1861 the gossipmongers of the courts of Europe *knew* that Queen Victoria was mad: her mind had given way in an excess of grief following the death of her mother. What they mistook for madness was extreme nervous collapse, exacerbated by the Queen's determination not to be distracted from her sorrow but rather to dwell on it, clasping it to her as a substitute for the loved one she had lost. In the Queen's emotional life were no half-measures: she mourned as she loved, possessively and energetically. At the death of the Prince Consort, the mourning overtures heard nine months earlier for the Duchess of Kent reached a climax. They found an echo in the poetry of Tennyson. Writing to her eldest daughter, the Queen quoted from 'In Memoriam': '"O Sorrow, wilt thou live with me / No casual mistress, but a wife, / My bosom-friend and half of life, / As I confess it needs must be ..." This is what I feel; yes, I long for my suffering almost – as it is blinded with him!'[25]

The Queen met the poet on Beatrice's fifth birthday and took the opportunity of telling him how much she had been comforted by 'In Memoriam'. Afterwards Beatrice also met Tennyson, in company with her sister Alice, and turned upon him what his wife described as a 'pondering, puzzled, horrified gaze',[26] perhaps disconcerted by some dishevelment in the poet's appearance or peculiarity of expression. The Queen was not mad, but the compass of her thoughts, enlarged by the Prince in life, at his death shrank to a single focus. This all-absorbing subject – the Prince sanctified by premature death – came to dominate the Queen's relationship with her youngest daughter. Nothing must distract her from her sorrow. Grown-up children had a way of obfuscating what mattered in a welter of lesser concerns and of losing sight of the Queen's suffering in the maelstrom of their own affairs. Only Beatrice was young enough to surrender wholeheartedly to a single obsession. And so, given no choice in the matter, she put on the nightshirt of her mother's 'paroxysms of despair and yearning and longing and of daily, nightly longing to die',[27] and embarked on the career as comforter that was hers by default. She would embrace that career with a single-minded devotion that never faltered. Her life henceforth was one of sacrifices, but one rewarded with the benison of her mother's sincere and often-expressed adoration.

FOUR

'The bright spot in this dead home'

·◆·

On 4 July 1865, Lewis Carroll gave Alice Liddell the first presentation copy of *Alice's Adventures in Wonderland*. The second copy he sent to Princess Beatrice.

Sir John Tenniel's Alice illustrations depict a spidery mid-Victorian girl with pretty eyes and blonde hair. As the Queen's line-drawing of her youngest daughter clasping her baby nephew William of Prussia shows, the young Princess Beatrice resembled that girl. She shared the fine features of her sisters Alice and Louise, only later succumbing to the Queen's heavier, more rounded physiognomy, which Helena and the Crown Princess had inherited. Her hair, which she wore loose, was of a rich strawberry blonde that the Queen was at pains to capture accurately in the numerous watercolour sketches she made of her. Despite being expected to spend much of her time outside the nursery sedentary at her mother's side, Beatrice retained for the moment her fairy-like, Alice-like grace in motion and a definitely childish restlessness and excess of energy. As the Queen recorded on 2 June 1865, 'Baby's liveliness and fidgetyness was beyond everything, and she ended by throwing all the milk over herself' – an unusually waspish tone for the Queen to adopt in relation to this adored youngest child.[1]

The Queen, we know, was fond of pretty children. 'The happy time is when children are six to five and three years old,' she declared, decided in this as in all her tastes.[2] Her pleasure was increased if, added to good looks, the child was well behaved. To her uncle Leopold the summer before Beatrice's birth, she had described Prince Arthur, her favourite of her children: ' ... he is not only so lovely and engaging, but *so* sensible and clever

30

and such a very good little Child – that it is a delight to have him with you.'[3] The Queen took the same delight in Beatrice, and for the same reasons. The 'darling little baby' of whom, at four months old, she had written to Princess Augusta of Prussia was already by her first birthday 'a great beauty'.[4] Remembering her fifth birthday twenty years later, Tennyson described her as 'a fair-haired child whom it was a pleasure to look upon'. [5] For her mother she would remain specially pleasing throughout her life.

Shortly after Beatrice's fifth birthday, the Queen wrote to the Crown Princess, 'Dearest Baby is the bright spot in this dead home.'[6] Overwhelmingly, the Queen regarded the Prince Consort's death in terms of its effect on herself. She lamented the Prince's loss to the country and deeply regretted for her children's sake the removal of a paragon among fathers, but the devastation was chiefly her own. No one else could fully comprehend her suffering, nor could any third person moderate the acuteness of her misery. As Queen her burden was one of lonely eminence; widowhood redoubled that loneliness. In her deep unhappiness, the Queen turned not towards her children – whose sorrow she could only acknowledge as secondary to her own – but away from them. Struggling to come to terms with their own bereavement, they in turn were predictably wrong-footed by their mother's attitude. They learnt that to say nothing was safer than saying what was wrong, and so homes that should have been cheered by the presence of a large family took on instead an eerie quiet; no laughter rent the shadows. Only Beatrice, too young for nuances, continued to behave with spontaneity and naturalness. Happily for her, her childish giggle was not irksome to the Queen, though even she learnt quickly to stop asking where her father was.

In her response to the death of her husband, as in all things, the Queen was a woman of contradictions. She wished to hear from her children that they missed their father as she missed him, though she denied that this was possible. She wanted them to support her in her terrible grief, but repeatedly asserted that no one could support her. With their father dead, she craved all their love for herself, as if being loved wholeheartedly by nine children would fill the void left by the removal of that single, quite different sort of love – though she knew that it could not. She demanded their feelings fall into the line she had determined on for them, but felt her authority dissipated by the death of him on whom she had relied in everything, so that she was herself reduced to the status of 'a deserted child'.[7] Her implicit insistence to all her children was that they idealize their father, though, as she admitted to her eldest daughter, she missed the physical love of the Prince as much as his finer feelings.

'I do not want to feel better. I love to dwell on her ... and not to be roused out of my grief,' the Queen had written after her mother's death.[8] So, too, she felt at the death of the Prince Consort. Her grief had about it an orgiastic quality, as if she delighted in the deep black borders to her writing paper, the widow's cap she had adopted, described by Beatrice as her 'sad cap', her shattered nerves, racing pulse ('constantly', she boasted, 'between 90 and 100 instead of being at 74!'[9]), and weak limbs. Throughout her life, at moments of high distress the Queen lost the use of her legs. The Prince Consort had carried her from her mother's deathbed; later, in 1871, threatened by republicans and feeling herself hounded from all sides, the Queen would again find herself unable to walk; without the Prince, John Brown carried her.

Year after year, the anniversary of the Prince's death stimulated his children haplessly to say the wrong things to their mother. On 19 December 1863, the Queen replied to the Crown Princess: 'You say how you wish to console and comfort and assist me. Dearest child – the only, only way is by trying to soothe, and weep as it were with me, not by trying to divert me from the one beloved object.'[10] Beatrice was by then six years old; already she had spent a third of her life under the shadow of her mother's grief. Unlike the eldest of her siblings she was too young to offer the Queen vain attempts at consolation, and so avoided those reproaches which in other cases threatened to sour relations between mother and child. Beatrice comforted her mother more simply, without any appeal to reason or good sense but straightforwardly, as one would tend a suffering child, soothing and kissing her. Every morning, Augusta Bruce recorded, 'Princess Beatrice spends an hour with Her, and is in agonies when She sees Her cry. "Dear Darling" as She calls Her, hugging and kissing Her so tenderly.'[11] In these morning encounters the roles of mother and child were reversed, Beatrice embarking on her long schooling in the self-denial that ultimately would appear to the outside world her principal characteristic. Once she had been encouraged to show off, her funny, clever ways applauded by family and courtiers alike. Now, though as yet she remained that precocious little girl, she was learning to subsume herself in her mother's concerns, responding rather than initiating, the active giving way to the passive.

It is possible that the Queen did not speak directly to Beatrice of her sorrow at all, but simply found in her a willing, kindly listener to an inexhaustible fund of stories about the Prince. Undoubtedly, Beatrice retained the ability to divert the Queen with her disarming pertness and childishly lopsided logic, which even in the darkest days still gave rise to intermittent laughter. On the Queen's part, she recognized that her delight in Beatrice was a permissible distraction for one whose life had become a waking death: the Prince had loved Baby and revelled in her ways, no guilt could attach to his widow's deriving similar pleasure. She instructed Helena to write to the Crown Princess relating Beatrice's funnier sayings. But the Queen's emotional well-being required more than the stimulus of a child's comical antics or the balm of her morning kisses, while Beatrice's development could not proceed along normal lines so long as her time was divided between the company of a mother overwhelmed by unhappiness and periods alone in the schoolroom. The Queen required adult solace, Beatrice the company of children and an atmosphere that embraced the present as well as the past. Neither requirement would be satisfied.

The Queen seems scarcely to have been aware of the needs of her youngest daughter – oddly, given that she herself had grown up fatherless and frequently lonely and unhappy. She was sunk so deep in self-absorption that she could acknowledge nothing beyond the demands of her suffering, her constant refrain that the extent of that suffering be recognized by others. She could not endure in silence and had no intention of sorrowing in solitude. Her family, her household, her ministers, her country – all must share her titanic grief. The Prince was irreplaceable and her children were no substitute, but this was no reason why one of them should not step into the breach at the Queen's side and help her shoulder her unmanageable burden. A daughter would be preferable to a son. Quickly the Queen remembered that it had always been the Prince's intention that one of their daughters remain at home to help her. As she wrote to the Crown Princess – married and living in Germany, off the hook both on account of distance and her 'great and high' position, the Queen being a respecter of thrones – 'I must never, during the few ... years still remaining, be left without one of you – and with five daughters this will be quite easy. Dear Papa said so himself.'[12]

With the Crown Princess safely out of reach, Alice was next in line. She had nursed her father with unflinching selflessness and afterwards, sleeping in the same room as her mother, maintained a nightly vigil that probably saved the Queen from complete nervous collapse. Alice was engaged, but her fiancé, Louis of Hesse, until he inherited the Grand Duchy of Hesse was a princeling of limited consequence. In the first years of their marriage, Alice and Louis's responsibilities in Germany would be trifling compared with the Queen's need for day-long secretarial assistance and sympathetic hand-holding. They then must live with the Queen. There could be no room for argument. The Queen had decided as early as December 1860 that Louis did 'not [have] any duties to detain him much at home at present'[13] and thus no reasonable grounds for objection.

When Louis became Grand Duke, Alice would leave her mother. Into her place would step Helena, or Louise. Or even, in due course, Beatrice. 'As long as life remains in this shattered body, it will be devoted to her children and her country,' the Queen promised her Prime Minister Lord Palmerston in May 1862.[14] In truth, she expected her children to devote themselves to her, and her country to exercise tolerance and understanding.

Alice did not remain with her mother. She was married on 1 July 1862 and Beatrice saw the family circle diminish further. The Queen did not miss her second daughter unduly: 'Much as she has been to me . . . and dear and precious as a comfort and an assistance, I hardly miss her at all, or felt her going – so utterly alone am I.'[15] The Queen had three daughters remaining. She had in fact already decided that Helena, 'Lenchen', not Alice was her ideal helpmeet; to Uncle Leopold she commended Lenchen's usefulness and the manner in which 'her whole character [was] so well adapted to live in the house'.[16] For the moment Alice and the Queen, between whom good relations would gradually deteriorate, continued on cosy terms. Alice used her parents as the model for the upbringing of her own children and in time wrote to her mother, 'I try to copy as much as is in my power all those things for my children that they may have an idea when I speak to them of it what a happy home ours was. I do feel so much for dear Beatrice and the other younger ones who had so much less of it than we had.'[17] Alice must have known of Beatrice's morning visits to her mother. Perhaps she would grow to feel uneasy at leaving behind her youngest sister to her mournful fate.

Just how much less of that 'happy home' Beatrice had than her elder siblings was immediately obvious to William Leighton Leitch, visiting Balmoral the summer after the Prince Consort's death. Leitch had been summoned to give painting lessons to Helena, Louise, Arthur and Leopold (Beatrice was still too young for watercolours). He was an old familiar of the Royal Family's and had spent three weeks at Balmoral the previous autumn teaching the Queen and her daughters. To his wife he described the wholesale changes he found at the castle:

> Everything was quiet and still. How different from my first visit here – the joyous bustle in the morning when the Prince went out: the Highland ponies and dogs; the ghillies and the pipers. Then the coming home – the Queen and her ladies going out to meet them, and the merry time afterwards; the torch-lit sword-dances on the green and the servants' ball closing the day. Now all was gone with him who was the life and soul of it all.[18]

The Queen would resume drawing lessons in 1863, then managing even to chat and occasionally laugh 'at the little difficulties and drawbacks',[19] but for the first widowed summer there would be no such distractions. With a heavy heart the Queen had made it through Alice's wedding, a small, decidedly funereal affair in the dining room at Osborne. Beatrice was a bridesmaid, a source of some excitement, but even Baby enjoying herself in her finery could not rouse the Queen. 'It was a terrible moment for me,' she confided to her Journal.[20] It would not be a happy summer.

The following spring came another wedding, that of the Prince of Wales to Princess Alexandra of Denmark. The Queen had wished initially that the service would take place on her own wedding anniversary, but objections were raised and the date was fixed for a month later, 10 March, at St George's Chapel, Windsor. Mourning was temporarily lifted, with the exception of 'the Ladies of Her Majesty's Household, who must be in grey, lilac or mauve', according to a memorandum sent to the Lord Chamberlain's office;[21] the Queen's unmarried daughters, who wore white with mauve ribbons and carried mauve and white wreaths; and the Queen herself, who remained in inkiest black and witnessed the ceremony from the partial seclusion of the Chapel's Royal Closet. Her distance from prying eyes did not serve to increase her enjoyment of the service – her only pleasure was in watching her adored Beatrice. 'When the procession entered', she wrote in her Journal, 'and our five fatherless children (the three girls and two little boys) came into view, the latter without either parent (at Vicky's wedding, they walked before, behind and near me), I felt terribly overcome. I could not take my eyes off precious little Baby, with her golden hair and large nosegay, and smiled at her as she made a beautiful curtsey ...'[22] The princess's appearance struck another less-than-impartial witness, Lady Augusta Bruce: 'You may suppose', she wrote affectionately, 'what a person [Beatrice] looked like with the wreaths, long silk stockings and gigantic bouquet.'[23] At the entry of the Prince of Wales, the Crown Princess burst into tears, followed by Princess Alice, then Princess Beatrice, who was still so short compared with her full-grown sisters that when the princesses came to kneel for the prayers, 'all that could be seen of [her] was a cloud of golden hair behind the altar rails,' according to eyewitness Mary Stanley.[24] Afterwards, cross-examined on the cause of her tears, Beatrice was unable to provide any explanation, but responded with characteristically vigorous indignation to 'the idea of its being because she saw the others weep!'[25] The Prince and Princess exchanged vows and up welled the chorale composed by the Prince Consort before his death, its solemn notes threatening further tears on the part of the bridegroom's family. Clear among the voices rose that of 'Swedish nightingale' Jenny Lind, the opera singer the Queen and Prince had heard first the year before Beatrice's birth in the Festhalle in Bonn.

When the service was over, the Queen did not attend the family luncheon for thirty-eight. She lunched quietly with Beatrice and the widow of the Prince of Wales's governor General Bruce. Her mood was coloured by the inevitable sorrowful memories of her own wedding day, Bertie's new-found happiness an unnecessary reminder of what she had lost. It is not difficult to imagine the verdict on weddings shaping in Beatrice's mind.

The Queen had commissioned William Powell Frith, chronicler par excellence of the mid-Victorian pageant, to paint the Prince's marriage ceremony. Much of Frith's work was undertaken at Windsor after the event, including, as the Queen noted in her Journal for 8 April 1863, 'Photographing of the girls and Baby for Mr Frith's wedding picture.' Significantly, Beatrice already merits special mention: it is not enough that she be included within 'girls' alongside the Queen's other unmarried daughters, Helena and Louise. Perhaps Beatrice's status as 'Baby' defied attributions of gender; she was outside all that, which was part of her charm for the Queen: not a girl but 'Baby'. Certainly in years to come the Queen would determinedly attempt to deny any attainment of sexual maturity on Beatrice's part. She would continue, too, to refer to her last baby in terms that marked her as distinctive and special – and cut off from her siblings.

Frith was working on likenesses of Helena and Louise when

Beatrice first encountered him. She burst into his temporary studio in the company of her new sister-in-law the Princess of Wales, the Crown Prince and Princess and her nephew William. The atmosphere of businesslike calm was shattered – 'of all the rows! those children shouting, laughing and romping with the Princesses'.[26] When the noise subsided, the artist asked six-year-old Beatrice if she would not have liked to be one of Alexandra's bridesmaids. 'Oh, no,' she replied. 'I don't like weddings at all. I shall never be married. I shall stay with mother.'[27]

The Prince Consort had been dead less than a year and a half. The previous summer, for the first and last time, Beatrice had been a bridesmaid, an excitement in a young girl's life. By the time of her brother's wedding that excitement was forgotten, confused by a growing apprehension that weddings were not necessarily happy events. Fifteen months' exposure to her mother's sorrow had begun already to change the last princess, her outlook distorted by a woman whose principal achievement to date was a resoundingly happy marriage.

FIVE

'Beatrice is quite well'

•◆•

Three of the ten Maori chiefs whose meeting at Osborne with Queen Victoria, Princess Helena, Prince Leopold and Princess Beatrice was reported in the *Australian and New Zealand Gazette* of 17 July 1863 were accompanied by their wives. The exotic appearance of the deputation of thirteen from one of their mother's furthest colonies impressed the royal children. Dusky-skinned, the Maoris were tattooed, they wore flax cloaks far removed from the customary dress of Queen Victoria's court, feathers in their hair and shark's-tooth and greenstone earrings.

The Queen received them in the Council Room, where they kissed her hand, and monarch and chiefs spoke through an interpreter. Even barriers of language and culture could not disguise from her visitors the Queen's continuing sorrow. Afterwards, from London, one of the chiefs, Kissling te Tuaha, wrote to the Queen: 'Your Majesty the Queen, I salute you and your children, who are widowed and orphans through the death of Prince Albert. It is well, your Majesty; he has gone to God's right hand. Pray rather, your Majesty, for those who are in the world.'

It was always the same: the Prince Consort, though no longer present, was never entirely absent; the thought of him occupied the Queen's waking day and her sleepless nights. Her children accepted it as so. They could have told Kissling te Tuaha that their mother would ignore his injunction to pray 'rather ... for those who are in the world'

The previous autumn, Beatrice had travelled abroad for the first time She accompanied her mother and siblings first to Belgium, where in the presence of King Leopold the Queen had been introduced to Princess Alexandra of Denmark and approved her as a bride for the Prince of Wales, and then, with the Queen's half-sister Feodora in tow, to Coburg and the Prince Consort's birthplace. It was not a holiday. The Queen had combined state business (the choice of a future queen consort) with fidelity to family ties (meeting Feodora, who she hoped at this point would come and live with her, two widows together, united in sorrow and memories of the past). Her journey was also a widow's pilgrimage: she revisited the hunting lodge of Reinhardtsbrunn in the Thuringian forest, 'one of the most beautiful spots imaginable',[1] where, on 27 August 1845, she and Prince Albert had rested a night. In 1863, after the meeting with the Maoris, the Queen and Beatrice were once more in Germany, visiting the married Princess Alice at her ancient, tree-girt castle of Kranichstein, and afterwards journeying to the Rosenau, the house in which the Prince Consort had been born. On a terrace at the Rosenau, Beatrice was painted by German portraitist Richard Lauchert: turning towards the viewer, she holds in both hands a miniature of her deceased father. Lauchert's is the prettiest image of the princess ever painted: she wears a flounced white lace dress, fleetingly out of mourning save for the dark ribbon in her tumbling hair. The Queen thought it 'lovely and so like', but disliked the background, the sky 'a leaden, lilacy blue – with no white clouds', which would 'not match with the fine turquoise-blue skies darling Papa made Winterhalter paint into our family pictures'.[2] Since the Prince's death the sun no longer shone even as a backdrop to children's portraits, a symbolic example of art imitating life.

Beatrice returned to Coburg with her mother two years later, in 1865, this time with all eight of her siblings. The Queen's purpose was to unveil a statue of the Prince Consort in the town's marketplace and for once she did not quash municipal plans for a day of pageantry and splendour. What followed was an impressive and colourful spectacle for the eight-year-old Beatrice, but one that as ever gave rise to mournful thoughts on the part of the princess's constant companion, her mother. Beatrice would have to wait another twenty years, until she herself was married, before being able to make any equation of travel and simple pleasure. For now, like so much else in her life, it was chiefly a compound of family piety and duty.

Alone in Beatrice's life her education proceeded much as it would have done had the Prince not died. Certainly she was overseen by one not two parents, and the Queen took to interrupting schoolroom hours as she had never done with her older children, but the educational regime followed by the princess, under the overall control of Lady Car, was essentially that pursued by all the Queen's children, 'from its earliest beginnings a truly moral and a truly *English* [education]', as its author Baron Stockmar described it.[3]

That 'English' education included lessons in French, under Mademoiselle Norèle, and German with Fräulein Ottilie Bauer, a relation of Stockmar's remembered by one (non-royal) pupil as a 'dried-up, withered little lady';[4] Fräulein Bauer, referred to by the Queen and her children as 'Bauerlein', remained part of the household beyond Beatrice's schoolroom days, later assuming the role of Reader to the Queen's Household. English itself was in the hands of Miss Hildyard, 'Tilla'. History was both taught and absorbed on visits to sites of particular historic interest, such as the Tower of London. In a letter of 14 May 1868, 'The Princess Beatrice thanks Lord De Ros very much for sending his interesting account of the Tower of London,' which served as a pleasant recollection of her visit there.[5] Four years later, in Edinburgh with the Queen, Beatrice was taken on a tour of the palace of Holyrood House and its ruined abbey by Duncan Anderson, Keeper of the Chapel Royal.

On the earlier occasion, the sloping italic hand that thanked Lord De Ros was precise and extremely neat, written on widely spaced lines that may have been assisted by a ruler. Though encouraged to express herself on paper from an early age, Beatrice was not taught this particular script until after her seventh birthday, the Hon. Mrs Bruce writing to the Dean of Westminster, Dr Stanley, in the autumn of 1864, 'Princess Beatrice ... has at last begun her long-delayed writing lessons, but struck work the other day after making a long line of the letter P. "It is so difficult to make their stomachs." Not a bad idea ..."[6] From this point onwards, for the remainder of her life, Beatrice wrote clearly and legibly, in marked contrast to her mother, whose amanuensis she was to become, and almost all her siblings. Her spelling, too, was consistently accurate, more so than the Queen's, though like all children she got off to an uncertain start. Lady Augusta Bruce, known to the princess as 'Guska' or 'Oguska', remembered an early attempt at letter-writing on the family trip to Coburg in October 1862:

> Princess Beatrice has bestowed a good deal of her company on us during these rainy days. Yesterday she was established writing on 'silk paper', having bespoken 'a nice little large silk envelope', when the footman came in to summon me to the Queen. You should have seen the look with which she turned round and with withering contempt exclaimed '*always*'. They might have known she was writing to Oguska, because she put a big O![7]

Aged only three, the princess had written to her father to congratulate him on his birthday, composing her letter with the help of Lady Car. Aged five, on her first holiday abroad, she wrote to a favourite lady-in-waiting, who was also of the party. Aged eleven, she wrote to Lord De Ros in the third person, a formal, already recognizably royal letter of a sort she would repeat hundreds of times. Queen Victoria was a passionate letter-writer and required that all her children share her habit. Princess Louise apologized to Prince Arthur in 1862, 'So you see, dear Arthur, how little time I have to write.' In addition to letters to her brother, Louise had to write to 'Mr Ogg twice a week, the Dean twice a week, and Mrs Anderson three times a week';[8] the royal siblings were respectively fourteen and twelve. From infancy Beatrice acquired the family habit, and found it easy and natural to express herself on paper. It would prove a useful skill. As early as 1872, when she was fifteen, she began writing letters on the Queen's behalf, in the first instance from the Queen to her cousin Princess Mary Adelaide, Duchess of Teck. With the passage of years further correspondents would be added, alongside new relations acquired by marriage and, eventually, friends of her own.

By then Beatrice had grown into the helper Queen Victoria required: quiet, attentive, unquestioning in her devotion and support. The transformation came about gradually. In January 1864 the Prince Consort had been dead two years. Lady Car wrote to Eleanor Stanley from Osborne describing what at that point was still a characteristic Beatrice incident. 'The draughts all over the house are not to be described; the German governess asked Princess Beatrice the other day what windows were made for? "To let in *wind*" was her immediate reply, and a more exact description of the Osborne windows there could not be.'⁹ In the same year, the Princess of Wales's lady-in-waiting Lady Macclesfield encountered the younger royal children at Windsor. She was unimpressed by Beatrice, whom she considered petted and spoilt. On that occasion Beatrice announced to Lady Macclesfield that the Queen had decided on the names 'Albert Victor' for the Prince and Princess of Wales's newborn eldest son. The Prince had yet to speak to the Queen about the matter, and his subsequent annoyance at Beatrice's prattle may have coloured Lady Macclesfield's recollection of his youngest sister. Incidents of this sort would later proliferate, Beatrice usually cast in the role of hapless bearer of bad news from sovereign to estranged heir. The long-term result, predictably, was a remote, unsatisfactory relationship between the Queen's eldest son and youngest daughter.

'I had such a funny thought today, just for my own amusement,' Beatrice confided to Lady Augusta Bruce shortly after the death of the Prince Consort, 'but it turned out an improper thought so I would not let it think.' 'No doubt', wrote Lady Augusta, 'the poor child was going to play or some such diversion which didn't suit a house in mourning.'¹⁰ At the outset of the Queen's protracted bereavement, Beatrice understood no more than the inappropriateness of herself feeling happy while her mother suffered. Too young to grapple with complex adult emotions, she trained herself simply in denial. If there is pathos in her statement, it was lost on the Queen. Beatrice expressed herself straightforwardly to Lady Augusta, whom she had known all her life and regarded as a friend, an artless confidence bestowed by a bewildered child on an alternative mother figure. As time passed, the bright, ebullient child of the Prince Consort's final years would be revealed in such passing snapshots only to her family and a small group of old familiars with increasing infrequency.

It is easy for the biographer to enmire in black crêpe those years of Beatrice's childhood following the Prince Consort's death. To do so is to illuminate only half the picture. Aged four and a half at the time of her father's death, after the initial surprise Beatrice would not ordinarily have missed him unduly; her nurse Mrs Thurston noted that she hardly mentioned him. She was a robust, high-spirited, tomboyish child. During the awful summer of 1862 she shut her governess into Prince Arthur's fort at the Swiss Cottage and roared with laughter as that enterprising instructress pretended to be a dog in a kennel and barked at her royal charge. To Augusta Bruce, Beatrice wrote, 'I have a broose on the side of my nee ... What fun to tumble on the floor did you mind it.'[11] Like her brothers and sisters before her, Beatrice had begun to learn to ride as a tiny tot, taking her first lesson on her second birthday at Osborne. At Balmoral the Queen and Princess Alice rode out with her, moderating their speed to the sedate amble of her pony Tommy. Her father's death did not put an end to her riding (in April 1865 Landseer produced a portrait in pastels of Beatrice on her pony), nor to the Queen's. Indeed it was on the pretext of providing herself with a familiar face to act as groom on her rides on her pony Flora that the Queen decided, in consultation with Dr Jenner and Keeper of the Privy Purse Sir Charles Phipps, to bring John Brown to Osborne in October 1864. For Beatrice there was still dancing, too. In June 1863 she wrote to her brother Arthur to thank him for his present of a tortoise: 'It runs very funnily and I like it very much ... Miss Lowe is here and I take dancing lessons twice a day with her.'[12] At Osborne in the summer there was also croquet, which Beatrice had mastered sufficiently by the age of seven to beat the Dean of Westminster. This may have been a victory of tact on the Dean's part rather than skill on Beatrice's, but its verisimilitude would have required at least a degree of competence on the part of the younger player.

Had it not been for the Queen's insistence on what for all her children became an unnatural prolongation of grief, Beatrice would soon have rediscovered the high spirits that came naturally to her. She was an intellectually curious child.

> The history of Lot and his wife was read to her yesterday and she was much taken up about the fate of the 'poor lady'. Today, when she was having her dinner at the Queen's luncheon table, and some salt on her plate – she exclaimed, perhaps this is a bit of Lot's wife – the little princess entered into a long discussion as to the kind of salt into which Lot's wife was turned – whether it really was like what was in the salt cellars, that the Queen at last said, 'Well, suppose you ask Bertie – he has been at the Dead Sea, you know.'[13]

She was happy, too, amid the rough and tumble of what, with Helena, Louise, Leopold and, intermittently, Arthur, still at home to share her pranks, should have been a rumbustious, laughter-filled childhood.

The Queen, of course, had other thoughts. One result of the attitude towards their father's death that she devised for her children was that, although their lives retained vestiges of the family childhood enjoyed by their oldest siblings, they did so in outward appearance only: in spirit they were quite changed.

'You must treasure her in your hearts as a *Saint* – one who is rare in this World!' the Queen wrote to her granddaughter Victoria of Hesse, on the death of the Queen's daughter, Victoria's mother Princess Alice. 'It is a great *privilege* to be her child, but it is also a great responsibility to become *really worthy* of her – to walk in her footsteps – to be unselfish, truthful, humble-minded – *simple* – and try and do *all* you can for *others* as she did!'[14] Seventeen years earlier, she might easily have rehearsed the same sentiments at daily intervals to those five of her children still under her care. It was too heavy an expectation to impose upon a child, and one that the three most sensitive children,

Louise, Leopold and Beatrice, addressed by withdrawing within themselves. In Beatrice's case, so complete would that withdrawal become that it shaped her personality. Much later, in the company of her husband, she escaped, but she did so in private and for all too short a time.

Faced with scriptural conundra such as the fate and composition of Lot's wife, the little princess asked pertinent questions for which she was rewarded with laughter and answers. But to those larger questions shaping her future her mother saw no need for answers; and the frustration of Beatrice's natural curiosity unsurprisingly engendered over time a lethargy about looking outside herself and beyond what was immediately obvious. 'I have not the moral strength to see you and hear you so constantly unhappy,' Princess Feodora told the Queen in 1864, cutting short her four-month stay with her half-sister.[15] For those children still at home, too young for the most part to comprehend the concept of 'moral strength', such escape would prove impossible. Constant unhappiness was simply a fact of life.

The children were cast upon themselves. They had lost in effect not one parent but two. 'Orphaned' in this way and cut off from other children of their own age, they grew increasingly dependent on one another and, to a lesser extent, the circle of their attendants. The Queen and Prince Consort's tendency had been to divide their large family by age or sex. As the number of their offspring grew, they commissioned from Winterhalter a series of group portraits: Bertie with his nearest brother Alfred, Alfred with his nearest sister Helena, Louise with her younger brothers Arthur and Leopold, and the four eldest princesses together. For the wedding of the Crown Princess, her four sisters, including the eight-month-old Beatrice, each gave her a brooch: the patterns were identical but each was set with different stones – diamonds, rubies, sapphires, emeralds. For Alice's wedding, the unmarried brothers Alfred, Arthur and Leopold joined forces to buy a present of 'three keeprings, diamond, ruby and emerald', while the junior princesses Helena, Louise and Beatrice jointly gave 'a locket and a pair of ear-rings in turquoise and diamonds'.[16] In November 1865 Beatrice addressed birthday wishes to the

Prince of Wales: 'Leopold and I together send you a present which we hope you will like.'[17]

Proximity in age and shared sex may have appealed to the orderliness of a mind like the Prince Consort's, but in truth neither guaranteed affection between the children in question. Beatrice and her nearest sister Louise enjoyed a lifelong troubled relationship while, despite the Queen's best efforts, Beatrice struggled in vain to secure any reciprocation of warm feelings from Leopold. 'Beatrice is quite well and so good ... she is not a "stupid little thing" as you call her,' Helena reproved her youngest brother in May 1862.[18] It was only one of a number of instances of Leopold's irritation at Beatrice, an irritation justified by his mother's declared preference for Beatrice, his nearest sister, and Arthur, his nearest brother. Pig-in-the-middle and missing his father, Leopold did not pause to consider that neither Beatrice nor Arthur was culpable of courting their mother's favouritism. 'I have had tea with Leopold, it was very nice,' Beatrice wrote to Arthur from Windsor on 11 December 1864.[19] Leopold's feelings are not recorded, but it is significant that even into adulthood he continued to refer to Beatrice by their mother's moniker for her, 'Baby', the usage combining contempt with envy at the closeness of mother and daughter and the ease of their relationship, so different from his own relations with the Queen.

Helena's intervention on Beatrice's behalf may have been prompted by an instinct for fair play alone, but third and fifth royal daughters were close both in affection and temperament. Before her marriage, Princess Alice had regarded her last sister with quasi-maternal protectiveness; now, in the short term, Helena looked on Beatrice in a similar light. Beatrice called her sister 'Na'. At the children's dance at Windsor in 1866 for Helena's twentieth birthday, her last before her marriage, it was 'dear little Beatrice ... [who] proposed "dear Na's health and many happy returns of the day, as it is her last birthday at home",'[20] a statement, Louisa Bowater recorded, that was greeted with shrieks of laughter from Louise, Arthur and Leopold, all of whom, unusually for guests at a dance, were then suffering from whooping cough. Beatrice would grow to share Helena's placid disposition and unswerving, partly fearful devotion to the Queen. Though it was Beatrice who throughout her life stayed at her mother's side, Helena, too, remained almost always on call, living close by the Queen's principal residences if not, like Beatrice, in the same building as her mother. 'Our darling little Baby ... is the only thing I feel keeps me alive, for she alone wants me really. She, perhaps as well as poor Lenchen, are the only two who still love me the most of anything,' Queen Victoria wrote to the Crown Princess in April 1863.[21] From early days the sisters' friendship successfully spanned their eleven-year age gap. After Alice's marriage it was Helena who helped the Queen, occupying much of the leisure time that the Queen did not devote to Beatrice. But in 1866 Helena, too, married. Louise became their mother's helper. Beatrice lost another mainstay of her tiny circle, and took a step closer to the role that was to be hers for life.

SIX

'A nervous way of speaking and laughing'

•◆•

The spring of Bertie's wedding, Beatrice met her future father-in-law for the first time. She was six. The Queen had invited to Windsor Prince Alexander of Battenberg, father of four sons and a daughter, the prince of royal Hessian blood, besmirched in the case of his children by Alexander's morganatic marriage to the non-royal Countess Julie von Hauke. By contemporary standards Queen Victoria was open-minded about such nice distinctions of princely rank. A soldier's daughter, she was also fond of fighting men and a handsome face. Alexander was not only strikingly good-looking – a benison he would bequeath to all his sons – he had served with distinction in the Austrian imperial army, notably at the Battle of Solferino. He was the uncle by marriage of the Queen's daughter Alice, who was expecting her first child at Windsor. In due course that child, a girl, would be christened, also in the Queen's house. Alexander's stay at Windsor would include the baptism of Princess Victoria of Hesse, his first great-niece, the Queen's fourth grandchild and Beatrice's second niece.

The Prince, whom the Queen found 'very clever and agreeable',[1] did not feel constrained by that injunction to discretion which, in principal, governed courtiers' correspondence. His letters to his sister Marie record his impressions of the Royal Family:

Bertie ... is exceedingly friendly and cordial to me. The younger sisters, Helena and Louise, are pretty and intelligent, especially the

49

former. The Queen's youngest child, Beatrice, is a dear little girl with flying golden curls down to her waist, but she seems to be thoroughly spoiled by everyone. The boys are nice: Alfred ... is a typical naval officer; Arthur is thirteen and rather shy, so is ten-year-old Leopold; they are strictly brought up.[2]

Until the last of her sisters left home, and Beatrice took on the task of full-time personal assistant to her mother, her lot was one of spoiling within a strict upbringing – at the time of Alexander's visit played out against a backdrop of prevailing mournfulness. With the passage of time that mournfulness less-ened, sunshine began to irradiate the shadows, the merest glimmer at first, waxing gradually, unnoticed as yet by outside observers such as Alexander of Battenberg. It was the misfortune of the Queen's children that all happiness was associated with the Prince Consort; the sting in the tail of every pleasant diversion was its coda of sorrowful reminders irresistible to the Queen. For her younger children, who had not experienced or did not remember the past happinesses to which their mother clung, this train of thought was alien and obscure, though none would have confessed as much.

In October 1865 the royal children staged a play at Osborne. That the play happened at all was indicative of the Queen's changing state of mind. The Queen humoured her children up to a point, watching a rehearsal rather than the performance itself. The entertainment attained noteworthiness in her eyes on account of a decorative recitation by Beatrice and the handsome appear-ance and footlights prowess of her other favourite child, Arthur. In her Journal she recorded,

> To please the children went down to the Council Room to see the rehearsal of a little Play the Boys are acting, 'Box and Cox'. It was a terrible effort, for it reminded me of so many happy performances, dearest Albert sitting near me, directing everything, and correcting the Children, applauding and encouraging them. Before the play, Baby made her appearance as a milkmaid, and recited 'Le Pot au Lait'. Arthur looked wonderful in a wig with black eyebrows, also Leopold. Arthur acted exceedingly well.[3]

The following month Colonel Stodare was invited to Windsor. He presented an evening of 'Magic and Ventriloquism', including 'The Sphinx' ('an entirely new and original illusion') and 'The Instantaneous Growth of Flower Trees'. It was the sort of entertainment that would have been familiar to the Queen's older children, but for Beatrice it represented an enchanted interlude, a previously unglimpsed world of children's party tricks, light-hearted amusement and harmless silliness.

The Queen was still struggling to resist any diminution of her sadness. She continued to rebut all efforts to divert her from her sorrowful and determinedly lonely course. But against her will, her emotions were slowly shifting. From beyond palace and castle walls, ministers and the mass of the people alike clamoured increasingly for her return to public life. Queen Victoria was not the woman to respond positively to demands – throughout her life she refused compliance with those who backed her into a corner. She did not concede the justness of the requests that she show herself in public which multiplied through the mid-1860s. Rather, in her justification of her refusal to satisfy those requests, she acknowledged implicitly their reasonableness as demands from a country to its sovereign, just not, at this juncture, this sovereign, in her own eyes a frail and sorrowing widow prematurely aged by tragedy and overwork. To one of her more sympathetic correspondents, the Prince Consort's future biographer Theodore Martin, she had written as early as 1863, 'It is not the Queen's *sorrow* that keeps her secluded ... it is her *overwhelming work* and her health ... From the hour she gets out of bed till the hour she gets into it again there is work, work, work – letter-boxes, questions, etc, which are dreadfully exhausting – and if she has not comparative rest in the evening she would most likely not be *alive*.'[4] The excuses of overwhelming work and her health would serve the Queen well through the next four decades when confronted with disagreeable requests; the crux of the matter was inclination. At the Prince Consort's death the Queen's inclination had been simply to mourn as she awaited her own demise, which she confidently anticipated following swiftly on its heels. Through the second half of the

1860s she inclined increasingly to a return to the life she had abandoned, though as yet only in the private not the public sphere and only up to a point: she did not, for example, set aside her mourning dress or resume her once eager theatre-going, and anniversaries associated with the Prince remained deeply pious, joyless occasions. Nevertheless, there were positive implications of this period of slow renewal – private theatricals among them – for the children the Queen had required to share her tenebrous incarceration.

In 1867, days after her wedding anniversary, the Queen wrote to the Crown Princess:

> My gratitude for what was, my love and admiration for – and devotion to – adored Papa are as great, and part of myself. But with the easing of that violent grief, those paroxysms of despair and longing and of daily, nightly longing to die which for the first three years never left me, and which were a rendering asunder of heart and body and soul – the power of realizing that married life seems gone.[5]

It had taken more than five years, but the unthinkable had crept up on the Queen: her grief was working out its course; despite her best efforts she felt it less keenly; even her memories of shared enchantment were dimming. In the Royal Household the Prince would continue to be spoken of in hushed tones; the life of the Prince the Queen commissioned from Theodore Martin was, on publication the following decade, a virtual hagiography of excellence; the Queen continued to erect monuments in memory of the man she loved so much more than did his adopted country – but now there was room for other interests and objects. Even Christmas, a celebration invariably marred by its proximity to the anniversary of the Prince's death, was happy that year.

On 27 December fourteen-year-old Leopold (habitually among the most disaffected of the Queen's children) wrote to Alice in Darmstadt, 'We are spending a very merry Christmas here, last night the tree was stripped ... and after the tree had been stripped we played at "Blind man's buff". We are going to act charades next week so we are very busy preparing for them.'[6] 'Homely' and 'Final' were the words chosen for the charades, the former tactful given the store set by the Queen on a full, obedient and uncomplaining participation in the family life of her peripatetic home by all her unmarried children. Three weeks later the children acted in closer accord with their natural tastes, offering 'Banditti' on 21 January. Far from objecting, the Queen mustered commendations even for Leopold's performances.

In 1864 the Queen had relaxed the mourning worn by her maids of honour, those junior ladies-in-waiting whose role was partly ornamental, partly one of assistance and diversion of the monarch. In place of black they were permitted to wear grey, white, purple and mauve. On 26 March, in anticipation of her seventh birthday, Beatrice was photographed sitting on a desk – as if to emphasize her smallness, her 'Baby' stature – wearing a full-skirted dress ornamented at the hem and on the bodice with stripes of black velvet, and with a black ribbon in her long hair. But the dress itself was white. The following year, when the Crown Prince and Princess of Prussia's visit to Windsor coincided with the Crown Princess's birthday, the family celebration took almost the form of birthdays during the Prince Consort's lifetime, with 'a juvenile party and magic lantern at five-thirty – a large dinner and evening party'.[7] Beatrice's own birthdays took on a similar festive atmosphere. Though she had to make do with tea-time children's dances at Windsor rather than the splendid children's balls previously held at night in the Throne Room of Buckingham Palace, she fared better than her brother Leopold. The programme for Leopold's fifteenth birthday in 1868, according to lady-in-waiting Lady Waterpark, included 'some sacred music in St George's Hall before dinner at which the Queen was present'.[8] One advantage of having a dance thrown for her was the necessity of Beatrice practising her dancing in advance, a source of pleasure in itself. As she wrote to Lady Car in 1868, 'Mes leçons de danse commenceront demains; elles m'amusent beaucoup.'[9]

Lady Waterpark was present at Beatrice's birthday dance in 1868. She took with her Charlie Anson, son of Frederick Anson, who lived in a house in the castle cloisters. Charlie Anson was a contemporary of Beatrice's and as such a precious and rare commodity. The Queen did not encourage her children to make friends outside the family and seldom invited children to court. By 1868, although the atmosphere of gloom in which her children had lived hitherto was lessening, their existences remained unusually lonely. By virtue of her position as youngest of the family, her nearest siblings both brothers, her closest sister almost a decade her senior, Beatrice was alone in the schoolroom. With half of her siblings married by her tenth birthday, she was also alone for much of her time outside the schoolroom.

In 1888 the Queen replied to a Miss Low, who wrote to her in the course of researching a book about historic dolls: 'The Queen has no hesitation in saying that she was quite devoted to dolls and played with them till she was fourteen ... None of her children loved them as she did.'[10] The Queen had overlooked that Beatrice played with dolls, and for the same reason as her mother: she became in effect an only child, with only inanimate companions to divert her. This arose not from an oversight on the Queen's part, but was deliberate.

In January 1869 the Queen told the Crown Princess, 'The Grosvenors come tonight till Monday. They bring their eldest girl [Elizabeth Harriet] – that Beatrice may see her – who they say is so lovely.'[11] There would, of course, be no question of Beatrice returning the visit, and whatever she may have thought of the loveliness of her mother's guest, the Queen took care that Beatrice and Elizabeth Grosvenor had little opportunity of becoming close friends. If this seems cruel on the Queen's part, it was indeed so, though possibly at this point her behaviour was subconscious rather than part of a considered plan. Later, with Louise's marriage and removal from court, the Queen would become preoccupied with the thought of losing Beatrice, the last daughter who remained to her. Then all her actions tended to bind Beatrice fast to her side, denying her chances of making friends and expressly prohibiting thoughts of marriage. But even at this early stage, before the Queen had thought of Louise marrying, her course is difficult to excuse. Repeatedly throughout her widowhood she had lamented the lack of a friend of her own age and sex who could in full measure understand and share her suffering. As in all her dealings with the youngest daughter she loved better than any other of her children, she never countenanced the possibility that Beatrice had similar needs, or appeared to consider that a life without friends was a wretched prospect for a girl already denied so many ordinary pleasures by virtue of her position as the Queen's daughter, surrounded almost exclusively by representatives of an older generation.

Seclusion was forced upon Beatrice: the results are easy to imagine. Encountering Beatrice aged ten at Osborne, in the context of an informal visit, Catherine Paget, an Isle of Wight neighbour and friend of Helena's, found her very quiet, with 'rather a nervous way of speaking and laughing'.[12] Despite this, Miss Paget admitted the princess's self-possession. What is remarkable about this assessment of Beatrice's character made at such a young age is that it held good for the remainder of her life, her quiet nervousness the result of her mother's behaviour towards her and the atmosphere in which she grew up, self-possession the corollary of her consciousness of her royal rank.

To seventeen-year-old Victoria of Hesse – that niece whose christening handsome Alexander of Battenberg had attended in 1863 – her grandmother the Queen wrote of the perils of making friends: 'You are right to be civil and friendly to the young girls you may occasionally meet, and to see them sometimes – but *never* make *friendships*; girl friendships and intimacies are very bad and often lead to great mischief – Grandpapa and I never allowed it.'[13] Significantly the Queen added, 'Besides ... you are so many of yourselves that you *want no one* else.' Beatrice was twenty-three by the time this letter was written, the Crown Princess, the Queen's eldest child, forty. Some forty years of motherhood had not altered the Queen's conviction (one perhaps that only an only child can hold) that it is impossible to be lonely within a large family. What the Queen overlooked was that, by the time Beatrice was approaching her teenage years, that large family had shrunk dramatically. With Louise's marriage to the Marquess of Lorne in 1871, of the Queen's nine children only two continued to live at home with her full-time, Beatrice and

Leopold. Even so the Queen did not see this as a problem: 'Beatrice is clever, and most amiable and I am sure in every family a Brother would like to be with his sister,' she wrote to her youngest son, at the same time forbidding him establishing over-friendly relations with members of the Household, equerries and maids of honour.[14] Leopold declined to be coerced and courtiers' diaries record few instances of prince and princess spending time together voluntarily – a game of bezique at Osborne one year, a shared supper alone in Leopold's bedroom the following winter.[15]

Leopold suffered from haemophilia. The illness, with its constant danger of internal bleeding, disqualified him from the boisterousness of much ordinary childish play, necessitating a degree of vigilance and, inevitably, periods in bed suffering, recuperating or resting. But when conditions were right and his mood sanguine, a combination obtained during the Queen's holiday to Switzerland in 1868, Leopold drew pleasure from the company of his youngest sister.

The Queen had taken a *pension* three-quarters of an hour from Lucerne, on a hill overlooking the lake, her purpose to escape the heatwave that held England in its grip. She travelled with Louise, Leopold and Beatrice, Lady Ely, Sir Thomas and Lady Biddulph, Sir William Jenner, Colonel Ponsonby, Leopold's tutor the Reverend Robinson Duckworth, and Beatrice's German governess, Fräulein Bauer. There were expeditions into the countryside, and picnic teas with delicious local blackberry tarts. The Queen was reminded of Scotland. Sadly, the heat that she had journeyed so far to escape had settled over Switzerland, too. With Louise and several attendants, the Queen retreated to a mountain inn, where the conditions were less comfortable but the air more bracing. Beatrice and Leopold remained at the Pension Wallis with Lady Biddulph, Colonel Ponsonby, Duckworth and Fräulein Bauer. Even the presence of their respective educators did not dampen the children's spirits, and the holiday-within-a-holiday became for both Beatrice and Leopold the high point of their Swiss sojourn. On 28 August Ponsonby wrote to his wife, 'Upon the "Cats away the Mice will play" principle, we are going it ... Today we went to Alpnacht and then drove to Lungern, had luncheon in a field and rambled in woods, Leopold and Beatrice quite delighted.'[16]

For the most part, Leopold resented Beatrice's special relationship with their mother. He was also devoted to Louise to the extent that he felt no need for close companionship with his younger sister. During one of his bouts of illness, Beatrice wrote to Louise, 'Mama has gently told dear Leopold that you might perhaps come ... and you ought to have seen his look of delight.'[17] It is characteristic that she stated the fact simply and did not demur from reporting to her absent sister Leopold's compliment. In her tone is no trace of grievance or complaint, only pleasure in Leopold's happy anticipation of Louise's visit. It was not a reaction that Beatrice would ever inspire in her brother.

What brother and sister did share was a love of music. Music would provide one of the chief distractions of Beatrice's lonely second decade, along with her position as aunt of an increasing number of English and Continental nieces and nephews, many of them closer to her in age than her own siblings, and her fondness for animals which, given her circumstances, living in a series of large houses each with an extensive outdoor staff, she was able to indulge fully.

Until her bereavement the Queen had been a regular and enthusiastic visitor to the theatre, the opera and even the circus. She had a particular fondness for the operas of Bellini and saw *Norma*, *I Puritani* and *La Somnambula* twenty times each. The singing lessons she began with Italian bass-baritone Luigi Lablache weeks before her seventeenth birthday continued until her pregnancy with Beatrice in 1856. Then the Prince Consort died, and there was no more music and no more singing. But in 1869, the year in which royal servants were at last permitted to discard the black crêpe armbands they had worn since December 1861, the Queen resumed playing the piano. She did so not because she derived any pleasure from the activity but for Beatrice's and Leopold's sakes. 'I do hear more music than I did some time ago,' she wrote to the Crown Princess in the New Year of 1870, 'and ever since this autumn have played myself again, with Beatrice and Leopold – to please them as they read so well at sight and are very fond of it. I am as fond as ever of it when I hear it, but I don't feel any very great enjoyment in listening to it. No that is gone.'[18] Over time, the habit would re-establish itself, and the Queen presumably resolved the apparent contradiction of being fond of hearing music but not enjoying listening to it, since she mentions that, during her stay at Inverlochy Castle near Fort William in September 1873, she 'played with Beatrice on the piano' in the morning and again in the evening of the same day.[19]

Music had been a shared passion for the Queen and Prince Consort; they took it for granted that their children would learn to play the piano and enjoy singing. In both Beatrice's and Leopold's cases, their talent far exceeded the requirements of a polite drawing-room accomplishment. Both read music easily from sight and would progress to master a number of instruments, Leopold playing the piano, flute and harmonium, Beatrice the piano, harmonium and organ. Such was Beatrice's facility at the piano from an early age that her teacher, Mrs Anderson, pre-viously the Queen's music mistress and the same Mrs Anderson to whom Louise in her letter to Arthur had described writing three times a week, suggested to the Queen that Charles Hallé give Beatrice more advanced lessons than she was able to do. Hallé arrived at Osborne in December 1867 and was rapturously received by Helena, Louise, Leopold and ten-year-old Beatrice, who kept him at the piano for an hour and a half, his next day being taken up with playing duets with Helena. Hallé was sufficiently impressed by Beatrice's skills to suggest they play a duet together for the Queen. Master and pupil rehearsed, but when the time came for the recital, Hallé swapped the music and presented Beatrice with an unknown piece. Despite her misgivings, Beatrice acquitted herself so ably that the Queen was unaware of Hallé's ploy.

In time Mrs Anderson made a second recommendation to the Queen about Beatrice's musical education, suggesting that singer and composer Paolo Tosti be invited to train the princess's voice. From Tosti Beatrice may have absorbed her talent for sentimental songs like 'Retrospection', her setting of a poem by Charlotte Elliott published after her marriage in a popular periodical for young women. It is in marked contrast to the earnest sacred works composed by her father, although its tone recalls in part the melancholy lieder Albert had written as a young man, with which Beatrice may have been familiar. Beatrice composed a number of such songs, mostly for her own entertainment, although several were performed in front of a wider audience, including at a party held in August 1892 to celebrate what would prove to be the last birthday of the Queen's old friend and fellow Isle of Wight resident, Alfred, Lord Tennyson.

On 14 August 1874 Lady Waterpark wrote in her diary, 'A young pianist came [to Osborne], accompanied by her mother, to play before Princess Beatrice. We all assembled in the Drawing room to hear her.'[20] As Beatrice grew up, there would be a series of similar 'command' performances, including on her twenty-fourth birthday, 'a young man of sixteen [who] played on the piano in the Evening beautifully ... His name was d'Albert.'[21]

Music provided Beatrice with a common interest with the only sibling who, after 1871, remained at home with her, and an absorbing pastime that offered her both an escape and a means of expression acceptable to the Queen. It is wrong for the post-Freudian biographer and reader to assume that Beatrice's enjoyment of music signals a struggle to find herself. At no point in her life did Beatrice suggest any uncertainty about who or what she was. Her father died when she was four and a half years old, and she became for her mother 'the bright spot in this dead home'. From earliest childhood Beatrice was made aware by the Queen of exactly who she was and what was to be her role in life. Children accept as normal the circumstances that surround them. Although Beatrice may have recognized in later life the extreme degree of her thralldom to her mother (certainly, her daughter Ena was in no doubt about it), no direct betrayal to any third party survives to suggest she considered either the circumstances or the effect of her upbringing peculiar.

Of loneliness Beatrice could not be unaware, but this, too, she accepted as normal. Happily, her fondness for music leavened the solitary hours. It was a fondness that endured lifelong. To commemorate her eightieth birthday in 1937, Beatrice received from the people of the Isle of Wight not a silver bibelot or trinket of jewellery but a Carolean organ of royal provenance in full working order. It was the present she had herself requested when she learnt of the islanders' intention of honouring her. Such was the quality of the piano she owned as an adult – a Steinway Duo-Art Pedal Electric Grand – that, on its removal from Kensington Palace after her death, it entered the collection of the Musical Museum and was used to make archive recordings for the BBC.

SEVEN

'Auntie Beatrice sends you
many loves'

•◆•

On 1 March 1877 Princess Alice wrote to her seventeen-
year-old niece Charlotte of Prussia. Charlotte was newly
engaged and about to be confirmed, an event her aunt would be
unable to attend. Expressing her disappointment at this, Alice
added, 'The Cousins – who being at lessons send you their love –
are so sorry that they know their Prussian Cousins so little – it
has been unfortunate that of late years you have been able to see
so little of each other.'[1]

Alice's letter encompasses important preoccupations of the
women of Queen Victoria's family: confirmation (usually taken
to indicate that a daughter had reached adulthood and might
henceforth be considered marriageable – in Charlotte's case she
had jumped the gun somewhat, hence the hasty concertinaing of
events); engagement (invariably the ultimate aim of mother,
daughter or the Queen, and in some cases all three); and the ties
of extended blood relationships. The Queen found it impossible
to interest herself in every new grandchild. To the Crown
Princess she described unsympathetically the birth of her seventh
granddaughter Princess Maud of Wales as 'very uninteresting ...
it seems to me to go on like the rabbits in Windsor Park!'[2] But
her interest would increase as Maud neared an age to be married,
and the Queen would never forget that Maud was her granddaughter and that she ought regularly to see her and be permitted,
if necessary, to meddle in her upbringing and her future.

As with so much of Beatrice's life, even these three cornerstones
of royal existence could not be taken for granted. She was from
birth part of a large family; there would be no question but that
she would follow her brothers and sisters and be confirmed into

the Church of which her mother was, in private, a vociferous head. But long before Beatrice's confirmation the Queen's determination crystallized that the event would not in the case of the last princess signify any readiness for marriage. The Queen had decided there would be no marriage. In order to be doubly certain, there would not even be any talk of marriage.

Queen Victoria was an only child; the Prince Consort had a single dissolute brother with no legitimate offspring; Beatrice and her siblings had no first cousins. What Beatrice soon acquired instead was numerous nephews and nieces – including Charlotte of Prussia, who was only three years her junior.

Beatrice could never remember a time when she had not been an aunt. She was twenty-one months old at the birth of the first of her siblings' children, William of Prussia, and full of condescension when, the following year, she met William and his tiny sister Charlotte. The meeting was taken up with a tussle for position characteristic of the future Kaiser. As Lady Augusta Bruce described it: 'Princess Beatrice very patronizing to "nephew and niece" and bearing his roughness with equanimity and wonderful goodness.'[3] William refused to call Beatrice aunt, preferring to taunt her with her parents' name for her, 'Baby'. Beatrice held her ground and, with a bad grace, William compromised on 'Aunt Baby'. For Charlotte, the Prince Consort had recommended Beatrice as a role model, amused by his daughter's precocious self-importance as she announced, aged three, that she must write letters to her niece. But Charlotte and Beatrice were never close, and Beatrice had the indignity, far from being a role model for her niece, of following rather than leading. This applied to small things as well as matters of consequence: in 1862 it was Charlotte's full-length portrait by Lauchert that inspired the Queen's commission of a similar portrait of Beatrice the following year; Charlotte became engaged to Prince Bernard of Saxe-Meiningen, a step-grandson of the Queen's half-sister Feodora, when she was only sixteen – Beatrice had to wait another eight years until, aged twenty-seven, she too was able to marry for love, an alliance that would be scoffed at by the 'foolish, frivolous little Princess' her niece.[4] Happily, Beatrice fared better with the Crown Princess's third child, Henry, who visited Osborne in 1867. Snow lay thickly on the slopes and terraces surrounding the Queen's seaside home, and even the Queen enjoyed long drives by sledge with Arthur, Louise and Lady Waterpark, sledging temporarily the only way of getting about. Beatrice joined in the fun, and five-year-old Henry's good graces earned him a commendation from his grandmother. 'Dear little Henry is very well and a great darling and everyone admires him,' wrote the Queen to her daughter.[5] Even the charmless William occasionally had his uses for his aunt: his fourth birthday, in 1863, was the first occasion on which Beatrice joined her mother for grown-up dinner; William's health was drunk, 'sweet Baby staying up on purpose'.[6]

Just as Queen Victoria had embraced her position as '*mamma d'une nombreuse famille*', so in time she came to relish her role as 'grandmama of Europe'. Her house filled with paintings, photographs and sculptures of her far-flung descendants, to many of whom she addressed a regular and more than perfunctory correspondence. She was particularly punctilious about birthdays. In later years it was Beatrice who would coordinate this cumbersome communications network, assisted in her task by her consciousness of herself as part of the Queen's sprawling inkblot of a family. This consciousness was not shared by her older siblings, for whom those nephews and nieces, who were all but Beatrice's contemporaries, were simply so many children of their brothers' and sisters' marriages, seldom seen and of passing interest. They had not, as Beatrice had, shared holidays with those children, whose visits to the Queen began in the 1860s and increased over the next three decades. Ever at their grandmother's side to welcome them were their uncle Leopold and their aunt Beatrice. Afterwards, in the Queen's letters to her departed visitors, Leopold and Beatrice continued to supplicate for their attention: 'I send you a photograph of Aunt Beatrice';[7] 'How very unfortunate your Uncle Leopold having hurt his leg!';[8] 'Auntie Beatrice sends you many loves';[9] 'Your Uncle Leopold was imprudent and overdid it fishing and had both legs bad! Why will he not listen? Auntie sends many loves.[10]' In due course, the visitors sent photographs – of themselves, their husbands and wives, eventually their children. These photographs and the extended dramatis personae they represented came to form part of the backdrop to Beatrice's world. At the Queen's death her houses and most of their contents became Bertie's property. His defiantly new broom swept away such debris of the past, and back to the sitters went the images sent in love and duty. It was an action that would have been inconceivable on Beatrice's part, but by then Bertie's life had been distinct from that of the Queen for almost forty years, from the time of his marriage: the relations who comprised Beatrice's extended 'cousinhood' were to her elder brother often only names and faces. Bertie had been painted by Winterhalter as a child and again on his marriage. Winterhalter painted Beatrice as a baby, but the picture the Queen particularly craved from him was never begun: 'of myself with Beatrice and perhaps a grandchild'.[11] That picture would have expressed tangibly the dislocation of Beatrice's position: a daughter of a granddaughter's age, an aunt more akin to a sister.

Growing up, Beatrice existed in a limbo-like middle ground, one foot in one camp, one in another, belonging wholly to neither. Her place at the crossroads of two generations augmented the isolation that was the inevitable result of her mother's special treatment of her. The Queen further muddied the water by referring to Beatrice as 'really almost as much like a sister as a daughter'.[12]

The Hessian children whose remote relationship with their Prussian cousins Alice had lamented to her niece Charlotte were on better terms with their Wales cousins and their aunt Beatrice. Victoria of Hesse's memoirs include this account of childish romps at Windsor Castle in the period following Bertie's recovery from typhoid in the winter of 1871:

We were not old enough to understand the anxiety Grandmama was going through when her son was at death's door, and were a very merry party of children. Our wild romps in the great corridor, in which Aunt Beatrice, a girl of thirteen, joined, were often interrupted by one of the pages bringing a message from the Queen that she would not have so much noise.[13]

In the heat of the moment, Beatrice clearly overcame the uncertainty and rather priggish disapproval of her Wales nieces she had expressed in a letter to Lady Car the previous summer: 'Bertie and Alix's two youngest little girls are here; I am sorry to say that Victoria is rather willful [sic], and very shy, but I hope that in time she will like us better.'[14]

'All our cousins', wrote Beatrice's niece, Helena's younger daughter Marie Louise of Schleswig-Holstein, 'were more like brothers and sisters than mere blood relations.'[15] But the illusion did not hold good when pushed. Due to the overlap of generations, when at last Beatrice married, she became sister-in-law to one of her nieces. She suggested to that niece that from now on she call her sister rather than aunt. The niece demurred, unable at that point to break long habit. Beatrice, after all, had sisters of her own. But they were not her contemporaries, and the absence of a sister close to her in age, any cousin, or a niece to live with her contributed to her loneliness and the shyness that, after Helena's marriage in 1866 and the shrinking of the Queen's family at home, gradually replaced the ebullience of the Prince Consort's golden-haired baby.

Public sympathy with Queen Victoria's mourning was of finite elasticity. By the end of the 1860s that elasticity had reached breaking point; it took the near death of the heir to the throne from typhoid fever in December 1871 to rally once again public sympathy behind the Queen, who appeared to have forgotten or to judge of no consequence the visible duties of monarchy. Before that turning point was reached, Bertie, along with several of his siblings and the Queen's ministers, had tried to point his mother towards a proper understanding of what was expected of her: 'If you sometimes came to London from Windsor, and then drove for an hour in the Park ... the people would be overjoyed ... The more *People* see *the Sovereign* the better it is for the People and the Country.'[16] As so often, the Prince's suggestion fell on deaf ears. The Queen did, however, undertake a brief sojourn in London in March 1869. Her purpose was not the good opinion of either the Prince of Wales or her disaffected people, but to visit the Albert Memorial in Hyde Park. Afterwards she drove through the park in a carriage with Beatrice and a lady-in-waiting. Beatrice, at nearly twelve, did not question the purpose of her mother's outing and was in no position – herself still a child – to formulate judgements on her mother's conduct of her royal role. She was accustomed to maudlin excursions. She understood her mother's predilections and the hegemony the Prince Consort's shade continued to exercise over his family. She had received anyway a sweetener the previous morning in the form of a trip with her mother to the Zoological Gardens.

A fondness for animals was among the shared tastes of mother and daughter. For the Queen, animals, notably Dash, the King Charles spaniel who brightened her teenage years, and the Duchess of Kent's parakeet and tame canary, had supplied the want of companionship that was such a feature of her solitary childhood. Four decades later, when the Queen refused to resolve the conflict of public and private duty, not acknowledging that any conflict existed, animals were the subjects whose affection never wavered, the children whose allegiance did not falter. For the Queen, Dash was only the beginning of a lifelong passion for dogs that she indulged in numbers of collies (associated in her mind with Scotland), dachshunds (invariably given German names, such as Däckel and Waldman) and, at the end of her life, Pomeranians. The Queen discovered animal painter Charles Burton Barber in the 1870s and commissioned from him a series of canine portraits to record these many friends, including a picture of herself and Beatrice with three collies and a dachshund on the slopes at Windsor. A pleasantly second-rate practitioner, Burton Barber enjoyed royal patronage until his death in 1894: in 1877 he painted Beatrice's collie Watts; the following decade he painted Spot for her; and in 1891 he painted her favourite collie, Oswald. The Prince Consort kept a finch in his dressing room; Beatrice grew up to love caged birds, a taste she in turn would pass on to her own children, whom the *Daily Mail* later reported travelling between the Queen's homes with their bird-cages in tow.

Animals returned affection unquestioningly; their wordlessness made them ideal companions for the adventurous role play of a lonely daydreamer. Beatrice kept cats as well as dogs and suffered the misfortune of having one of her cats shot by a keeper in Windsor Park. This could not have happened to a cat belonging to her mother, the Queen wrote comfortably to the Crown Princess: the Queen's cats wore collars with her royal monogram, 'and that preserves them'.[17] History does not relate what happened to the birthday tortoise for which Beatrice had thanked her brother Arthur in 1863; hopefully its heavy shell offered protection from the zeal of the Queen's keepers.

Animals provided Beatrice with an outlet for her abundant energy as a growing child. Only gradually did she adapt herself fully to the somnambulant pace of her mother's widowhood. In 1869, while Louise sketched with the Queen on the banks of Loch Ard in view of Ben Lomond, 'Beatrice [ran] about merrily with Jane Churchill'.[18] She needed exercise and activity, and this animals, particularly horses, supplied. Tommy, the solid Shetland pony of Beatrice's earliest rides, was quickly outgrown. He remained at Windsor and was later given to Beatrice's niece Victoria of Hesse, who renamed him Dread after the character in Harriet Beecher Stowe's *Uncle Tom's Cabin*. Tommy was succeeded by Beatrice, named after her owner, the correspondence of name of rider and mount no doubt simplifying the life of the royal grooms. Riding played the largest part in Beatrice's life at Balmoral, where the Royal Family spent as much time as possible outside, the Queen determinedly fostering the illusion that she was not a working monarch but a laird's widow deeply attached to the country and the people surrounding her house. Sometimes Beatrice rode while the Queen travelled by carriage; on other occasions, as before the Prince Consort's death, the Queen accompanied Beatrice on horseback. Often they took with them a dog, which added to the bustle and enjoyment of the excursion. At Balmoral the collie could be sure of encountering others of the same breed at the cottages the Queen and Beatrice visited with blankets and baskets of food, or to witness a christening or the laying out of a dead baby.

In his sitting room at Osborne, Leopold hung portraits of a dachshund and a Dandie Dinmont. Both were painted by Landseer, who in 1867 also contributed a pen-and-ink sketch of a dog at rest to the Prince's autograph book. In Beatrice's sitting room hung an earlier painting by Thomas Woodward of a chestnut charger bearing the Queen's side saddle. Animals were integral to the life of the Royal Family; they surrounded them in art as well as in the flesh. In the case of the Queen's youngest, lonely children, their role is obvious.

EIGHT

'Youngest daughters have a duty
to widowed mothers'

•◆•

*B*eatrice was nineteen when the Queen wrote, with complacent affection, 'She well deserves being loved, for a dearer, sweeter, more amiable and unselfish child I have never found, and she is the comfort and blessing of my declining years.'[1]

The Queen had never disguised her adoration of her youngest daughter. At fifty-seven she had been, in her own words, 'a woman, no longer young' for five years, and was happy to lean on this prettiest of props. She was, one observer noted, 'very large, ruddy and fat',[2] with a hearty appetite and robust constitution, but fretted continually about her health. Beatrice was taller than her mother, at this stage still slender, with a fine complexion and rich red-gold hair that tumbled over her shoulders. Estrangement from the company of her contemporaries had not lessened her natural girlish instincts: she enjoyed pretty clothes and lace, which she later collected. Over time she had grown up pliant and gentle, no longer the harum-scarum tomboy of her childhood: pliancy, gentleness and an overriding equability made her the Queen's ideal companion, and would earn her much praise in her mother's correspondence.

Beatrice's curious childhood had effectively ended three weeks short of her fourteenth birthday. It ended with a marriage, not her own – for that she still had many years to wait – but that of her sister Louise to the Marquess of Lorne, heir to the Duke of Argyll, on 21 March 1871. The Queen used the ceremony to indicate that she had taken a further Lilliputian step towards overcoming her misery of 1861: with her coal-black, jet-sparkling dress she wore not only her customary diamonds but rubies, an unprecedented splash of bright colour. Beatrice wore a dress of rich rose pink that brought out the burnished highlights of her hair. With hindsight it ought not to have been a day of celebration for Beatrice: Louise's marriage and departure from court – though she continued intermittently to assist her mother – left the Queen with one last daughter to take on the role of informal secretary with which she could not dispense and without which the onerous burden of sovereignty became insupportable. That daughter was Beatrice, and in the matter of securing her compliance, the Queen – rubies and epistolary blandishments notwithstanding – was resolved to brook no gainsaying. 'Youngest daughters', she wrote to the Crown Princess, 'have a duty to widowed mothers.'[3] Eight days after Louise's wedding, accompanied by six of her children, the Queen opened the Royal Albert Hall. On this occasion Beatrice wore not pink but a shade the newspapers described as 'the fashionable green', a foil for her mother's impenetrable black. It was the nearest thing to independence she would be permitted.

The Queen's anxiety was understandable. Alice, Helena and Louise had each in turn taken on the duties that now fell to Beatrice. Even Louise, the Queen's least sympathetic daughter and initially her least promising helpmeet, long before her departure had become '(and who would some years ago have thought it?) a clever, dear girl',[4] whose passing her mother regretted. But each daughter had longed for marriage, and with marriage each had left her mother. Louise, by marrying one of the Queen's subjects, remained in Britain. Helena, too, on account of having married a princeling without a throne, Christian of Schleswig-Holstein, stayed close to her mother's side, her first married home being Frogmore in Windsor Great Park. But Helena and Christian produced four children in five years, and the obligations of their growing family completed Helena's temporary withdrawal from her mother's service. Alice lived in Germany. With the accession of her husband to the Grand Duchy, she would be known as the *Landesmutter* ('mother of the country'); she could not, under such circumstances, also take on the role of playing mother to her own mother across the sea. Beatrice was the Queen's last chance, 'the only one who needs me now',[5] as she spun it to herself. The reality was quite the opposite, and the Queen formulated her plans without reference to Beatrice herself. Beatrice's role was acquiescence. There must be no thoughts of independence or escape.

That escape meant marriage was a synonym Louise had recognized only too clearly. Marriage was a daughter's passport to an independent establishment. More significantly for the Queen, it represented inevitably divided loyalties and the down-grading of the Queen from her daughter's first priority to her second (after her husband) and, with the arrival of children, third, fourth and so on. In late 1872 Lady Augusta Bruce, now herself married and no longer in attendance at court, visited the Queen at Windsor. She found her 'in despair over the fact that her daughters were married and filled with their own interests, from which she was excluded. The Queen's one comfort was Princess Beatrice, "and I'll take care that She never marries ... She is quite happy at home and contented and sweet tempered ... and without jealousy".'[6] In reply Lady Augusta suggested that Beatrice 'had no one to be jealous of'.[7] Whether or not she intended this as a compliment to her erstwhile royal mistress, her statement points to the bleakness of Beatrice's position. Beatrice enjoyed the questionable blessing of her mother's wholehearted preference and this was the single boon of her extraordinary existence. She had seen so little of life. Her perception of her siblings' marriages had been distorted by the Queen's funereal response to each happy event. Beatrice could not know that life held greater rewards than to serve her mother as handmaiden. The challenge the Queen set herself was to prolong access to this knowledge for as long as possible.

That the Queen should have experienced anxiety about Beatrice's loyalty as early as 1872 amounts to nothing less than paranoia. Beatrice, she knew, was 'amiable and unselfish', words that on the Queen's lips denoted total concurrence with her wishes and her assertions, and a willingness on Beatrice's part to put everything relating to the Queen before her own concerns – the very course towards which Beatrice's life had tended since before her fifth birthday. Beatrice harboured no secret desire to escape her mother. She was still a child, after all. Her mother was all she had. She had no friends outside court and would not have conceived of leaving her mother to live with one of her siblings, even had she enjoyed so intimate a relationship with them, which she did not. Her brother Arthur, she had seen, lived semi-independently of the Queen, in the nominal charge of his tutor, or 'governor', Major Elphinstone. But this was not a daughter's role. Daughters behaved as Alice, Helena and Louise had behaved, and remained at home to help their mother for as long as they could. While the Queen connived to find ways of preventing Beatrice from leaving her, Beatrice accepted as inevitable the position she now occupied. It was part of the natural order of her mother's (very unnatural) family. In this sense, the Queen's assessment of her last daughter's character is entirely correct: Beatrice *was* unselfish, because she understood that she was a cipher in an equation in which, except on the Queen's part, there could be no 'self'. She was still too young to think of marriage; she had never experienced or perhaps even conceived of independence; she had no home except with the Queen. Any role the Queen allotted her became simply the modus vivendi of Beatrice's home.

The summer before Louise's wedding, Beatrice had written to Lady Car, 'As it is not my turn to go out with Mama, I will take the opportunity of writing to you.'[8] Louise was still her mother's helpmeet, but Beatrice knew already that the opportunity of writing to her governess existed only because it was *not* her turn to dance attendance on her mother. She had begun her training early.

The Queen was quick to censure an 'unamiable' nature, less quick to commend its reverse. She made an exception in Beatrice's case, but even with Beatrice could not bring herself to believe that an amiable nature alone would guarantee her submission in the long term. And so by failing to trust, the Queen placed herself at an impasse of her own making, a situation full of the contradictions at which she excelled. She required a grown-up daughter at her constant beck and call, but could only be certain of that daughter's acquiescence by forbidding her the sort of grown-up thoughts that she had seen led inexorably towards marriage. Without a degree of intellectual and emotional maturity, no one could adequately take on the task of the Queen's extensive correspondence or successfully act as go-between from monarch to minister, matriarch to child, but the intellectually mature had a habit of independent thought that was anathema to the Queen. Five years earlier it had accounted for her reservations over the suitability of Louise as Helena's successor: 'She is not very discreet, and is very apt to take things always in a different light to me.'[9] Beatrice, the Queen must have known, was not Louise: for a decade the Queen had schooled her to entertain no thoughts but her own. Still the Queen worried. She had a single solution: her 'Baby' must remain her baby, unspoilt by worldly or romantic thoughts, preserved in unnaturally prolonged childishness as she had grown up in an environment of unnaturally prolonged grief.

The atmosphere at court, in which sober, decorous amusements were the order of the day, assisted the Queen in her plan. As early as 1865 she had forbidden her daughters to read novels. She preferred instead poems 'in all shapes'[10] on account of their more elegant, less perfervid expressions of emotion than those found in contemporary fiction. But poems, too, were subject to censorship, even Tennyson causing the Queen concern on occasion. On reading his 'Queen Mary' – 'I am not so set on wedlock as to choose / But where I list, nor yet so amorous / That I needs must be husbanded' – the Queen admired it 'immensely excepting the coarseness which ought to have been omitted ... Beatrice read it (with all those parts omitted) ...'[11] Beatrice was eighteen at the time. Predictably, with the human instinct for hankering after forbidden fruit, she would later claim she could not bear poetry, preferring prose.[12] In 1868 the Queen had published *Leaves from the Journal of Our Life in the Highlands*. In its first year, the book sold 103,000 copies in a cheap edition published at 2s. 6d,[13] and the Queen henceforth considered herself an author, her Highland home not merely a peaceful retreat but the inspiration for a *littérateuse*. 'Rather amusing,' wrote Mary Ponsonby, 'the literary line the Queen has taken up since her book was published.'[14] The Queen had begun to paint again, she knitted and crocheted. 'I am so fond of painted flowers,' she wrote to the Crown Princess in January 1871, 'and have taken to do [sic] them myself which I don't think I told you – and really I was surprised at my own comparative success. I will try to do some for you ... Do tell this to dear Fritz. I have just croche'd him a comforter which it gave me much pleasure to do, and I sent it to him today and hope he may use it.'[15] In years to come conflict in the Near East would see the Queen's ladies, under Beatrice's management, involved in a flurry of bandage-making, the sort of parlour relief work the Queen considered a suitable feminine contribution to the male arena of war. Added to music, riding, skating in the winter, yachting excursions at Osborne in the summer and a constant stream of visiting relatives, along with lessons, which continued until she was sixteen, and her work for the Queen, this left Beatrice limited time in which to entertain the thoughts so worrying to her mother. As Beatrice wrote to Disraeli early in 1881, thanking him for his gift of his latest novel *Endymion*, 'I have had so much writing to do lately, that I am sorry I could not read the book as steadily as I should have liked, but I can assure you that it has not rendered it the less interesting ...'[16] Objects of interest were in short supply and the only potential fly in the ointment as far as the Queen was concerned was whether Beatrice could adapt herself to the stultifying boredom. 'I must say I pity you as it must be very dull there,' Bertie had written to Louise about the long New Year's stay at Osborne in 1869.[17] Louise had hungered for the world outside her mother's walls and even, in 1868, successfully persuaded the Queen to allow her to enrol in sculpture classes at the National Art Training School in South Kensington. Bertie did not write in similar vein to his youngest sister. Unlike Louise, Beatrice knew nothing else and looked no further.

Beatrice's initiation into her duties towards her mother took the form of a baptism by fire. The summer of 1871 was the most difficult of the Queen's reign, characterized by family squabbles and demands from her ministers, chief among them the Prime

Minister, Gladstone, to which she was at first reluctant and ultimately physically unable to accede. The problem that exercised the Queen's children and her government was the same: the rising tide of republican feeling in the country, fuelled by the Queen's continuing withdrawal from public life and her apparent dereliction of her duty.

The Crown Princess was at Osborne for the summer, with her husband and four of her children. She discussed the problem separately with Gladstone and her siblings, and in August wrote a letter to her mother. 'We have each of us individually wished to say this to you ... but we refrained for fear of offending ... Had not the conviction come upon *us all* (moving as we do in different circles), with an alarming force, that some danger is in the air, that something must be done ... to avert a frightful calamity.'[18] Not only the Crown Princess but all the Queen's children and even their spouses signed the explosive missive. All except Beatrice. She had been the Queen's lone helper for five months; already in her siblings' minds she was too close to their mother to be involved in something that challenged her so directly. Perhaps the Crown Princess was reluctant to place Beatrice in an awkward and untenable position, or thought her still too young for something approaching a palace coup; perhaps Beatrice was invited to sign the letter and refused. Whatever the reason, the result was the same, with Beatrice singled out for special isolation within the family, an isolation she shared only with the Queen. It was an important and potentially damaging precedent.

The Crown Princess's letter was never sent. By the middle of August the Queen complained of feeling unwell and excused herself from family meals. Children, ministers and journalists united in choosing not to believe her. Her unwellness did not prevent her departure for Balmoral, as planned, on 17 August, Beatrice and Leopold at her side. Swiftly, however, it became clear that the Queen really was unwell. On 22 August she wrote, 'Never since I was a girl, when I had typhoid fever at Ramsgate in '35, have I felt so ill.'[19] The Queen had a throat infection, which was followed by an abscess on her arm. On 4 September

Joseph Lister lanced the abscess, having been specially summoned from Edinburgh for the purpose. In its wake came a severe attack of gout and rheumatoid arthritis. At the beginning of September the Queen was unable to walk, her only exercise being pushed around the castle garden in a chair, Beatrice walking beside her. Her arm was so painful that throughout much of August, September and October she dictated her Journal to Beatrice, a foreshadowing of things to come when, towards the end of the Queen's life, Beatrice acted as her full-time amanuensis, not only writing but also reading for her mother. Unable to move even across her sitting room, and too heavy to be lifted by Beatrice, her maids or dressers, the Queen was carried up and down stairs and even lifted into bed by John Brown.

Unsurprisingly the Queen's physical sufferings affected her state of mind. Her irritability of the beginning of the summer gave way to serious depression. It was not an enjoyable atmosphere for a girl of fourteen. Beatrice welcomed the arrival at Balmoral of Alice and her children. Two months earlier Alice had given birth to her sixth and penultimate child, named after the Queen's daughters Alix Victoria Helena Louisa Beatrice, but she slipped uncomplaining once more into her role of nurse. Alice's attendance on her mother was even more exacting than Beatrice's, since the latter continued to be sent to bed early and did not, as a matter of course, spend evenings with the Queen, part of a deliberate policy the Queen confided to the Crown Princess on Beatrice's sixteenth birthday to 'keep her as young and child-like as I can'.[20] To her mother-in-law, Princess Charles of Hesse, Alice described what she found awaiting her at Balmoral:

> Mama was weak and unwell when I arrived, as she was getting over two serious illnesses – a very bad throat infection, and then the abscess ... on her arm which had to be operated on. Four days after our arrival, a third illness appeared, by far the most painful – rheumatoid arthritis ... and she was confined to the sofa and could not move at all without help ... I often sat with her ... I play to her every evening, either alone or with Leopold.[21]

Though Alice's ministrations soothed the Queen, her recovery was slow. In the second half of October she was still confiding to her Journal, 'A most dreadful night of agonizing pain. No sedative did any good ... Had my feet and hands bandaged. My utter helplessness is a bitter trial, not even being able to feed myself ... Dictated my Journal to Beatrice which I have done most days lately ... Was unable all day hardly to eat anything.'[22] The Queen chafed in equal measure at her forced inertia and the indignity of her condition: 'I can't help thinking that anyone, even inactive, would not like ... to be fed like a baby which lasted three days and a half – the food being put into your mouth, your nose blown and everything done for you.'[23] She did not appear in public until 5 November, when she attended a kirk service; even then she required John Brown's help to negotiate the steps into the building.

During Alice's stay Beatrice had enjoyed, in the company of her Hesse nieces, a reprieve from the unremitting dourness of this first summer with no sisters at home to divert her. It was to be all too brief. Quite by chance she and her mother had again fallen into that reversal of roles they played out in the tear-stained mornings after the Prince Consort's death, the Queen reduced by illness to infantilism, Beatrice watching and comforting, walking at the side of her mother's wheelchair, writing her diary. Again Beatrice's position was one that contained no element of choice; again her role was to react rather than anticipate or initiate. If in later life she was criticized for indecision or, as one maid of honour would have it, lack of imagination, it is easy to see how that suppression of her own instincts came about. No loving daughter could have responded any differently to a mother so afflicted. Only on 22 November was the Queen able to record in her Journal, 'Breakfasted for the first time again with my children, and felt it was a step forward and I was returning to ordinary life.'[24]

But if the Queen and Beatrice imagined their difficulties at an end, they had one further grim surprise in store. The very same day, the Queen 'heard dear Bertie had "mild typhoid fever" ... Felt very anxious.'[25] A week later, reports of the Prince's condition were sufficiently alarming for the Queen to set off for Sandringham, the Waleses' country house in Norfolk. By 8 December, 'It was decided to send for Leopold and Beatrice, as the danger seemed so great.'[26] Beatrice had been too young for her father's typhoid deathbed, but she was not too young to witness the similar demise of her eldest brother. Such was the pressure of space at Sandringham, on which the Royal Family had descended in numbers, not only Bertie's siblings but such peripheral relations as the Queen's cousin the Duke of Cambridge, that Beatrice had to share a bed with Louise. But despite the overcrowding and atmosphere of despondency, the Queen organized her days much as she would in her own home, overruling the Princess of Wales on all domestic matters and dining alone with her two youngest children, an arrangement that further taxed the house's already overstretched staff.

Matters reached a head on 13 December, and it seemed certain that the Prince would die – if not then, the following day, the tenth anniversary of the Prince Consort's death. Almost miraculously, at the eleventh hour the Prince's condition took a turn for the better. Like that of the Queen, his recovery was slow, and the Queen decided to alter her Christmas plans, remaining at Windsor rather than removing to Osborne. There the Christmas festivities hardly merited the name. 'This was the first Christmas the Queen had spent at Windsor since the death of the Prince Consort,' Lady Waterpark recorded in her diary on Christmas Day, 'but she would not go to Osborne on account of the Prince of Wales's illness. He continued so ill, there were no Trees as usual or Christmas festivities. Our presents were sent to us in our rooms.'[27] Even to so amiable and unselfish a child as Beatrice it must have seemed a long year.

The idea for a public service of thanksgiving for the Prince's near escape probably originated with the Prince himself; it was enthusiastically taken up by members of his family, Gladstone and the government – all, in fact, except the Queen, who disliked the sort of spectacle proposed above all and behaved with singular obstructiveness throughout the two-month-long planning period. She successfully insisted, against all precedents, that the occasion be a semi-state affair, allowing her to wear ordinary morning clothes and travel in an ordinary carriage without the accompaniment of bands and massed soldiery. She was also adamant that the Prince and Princess of Wales not have a carriage of their own, but travel with her – in an open landau shared with their eldest son, eight-year-old Albert Victor and the Queen's youngest daughter Beatrice, the two children flanking the Prince. On other matters, such as increasing the number of guests invited to the cathedral, she was forced to give way, to the greater success of the occasion, as *The Times* reported when all was finished: 'Those who say the British people do not love shows mistake them sadly.'[28] As it turned out, the Queen enjoyed herself thoroughly, describing 27 February 1872 as 'a day that can never be forgotten!' 'Could think and talk of little else, but today's wonderful demonstration of loyalty and affection, from the very highest to the lowest.'[29] With the Prince's recovery, popular support for republicanism dissipated overnight. 'Thank God for this! Heaven has sent this dispensation to save us,' as the Duke of Cambridge wrote to his mother.[30] At the Queen's side throughout the celebrations was her youngest daughter, looking 'very nice in mauve, trimmed with swan's down' and carrying a swan's-down muff.[31] Afterwards, enjoying the loud cheers of the crowd from the balcony of Buckingham Palace was a family reduced to five: the Queen, Alfred, Arthur, Leopold and Beatrice, or, as the Queen put it in a phrase that betrays the hierarchy of her affections, 'Beatrice and my three sons'.[32] Firmly established beside her mother, with none of her sisters present, the last princess had become, in the eyes of the crowd below, the only princess. For the remainder of her mother's life Beatrice would occupy such a position of prominence in the public imagination, an unusual degree of notability in a family over which the Queen cast an exaggeratedly long shadow.

NINE

'The flower of the flock'

·•·

A combination of guilt and pity inspired the extremely generous confirmation present Beatrice received from her siblings in January 1874. With the exception of the Crown Princess – the richest of her sisters – Beatrice's brothers and sisters joined forces in order to buy her a single significant gift. Leopold coordinated the purchase, writing to his favourite sister Louise on 18 December 1873,

> I must now ask you about a confirmation present for Beatrice; we have all agreed to give one present together, so as to give a handsome one. We have selected a most lovely bracelet, pendant and earrings from Phillips', costing £150 [equivalent to £9000 in 2005] – Bertie and Alix meant to give £49, – Affie and Arthur £25 each, I £15 and Alice and Lenchen each £12, and I was asked to write to you about it. I suppose you are sure to agree to this arrangement but all the same I should like an answer.[1]

Louise did not refuse her contribution of £12.

Robert Phillips of London's Cockspur Street was a fashionable West End jeweller working in the so-called 'archaeological' taste. His customers included Sir Austen Layard, archaeologist and excavator of the Assyrian city of Nineveh, who commissioned from Phillips necklaces made from ancient coins and Assyrian cylinder seals; and Louise's husband the Marquess of Lorne, whose wedding gifts to the princess had included a tiara by Phillips in the form of leaves and buds of bog myrtle, the emblem of the Campbell clan. Beatrice's present was not of course a tiara, a piece of jewellery, as in Louise's case, particularly associated with marriage; but the suite of modish, finely made jewels may have been intended by its donors as a token compensation for their youngest sister's exclusion from that state, as well as an acknowledgement that – her mother's 'Baby' notwithstanding – at almost seventeen, she was indeed an adult. With the diamond necklace and matching long earrings that, in similar designs, had been the Queen's confirmation present to all five of her daughters, and the Duchess of Kent's pearls, which the Queen herself had worn since her mother's death – the last a token of singular esteem on the Queen's part – Beatrice would from now on have a choice of grown-up gew-gaws to wear at the Queen's dinners she had begun attending irregularly at the age of fifteen.

The service took place on 9 January, 'a rainy dull day',[2] at St Mildred's Church, Whippingham, close to Osborne on the Isle of Wight. Rumours of the imminence of Beatrice's confirmation had reached her godmother, the Crown Princess, in Germany as early as March 1872. At that point, with Beatrice not yet fifteen, the suggestion had horrified the Queen, who was determined, for reasons of her own, to put off the event for as long as possible: 'I shall certainly not have [Beatrice] confirmed till after she is sixteen for all of you sisters have come out too early and been made to grow up too soon. I mean to keep her back much more.'[3] In the event, Beatrice was confirmed, like her sisters, at the age of sixteen – though the absence of her eldest sister and the latter's husband meant that the milestone was passed without the customary prop of a single godparent (the Duchess of Kent had died in 1861). Officiating were the Archbishop of Canterbury, the rector of St Mildred's, Canon Prothero, and the Reverend Robinson Duckworth, from 1866 to 1870 Leopold's governor, retained by the Queen as a chaplain to the Household since he was 'so enlightened and so free from the usual prejudices of his profession ... an excellent preacher and good looking besides'.[4] It was Duckworth who had prepared Beatrice for this important rite of passage. The triumvirate of clergymen was familiar to Beatrice, since all had officiated at the most recent royal con- firmation, that of her brother Leopold in 1869, while St Mildred's, which the Queen reported 'very full' on this occasion, had been the Queen's preferred venue for all her children's confirmation services since the death of the Prince Consort. Also present were Lady Car, who wrote an account of the service to the Crown Princess, and Mrs Thurston, Beatrice's child-hood nurse, who had retired from royal service in 1867 to a house near Kensington Palace, where Beatrice continued to visit her.

If Beatrice's siblings, with their munificent present, had hoped to offer her not only some recompense for her lonely servitude at the Queen's side but also recognition of her confirmed adult status, their intent was in direct opposition to the Queen's. The Queen rejoiced that Beatrice, far from seeming grown-up, appeared quite the opposite at her confirmation service. Eighteen years earlier, for her confirmation, the Crown Princess, then Princess Royal, had worn what *The Times* described as a 'rich silk glacé gown, with five flounces pinked, the body richly trimmed with white riband and Mechlin lace'.[5] The effect of Beatrice's much more simple gown and her undressed long hair was very different, but exactly what the Queen wished (just as on that previous occasion she had intended her daughter to appear older than her sixteen years and hence prepared for the daunting political alliance into which the Queen and Prince Albert had hastened her in betrothing her to the future king of Prussia). With questionable tact the Queen wrote to the Crown Princess, 'I never saw anyone look more simple, pure, innocent and sweet than this dear good child did. She looked so very young – and her very plain white silk dress – beautiful complexion and very fine fair hair which she wears quite simply and plainly (and wishes to continue to do) was very suitable.'[6]

Beatrice herself was more ambivalent about her appearance Sending a photograph of herself in her confirmation dress to Lady Car, she expressed the hope that Lady Car would like the picture, but added quickly, 'Photographs taken in a room are never very good.'[7] As for wishing to continue wearing her hair 'quite simply and plainly', in the portrait of Beatrice Henry Richard Graves painted for the Queen in the first quarter of 1874, she wears her hair up, decorated with flowers, with soft ringlets falling on to the back of her neck and one shoulder. Also in this very pretty, defiantly grown-up picture, Beatrice wears pinned to the fichu of her low-cut gown the Royal Order of Victoria and Albert. The jewelled order, alongside an 'Indian shawl', had completed the Queen's confirmation presents to her daughter. Taken as a whole, they comprised a consolation prize to Beatrice for not being allowed to attend the wedding, in St Petersburg, of her second brother Affie to the Grand Duchess Marie of Russia. An occasion of some splendour, the wedding took place on 23 January and was attended by a number of Beatrice's siblings. (In a long-distance courtesy, the Russians added to Beatrice's new trawl of decorations and marked the occasion of the uniting of the two families by awarding her the Grand Cross of the Order of St Catherine.)

Beatrice wore the Victoria and Albert Order again in her portrait by Heinrich von Angeli, painted the following year to commemorate her eighteenth birthday. In both portraits the jewel serves as a reminder of Beatrice's rank. It also brands her clearly in the viewer's eye her mother's daughter, as a farmer tags his cattle or marks the fleece of his sheep, a symbol of possession as much as an ornament.

Despite the Queen's determination that Beatrice remain for ever childlike, she considered Graves's portrait 'charming'.[8] She instructed that it be shown publicly at the Royal Academy the following summer, her pride in her last daughter's prettiness momentarily outweighing any concern she may have felt that Beatrice was undeniably growing up. As a further token of affection the Queen presented Beatrice with Graves's picture of herself, painted at the same time as Beatrice's own portrait. This 'very nice picture and good likeness'[9] hung in Beatrice's sitting room at Buckingham Palace. Even in moments of repose during her rare trips to London Beatrice would not escape her mother's gaze, for ever fixed in paint.

Graves's portrait encapsulates a typically 'Victorian' contradiction. Its presentation of Beatrice is not one calculated to deter the advances of romantically inclined young men, combining as it does good looks with strong intimations of a sweet and gentle disposition, the very acme of later Victorian feminine

desirability. Nor is it the result of any decision on Beatrice's part
to exploit Graves's talents to signal to the world her accession
to womanhood, a considered defiance of her mother. The Queen
habitually interfered with all the portraits she commissioned. It
is impossible that Beatrice could have sat for Graves without her
mother at some point interesting herself in their sittings. Indeed,
such was the extent of the Queen's interference with Graves's
work, and so badly did Graves respond to it, that the Queen's
private secretary Henry Ponsonby had occasion to write to his
wife, 'Henry Graves ... says he cannot do [the portraits] yet as
his nerves are gone ... I suspect that incessant Royal criticisms
are more than he can bear.'[10] Undertaken after Beatrice's confirmation, the portrait, like that event, might have been expected
to herald Beatrice's entry into society and her availability for
marriage. But the Queen did not wish her daughter to enter any
society save that of her heavily vetted court and that only
sparingly, telling the Crown Princess that she did not intend either
confirmation or Beatrice's seventeenth birthday three months later
to be marked by Beatrice beginning to appear at state parties.
She also meant strenuously to prevent her marriage. Yet she
commissioned from Graves this dewy-eyed coming-of-age portrait
and exhibited the results to the fashionable world at the Royal
Academy.

In the matter of Beatrice's spiritual preparation for her journey
through life the Queen had not been remiss and, in this respect,
she was happy that the service of 9 January marked a new
maturity. During the royal visit to Balmoral the previous autumn
the Queen and her daughter had encountered the new minister
of Crathie kirk, Dr Campbell from Lonmay in Aberdeenshire,
who made a strong impression on both. The Queen described in
her Journal a Sunday visit to Glencoe: 'Rested, wrote, and then
read prayers with Beatrice, and part of Mr Campbell's sermon,
which Beatrice was so pleased with that she copied it entirely.'[11]
Except in the unlikely event of Dr Campbell having inspired a
schoolgirl crush, this is not the typical occupation of a teenage
girl yearning for romance and escape. Beatrice approached religion with a degree of seriousness: it would remain throughout

her life one of her chief comforts and she would later count a number of clergymen among her more intimate correspondents. Maid of honour Marie Mallet, who encountered Beatrice during the 1890s, claimed that she delighted 'in theology and all religious questions. Science is a dead letter,' and found her 'more fitted to be a clergyman's wife than a Princess, except of course in matters of finance'.[12]

Other onlookers than the Queen considered Beatrice's confirmation proof not of her age but her innocence. Such purity of mind and body did her appearance and behaviour suggest to her French governess Mademoiselle Norèle that she was reminded of a lily – as any nineteenth-century Catholic Frenchwoman must have been aware, a symbol of the Virgin Mary. Mademoiselle Norèle gave vent to her feelings in poetry, composing sentimental verses, which the Queen forwarded to Sir Theodore Martin with the comment,

> She did look so like a lily, so very young, so gentle and good. The Queen can only pray that this flower of the flock, which she really is (for the Queen may truly say she has never given the Queen one moment's displeasure) may never leave her, but be the prop, comfort and companion of her widowed mother to her old age. She is the Queen's Benjamin.[13]

Two years later Beatrice was the unwitting cause of the dismissal from Balmoral of a cousin of John Brown's, piper Willie Leys. Drunkenness was the nominal cause of Leys's dismissal; his offence in fact was to have frightened Beatrice, who came across him in this condition. It says much for the success of the Queen's policy of overprotecting her daughter that nineteen-year-old Beatrice's response to a drunken Highlander encountered in a castle corridor should be such as to merit his sacking despite his close kinship with the Queen's favourite servant. Perhaps the roses Beatrice wears in her hair in Graves's portrait were not, after all, an unintentional coquetry, but on the contrary a symbolic reference to her unspoiled virgin purity, a royal rosebud not yet ready to bloom.

*

Though she herself may not have recognized it until later, a single seed of romance had already been sown by the time of Beatrice's 'lily'-like appearance at her confirmation.

The Second Empire of Napoleon III and his Empress Eugénie collapsed on 5 September 1870. Eugénie and her son Louis Napoleon, the Prince Imperial, fled to England, where, on 20 March 1871, they were joined by the defeated Emperor. The British Royal Family was quick to sympathize with the imperial exiles: the Prince of Wales offered Chiswick House as a London residence (an offer which, for political reasons, he was forced to rescind), and the Queen lavished on the Emperor and Empress many 'delicate attentions'.[14] The imperial family settled at Camden Place, near Chislehurst in Kent. When, in February 1872, they made plans to watch, from the Army and Navy Club, the Royal Family's procession to St Paul's for the service of thanksgiving for the Prince of Wales's recovery, an invitation to Buckingham Palace was quickly issued; and the exiled sovereigns watched the procession set off from the vantage point of the main palace balcony on which, afterwards, the Queen would receive the acclamation of the cheering crowds.

Queen and Empress were near contemporaries, but Eugénie did not give birth to her only child until the relatively late age of thirty, with the result that the Prince Imperial was only a year older than Beatrice. Once Queen Victoria had found him 'short and stumpy'[15] – 'The boy is a very nice child but excessively short – shorter than Beatrice who is a year younger than him'[16] – but with the Prince and his parents now near neighbours, and the Prince's attainment of manhood cloaked in a mantle of romantic tragedy, that opinion began to change. In October 1871 the Prince entered the Royal Military Academy at Woolwich as a gentleman cadet. The following year he was invited to a military review at Bushey Park, also attended by the Queen. At the Queen's invitation he spoke to her while she remained in her carriage, he on horseback alongside. When he had finished speaking to the Queen, he rode round to the other side of the carriage to speak to Beatrice, as always since Louise's marriage her mother's companion. Quickly the society journal *The World* seized upon the meeting as proof of an imminent engagement. On 20 May 1874 a Royal Artillery review was held on Woolwich Common, attended by the Prince in the entourage of the guest of honour, Tsar Alexander II. The Prince Imperial was all but mobbed by the crowd, who broke through the police cordon to shake hands with the man they believed destined to be the Queen's last son-in-law. Rumours of his imminent marriage to the Queen's youngest daughter would continue until his untimely death five years later.

At Bushey the Queen had revised her opinion of the Prince's 'short and stumpy' appearance, finding his looks instead 'very nice'. Louis Napoleon, though like his father undeniably short, had inherited much of his mother's legendary beauty, including her downward-slanting eyes, long, straight nose and wide, sensuous mouth. The Cardinal de Bonnechose, a friend of the imperial family, commended his 'gentle, dreamy face, blue, melancholy eyes, and thoughtful, open brow'.[17] To this the Prince added his father's dark colouring and considerable charm, and an aura of exoticism derived from his family's circumstances; the inherited bravura of two generations of imperial adventurers; Eugénie's impetuous Latin blood and her connection, albeit small, with the royal house of Stuart; and his overwhelming self-confidence. The Prince was one of only two people Henry Ponsonby encountered who were not afraid of Queen Victoria; the other was John Brown. Later, Ponsonby might have added to his list Beatrice's husband, Henry of Battenberg, whom, save in height, the Prince strongly resembled. Time would reveal other parallels between the two men linked with Beatrice by fact or rumour.

Napoleon III's death in January 1873 served further to strengthen the bond between Queen Victoria and the Empress Eugénie. One manifestation of their friendship was the interest the Queen took in the Prince Imperial, who was soon established as a favourite at court. Lady Waterpark was in waiting when, on 9 August 1876, the Prince dined at Osborne: 'I thought the Prince Imperial very pleasing with remarkably good manners,' she wrote in her diary.[18] We cannot know if Beatrice, too, at this stage found the Prince 'very pleasing' since she did not entrust feelings of so private a nature to posterity, but it would be surprising if she had been entirely immune to the Prince's charms. He was the first man of her own age whose presence at court the Queen had encouraged, and unlike her brother Leopold, her only other regular young male companion, the Prince appears to have behaved towards Beatrice with consistent affection and good humour. The Queen had certainly come close to having her head turned by Louis Napoleon's father on her state visit to Paris in 1855; the Prince not only shared his father's charisma, but bore a strong facial resemblance to the handsome, dark-haired foreign prince whom Beatrice would eventually marry for love.

In her biography of the Empress Eugénie, written in 1906 when both the Empress and Beatrice were still alive, Jane T. Stoddart wrote: 'On the Prince Imperial's tomb lies a wreath of white immortelles given by Queen Victoria, and a bunch of purple heather recently laid there by Princess Beatrice. It had been gathered on the common by the Princess when she was the guest of the Empress Eugénie.'[19] This action on the part of the widowed, middle-aged Beatrice is not proof positive of a romantic attachment thirty years earlier – as we have seen, she had been brought up from earliest infancy to revere and commemorate the dead, and in later life she had a deep sentimental attachment to those connected with the scenes of her youth – but it is certainly suggestive.

Whatever the nature of Beatrice's and Louis Napoleon's feelings, they were never to be consummated in marriage. In 1879 the Prince Imperial joined British reinforcements sailing for Natal in South Africa to quash a Zulu uprising. His presence in the theatre of war – irksome to the Prime Minister, Disraeli – had been brought about by the combined efforts of the Queen and the Empress. They acted in concord to realise the Prince's strong desire to join the fighting party despite their separate reservations – the Queen acknowledging that the Prince was 'very venturesome' – and those of the British government and military authorities.[20] As events turned out, it was not the Prince's venturesomeness but misfortune and sheer force of numbers on the part of the enemy that brought about his death – on 1 June, on the banks of the Ityatosi River. In company with a small scouting party the Prince was surprised by Zulus. Quickly his commanding officer Captain Carey mounted his horse and rode off, taking with him as many of the party as were able to follow. But the Prince's horse first reared and plunged then bolted, trampling on his right hand. Though he ran after the animal, holding on to the stirrup, the leather tore and the Prince had no choice but to turn and face the enemy alone. In vain he fired three shots with his left hand. The Zulus closed in on him and killed him with their assegais, seventeen fierce wounds horribly mutilating his body.[21] 'He who belongs to a race of soldiers can make himself known to the world only by military exploits,' Louis Napoleon had written to his childhood friend and fellow cadet at Woolwich, Louis Conneau.[22] Happily, Beatrice was not privy to the friends' correspondence. Less than twenty years later the words would have a cruelly prophetic ring.

The Queen's grief was pronounced, and she related its course, as ever, to her Journal. Though she was habitually selfish in her indulgence of sorrow, she took time to mention Beatrice's unhappiness: 'Dear Beatrice, crying very much, as I did too, gave me the telegram ... It was dawning and little sleep did I get ... Beatrice is so distressed; everyone quite stunned.'[23] That these Journal entries survive to indicate Beatrice's affection for the Prince, and were not expunged by Beatrice during her 'editing' of her mother's Journal, can have three explanations: the princess's grief was the same as she would have felt for any young man known to her killed in his prime; her affection for the Prince was so pure that its admission to posterity could involve no shame or scandal; she continued to cherish her feelings for the Prince and his memory, and could not bring herself to destroy all evidence of a former happy attachment.

In support of the last explanation is a further entry in the Queen's Journal – for 18 August 1880.

[The Empress] asked me to keep [a] small packet, which I was only to open after her death, and then said, would I like perhaps to open it and "de l'avoir de mon vivant", which I said I would, and she undid the parcel, and took out a most splendid emerald cross, cut out of one stone, without any joints, and set at the points with fine diamonds, with two magnificent large ones at the top. It had been given her by the King of Spain when she married. When I asked her if she would not still wear it, she answered, "non, non, jamais plus de pareilles choses", that it was one of the few things she had kept and reserved for the future wife of her dear son. Alas! she gives everything away now.[24]

Either the Queen or Princess Beatrice (or both) appears to have overlooked the significance of the Empress's statement that the cross was among the few pieces of jewellery she had kept for her future daughter-in-law. Since the Empress's gift was made fourteen months after her son's death, it is unlikely that the action was wholly unconsidered on her part, arising simply from the excess of her grief. Though it reveals nothing of Beatrice's feelings, it points to a desire on the part of Eugénie – who would remain a lifelong friend of Beatrice's – that her daughter-in-law should have been closely connected to the Queen. The Queen accepted unquestioningly the munificent gift – the cross weighed a staggering forty-five carats – as a tribute paid by one friend to another. She referred to Eugénie as 'dear sister' and the women remained such until the Queen's death. In 1883 the Queen commissioned from her newest portraitist, Carl Rudolph Sohn, a portrait of the Empress, which she hung in her sitting room at Osborne. On her death she bequeathed the picture to Beatrice.

Theo Aronson, in his *Queen Victoria and the Bonapartes*, claimed that on the Empress's death in 1920 at the age of ninety-four, Beatrice wrote to Eugénie's lady-in-waiting requesting the immediate destruction of a number of her letters to Eugénie. He also repeats two rumours: the first, unsubstantiated but also repeated by David Duff, that a photograph of the Prince Imperial stood on Beatrice's desk until her death; and the second, that Beatrice had confided to her eldest son, the Marquess of

Carisbrooke, at the end of her life that she had been in love with the Prince Imperial, a rumour denied by Lord Carisbrooke in his lifetime.

Opportunity and good looks do not inevitably lead to love. That Beatrice should have fallen in love with her future husband at twenty-seven is not proof that at seventeen she conceived similar emotions for a man who resembled him physically. But it is hard to see why the Prince Imperial should not have caused some disturbance in the tranquil heart of a lonely, isolated young woman whose mother's machinations had hitherto excluded from her line of vision any other suitable object for her natural outpourings of affection.

TEN

'A good, handy, thoughtful servant'

·◆·

$\mathcal{T}$ he week before Christmas 1876, the court was at Windsor. The Queen and Beatrice walked to the Prince Consort's Mausoleum to pray before the annual departure for Osborne. Beatrice had been spending her days restoring order to certain of the Queen's papers. In her Journal, the Queen recorded:

> Walked with Beatrice down to the Mausoleum and back. She has been very busy these last days sorting old music of mine, amongst which treasures have been found. After my dreadful misfortune in '61, everything was left untouched, and I could not bear to look at what my darling one and I used to play together. Only within the last five or six years have I looked at my music again, and only quite lately re-opened my duet books and others. The past has seemed to rush in upon me in a strange and marvellous manner.[1]

This trivial-seeming occupation, imposed upon a quiet, musical nineteen-year-old whose life held few distractions, is significant: just as when the Queen dictated her Journal to Beatrice in the terrible summer of 1871, her entrusting her daughter with the music she had once enjoyed with the Prince Consort represents a step taken towards complete confidence between the two women, confidence the Queen would share with no other child. The rediscovery of former pleasures also afforded the Queen further indulgence of memories of a happy but departed past, another instance of the overshadowing by bygones of Beatrice's cloistered existence.

What began with duet books culminated in the Queen's Journal. After the Queen's death, Beatrice devoted more than thirty years to 'editing' her mother's diaries, omitting passages she considered unsuitable for the eyes of any third person, rewriting entries, copying her revised version into a series of blue notebooks and destroying the originals. It was a task towards which the whole of her adult life had tended. Her training began with writing the Queen's Journal when illness incapacitated its author, and organizing long-neglected music scores the Queen had laid aside, abandoned and forgotten. Such tasks bound mother and daughter ever more closely together, their relationship in both cases an outlet for emotions denied any more 'normal' channel, the Queen through her early widowhood, Beatrice because the Queen refused her friends or companions of her own age. By the second half of the 1870s, with Beatrice no longer a child except in a specifically emotional and by extension sexual sense in her mother's estimation, the Queen and her daughter looked on the world with one mind. Beatrice's apprenticeship had been exacting and ruthless: undertakings such as organizing the Queen's old music may have been presented as a diversion – may even have been a diversion – but for Beatrice there was nothing voluntary in the occupation. She had learnt already that her mother's wishes were also the request of a sovereign to a subject: the work Beatrice carried out for her mother had an aspect of sacred duty that permitted neither shirking nor flippancy. It was this seriousness of purpose that Beatrice would later apply to editing the Queen's Journal. By then she had long ceased to question the Queen's dictates.

No wonder the Queen could describe Beatrice as 'the flower of the flock', the only one of her children who had 'never given [her] one moment's cause of displeasure'.[2] During her marriage the Queen had struggled to submerge her sense of self in the Prince Consort, making his thoughts her thoughts, his way of encountering the world her way; so, after the Prince's death, she strove to subjugate Beatrice. She was not motivated by malice or even conscious selfishness, but by her terror of being finally alone – her husband, her mother, her first mentor Leopold of the Belgians and her childhood confidante Baroness Lehzen were all dead by 1870, while four of her nine children were married, with others certain to follow. Beatrice had not even been the Queen's first choice for the position of constant companion and emotional crutch: she had been too young at the time of the Prince Consort's death and the Queen had convinced herself that, as she would shortly follow her husband to the grave, only a child already adult in 1861 could help her. The Queen had tried to fashion from each of her daughters her ideal helper and had demanded from her sons unremitting indulgence of her sadness. In each case she had failed. Only with Beatrice did her tenacity reap dividends. 'Thank God she is not touchy and offended like several of her brothers and sisters are,' she wrote in October 1873.[3] Repeatedly the demanding Queen would thank the Almighty for this child whose tractable nature was little short of a divine gift. In the summer of 1876 Lady Waterpark accompanied the Queen and Beatrice 'to a school feast at Whippingham. Her Majesty stayed some time and both she and Princess Beatrice seemed much amused.'[4] There is a clear inference that Lady Waterpark did not appreciate, or was not privy to, the amusement of her royal employers. The communion of mother and daughter was so close as to exclude outsiders. Even within the Royal Family Beatrice and her mother came to be viewed – as the Queen herself had once described them – as inseparables. Alone of the Queen's children, Beatrice had not signed the Crown Princess's inflammatory letter in the summer of 1871. Henceforth her siblings would view her as effectively of one substance with their mother. 'This letter is only for you and Beatrice! Please don't have it copied,' Alice wrote to her mother shortly before the former's death.[5] Her relationship with Beatrice was the most enduring pleasure of the Queen's widowhood and, until her mother's death, provided Beatrice's *raison d'être*. What would happen to the princess next her mother does not appear to have considered. Only two people had previously enjoyed such intimacy with the Queen: the Prince Consort and John Brown.

John Brown died of erysipelas in March 1883. To her grandson, the future George V, the Queen wrote, 'I have lost my *dearest best* friend who no one in *this World* can *ever* replace … *never forget* your poor sorrowing old Grandmama's best and truest friend.'[6] Eighteen-year-old George had not been born at the time of the Prince Consort's death; unlike many of the Queen's family, he at least could not say he had heard it all before. The Queen was ill herself. Having slipped on stairs at Windsor, she was unable to walk; with the shock she found herself unable even to stand, and only managed to attend Brown's funeral leaning heavily on Beatrice's arm. As in 1861 her physical and emotional recovery were slow. At the beginning of June Arthur wrote to Louise, 'Poor Mama has been terribly upset by Brown's death – and her knee has given her so much trouble, she is still very lame',[7] while almost a year later the Court Circular lugubriously quibbled: 'Her Majesty is able to take short walks out of doors, but she can stand only for a few minutes.'[8] Brown's death was sudden and, to the Queen, unexpected. To his sister-in-law, she wrote that she '[knew] not how to bear it, or how to believe it possible.'[9] She employed the service of a masseuse, Charlotte Nautet, to assist with her recovery and required the constant presence of her new physician, Dr James Reid. Neither was enough, and the death of 'The Queen's Highland Servant' added an extra burden to Beatrice's already full-time duties. As the Queen wrote to Brown's sisters-in-law: 'You have your husbands – your support – but I have no strong arm to lean on now. Dear Beatrice is my great comfort.'[10] Now Beatrice's workload was physical as well as clerical and emotional. If she felt the shades of the prison house moving ever closer, Beatrice kept her fears well hidden.

To date no record of Beatrice's relationship with John Brown has surfaced, but she, more than any of the Queen's children, had extensive dealings with the abrasive Scotsman who shared with her the role of Queen's shadow. Beatrice, more than her siblings, understood exactly what John Brown did for their mother. She saw that, though the Queen treated Brown with injudicious favouritism that gave rise to ill feeling among other servants, courtiers and even the Royal Family, she could not survive without the duties he performed for her, menial tasks for the most part that would otherwise have been the business of a number of different servants – as the Queen herself expressed it, 'the offices of groom, footman, page and *maid*, I might almost say, as he is so handy about cloaks and shawls.'[11] The stable boy-turned-ghillie had been entrusted by the Prince Consort with the particular charge of overseeing the Queen's comfort and safety. From his summons to Osborne in 1864 until his death nineteen years later his unswerving attentiveness, which contained no trace of the courtier's deference but suggested rather a lover-like tenderness, consistently inspired in the Queen feelings of comfort and safety. For Beatrice, auditor of all the Queen's woes, it must have been a source of some gratitude that at least one important aspect of the Queen's private life was taken care of by someone else. His 'only object and interest is my service, and God knows how much I want to be taken care of', the Queen had written to the Crown Princess on 5 April 1865.[12] At the time, Beatrice was one week short of her eighth birthday, too young to take care of her mother. Nineteen-year-old Helena would shortly leave the Queen to be married; seventeen-year-old Louise was unsympathetic, fifteen-year-old Arthur training to be a soldier, while Leopold at thirteen was a part-time invalid. No child could satisfy the twin requirements of caring for their mother and making her service their only object and interest. Seizing on John Brown as a familiar face endorsed by the Prince Consort, the Queen directed the man to fit the job. As the years passed, Beatrice would see too much of what that job entailed to experience the misplaced jealousy several of her siblings felt towards John Brown.

All the Queen's sons enjoyed acrimonious relations with the Queen's ubiquitous Highlander. In her dealings with John Brown, Beatrice had three advantages over her brothers. First, she was a girl, and the Queen's daughters fared better with Brown than her sons, perhaps because the position he appeared to usurp was one that belonged to a man not a woman, and was hence resented to a greater degree by those who considered themselves contenders. Second, she enjoyed the singular esteem and affection of the Queen, who delighted in her; and Brown, for all his faults, was not disinterested when it came to the Queen's happiness and well-being. Third, Beatrice at this stage in her life was noticeably less 'royal' in her actions and self-perception than her elder siblings. She did not, as a knee-jerk reaction, balk at what others considered the inappropriate closeness of the relationship enjoyed by a servant with his sovereign. Even the favourite Arthur was guilty in this respect, and the Queen felt compelled to write to his governor, 'Reserve is not necessary towards the faithful devoted confidential servants who have known him from child-hood … If any of the Queen's sons put on a tone of stiffness in her presence towards her people when she does not do so, it is as if they meant to show their mother and the Queen that they disapproved HER MANNER.'[13] This injunction applied 'especially to my excellent Brown, who *ought* to be treated by *all* of *you*, as he is by others, *differently* to the more ordinary servants'.[14] Beatrice never expressed disapproval of her mother's manner, and she and John Brown were too much in one another's company – often in circumstances of extreme confinement – for her to behave with reserve towards him. Such a course would have been akin to her conceiving a pronounced antipathy for the Queen's favourite lady-in-waiting: an unworkable stance even had it been in Beatrice's nature, which, where her mother was concerned, it was not.

John Brown's usefulness to the Queen was initially of a practical nature: he was 'a good, handy, thoughtful servant'.[15] More than this, since he held the Queen in no awe, and had no qualms about addressing her on terms of near equality and sharing with her his forthright opinions, he quickly assumed something of the role the Queen had first devised for her children. He offered her the support that she had seen no daughter but Beatrice could give her; unmarried, his loyalty to her was absolute. 'There is one person whose sympathy has done me – and does me more good than almost anyone's,' the Queen wrote to her eldest daughter in 1866, 'and that is good, honest Brown … He has, when I have been very sad and lonely – often and often – with his strong, kind, simple words – so true, and so wise and so courageous, done me an immensity of good – and so he would to anyone in sorrow and distress.'[16] This sympathy, felt by the

Queen to be of a loving nature, remained a part of the relationship of mistress and servant. With the passage of time and Beatrice's growing maturity, this aspect of the Queen's needs increasingly became Beatrice's province. But it is possible she did not address it as satisfactorily as the less inhibited Scotsman. As a four-year-old, Lady Augusta Bruce had noted, Beatrice had been noticeably distressed by the Queen's grief during those morning visits she paid to her mother in the aftermath of the Prince Consort's death. But one result of growing up alongside her mother's effusions of sentiment was that, except at moments of crisis such as the death of the Prince Imperial, Beatrice learnt to hold her own emotions in check: the Queen's sorrow burned greedily, admitting no parity in the feelings of those close to her. So Beatrice, always supportive of her mother, may have expressed her sympathy in quiet gestures. John Brown, by contrast, where the Queen was concerned wore his heart on his sleeve. As she wrote to his brother Hugh after Brown's death: 'My beloved John would say: "You haven't a more devoted servant than Brown" – and oh! how I felt that! Afterwards so often I told him no one loved him more than I did or had a better friend than me, and he answered: "Nor you – than me. No one loves you more."'[17]

If, inadvertently, John Brown's presence lessened the burden of care and comfort imposed upon Beatrice, it is unlikely that she analysed its import until much later, if at all. Brown had been a ghillie at Balmoral before he became the Queen's full-time attendant. At Balmoral his role was less circumscribed than it would afterwards become: when Leopold first visited the castle in the summer of 1860, it was John Brown who led him on Topsy the pony, the Queen not then claiming his full attention. John Brown was a part of Beatrice's life almost from her earliest memories. He shared her attendance on the Queen to the extent that only after his death, when imagining became reality, could she conceive of her life with the Queen without him. He rode on the box on the front of the carriage when the Queen took her daily drive with Beatrice and her ladies. He accompanied the Queen on her holidays abroad, though he detested foreigners and was forcibly immune to the variety and blandishments of foreign landscapes. And at Balmoral, where the Queen and Beatrice spent up to four months a year, he was ubiquitous. He accompanied them, for example, on their visits to cottagers, when the Queen attended a Highland christening or, with her customary mournful tastes, took Beatrice to see the dead body of a 'poor sweet innocent bairnie, only three years old ... I ... was glad she should see death for the first time in so touching and pleasing a form'[18] – as if the story of her whole life had not been written in the vocabulary of death.

When, in the early 1870s, the Queen resumed the expeditions from Balmoral she had begun with the Prince Consort, John Brown was always of the party. In the evening he waited at table. Invariably the travellers lodged in somewhat cramped conditions, and Brown's room was never far away from either the Queen's or Beatrice's. At Dunrobin in 1872 the Queen recorded, 'I went to see Beatrice's room, which is close by [mine], down three steps in the same passage. Fräulein Bauer, and Morgan, her dresser, are near her. Brown lives just opposite in the room intended for Albert's valet.'[19] Five years later, the Queen and her party put up at the Loch Maree Hotel: 'Up the short but easy small winding staircase came small, though comfortable, rooms. To the left Beatrice's, and Brown's just opposite to the right.'[20] Living so regularly cheek by jowl like this would quickly have exposed any tensions in the relationship between Beatrice and John Brown. Since no source mentions any such unpleasantness, we must assume none existed. Indeed, it would be surprising if two people whose whole lives were devoted to the Queen's comfort had not endeavoured to work together amicably, setting aside personal grievances and antipathies. That it was possible to exist on amicable terms with the vilified Scotsman is suggested by a letter the Queen wrote to her granddaughter Victoria of Hesse, following a visit of Victoria and her sister Ella to Windsor: 'Brown said on Friday morning that it seemed all wrong without you and as if "a Blight had come over us".'[21] Since he rarely dissembled, Brown evidently liked the Hessian princesses. Victoria and Ella were close to Beatrice in age, and the three girls were friends. It is unlikely that John Brown would have got on with her nieces if his relationship with Beatrice had not been cordial.

Among the significant alterations we know that Beatrice made to Queen Victoria's Journal after her death is the excision of much material relating to John Brown. This was influenced by a number of factors – Beatrice's knowledge that scandal-mongers considered the Queen and Brown lovers, and her awareness of the deep dislike for Brown felt by several members of her family, in particular Bertie, who was certainly king when Beatrice began working on the Journal. It is also the case that a characteristic of Beatrice's reworking of the Journal is her downgrading of the prominence and significance accorded to servants. The Queen took an active interest in the lives and welfare of her servants; in her Journal as bequeathed by Beatrice all assume the status of background figures. Benita Stoney and Heinrich C. Weltzein, in their compilation of the letters of Frieda Arnold, one of the Queen's German dressers, compare before and after Journal entries for 9 August 1845, the former having survived in a copy made in the Queen's lifetime. The former reads, 'I undressed as quickly as possible and then Singer, Peneyvre, Rebecca and Dehler set off for Woolwich. Skerrett and Margaret return to Osborne.' (All those named are maids or dressers.) Beatrice's transcription reads: 'Undressed as quickly as possible, the maids having to leave for Woolwich.'[22] In this case, the servants expunged, with the exception of Miss Skerrett, were not known to Beatrice; her deletions do not indicate personal animosity. Nor should her excision of so much material concerning John Brown be interpreted in such a light.

As at the death of the Prince Consort, the Queen turned to Tennyson in March 1883. Of John Brown she wrote to the poet, 'He was part of my life and quite invaluable.' She added, 'I have a dear devoted child who has always been a dear unselfish companion to me, but she is young and I can't darken her young life by my trials and sorrows. My other children, though all loving, have all their own interests and homes.'[23] For more than twenty years Beatrice's life had been darkened by her mother's trials and sorrows. During that period, she had mutely watched as all eight of her siblings acquired 'their own interests and homes'. We do not know if she ever wondered whether her turn would come, if she would be allowed to marry and experience life outside the narrow confines of the Queen's houses.

With John Brown's death her turn was both closer and more remote than either the Queen or Beatrice imagined.

ELEVEN

'She is my constant companion'

·◆·

On Beatrice's eighteenth birthday the Queen gave thanks for the special joy her favourite child had brought her.

How many prayers and thanks went up to our Heavenly Father for this darling child, whose birth was such a joy to us, and who is my blessing and comfort, whom God will, I know, keep near me and preserve! I could but feel my heart full in thinking the little Baby my darling one loved so much, to whom he almost gave his last smile, had grown up to girlhood and to be of age, and *he* never have been there to guide and protect her![1]

Anointed with the Prince Consort's dying smile, Beatrice had had no choice but to grow up as her mother's particular comfort. Happily, she had developed 'the sweetest temper imaginable' and became 'very useful and handy ... She is my constant companion and hope and trust will never leave me while I live. I do not intend she should ever go out as her sisters did (which was a mistake) but let her stay (except of course occasionally going to theatres) as much as she can with me.'[2] That year the Queen wrote a memorandum concerning the procedure to be followed in the event of her own serious illness or death. 'Supposing she was too ill to be herself consulted,' she wrote in her customary third person, she nominated Beatrice as her lieutenant and alternative sounding box. 'Princess Beatrice, from living always with the Queen, is the one who is to be applied to for all that is to be done.'[3] Clearly, in black and white, the Queen expressed her certainty that Beatrice would never live anywhere but with her.

In her determination not to lose this daughter on whom she leaned so heavily, the Queen summoned to her aid God's will.

Together, the Queen decided, monarch and maker would collude to prevent Beatrice from leaving her mother. The first seeds of potential discord were sown not by Beatrice or by the Queen but by two other of the Queen's children, one living, one dead.

It was not enough that 14 December had carried off the Queen's husband and very nearly, in 1871, her eldest son. In 1878 it wrought again its cruel havoc with devastating effects. Aged thirty-five, Princess Alice, Grand Duchess of Hesse, died of diphtheria on the seventeenth anniversary of the death of her father. She left behind her, besides her widower Louis, four daughters and a son, aged between six and fifteen.

Relations between the Queen and Alice had latterly been strained, but the Queen took a close interest in her Hesse grandchildren. After what 'must have been a dreadful Christmas and what a New Year!'⁴, the Queen invited the family to Osborne. They arrived on 21 January. The following day, writing to the Queen's cousin Mary Adelaide, Duchess of Teck, Beatrice described their first meeting: 'I cannot tell you how sad the meeting yesterday with Louis and the Children was. For the first time to miss darling Alice, and to see him alone. It all brought our terrible loss so vividly before us.' Happily, the Grand Duke's grief was all his sister-in-law required it to be: 'It is such a comfort that he likes to speak of dear Alice and of all she did.'⁵ When the mournful party departed six weeks later, Beatrice recorded predictably, 'The parting from dear Louis was very sad ... We miss the dear Children so much, the house feels quite empty without them.'⁶ Even taking account of the circumspection Beatrice would wisely have employed in writing to this most garrulous of the Queen's relations, there is little here in these conventionalized, formal, even distant expressions of regret to suggest that she had conceived for her grieving brother-in-law anything more than the sympathy his circumstances inevitably inspired – as indeed she had not. Nor did anyone else in her family think otherwise. But it occurred to Bertie, whose voice for once found an acquiescent echo in the Queen, that a solution offering comfort and convenience all round (if not a recipe for happiness), was that Louis remarry – directing his choice to his sister-in-law Beatrice. The couple would live between Darmstadt and the Queen's homes, with the greater part of their time spent with the Queen, who would thereby not only not lose the daughter she had no intention of releasing but be able to oversee the upbringing and education of her four granddaughters and Louis's heir. Victoria and Ella, the eldest of Alice's children, were Beatrice's near contemporaries, whom we know she accounted friends. Among Louis's recommendations was his marked fondness for Balmoral – so rare among the Queen's children and their spouses – on account of its shooting and stalking. Contradictory in this as in so many of her plans, the Queen does not appear to have anticipated difficulties in reconciling her frequently expressed determination to keep Beatrice 'very quiet and at home'[7] with the imposition upon her of stepmotherhood to a family of five and marriage to a man twenty years her senior with whom she had no shared interests. It is unlikely that the Queen solicited Beatrice's feelings in the matter. Nor did she draw pause for thought from her excessively sheltered daughter's singular lack of qualifications for the task she so glibly allotted her. Only one obstacle blocked her path: the law.

That it was illegal for a husband to marry the sister of his deceased wife did not unduly concern either the Queen or the Prince of Wales. Bertie threw himself behind the Deceased Wife's Sister Bill's passage through Parliament, and the Queen kept the matter at the forefront of her conversations with the Prime Minister, Disraeli. On 6 May 1879, having successfully passed through the Commons, the bill reached its second reading in the House of Lords. The Prince was in the house to make a speech in favour of the change to the law; with him he carried a petition signed by 3258 Norfolk farmers praying that the prohibition be ended – an eccentric attempt to strengthen his cause given that the majority of the objections to the bill were raised by Church of England bishops in the Lords who were unlikely to be swayed by this or any other evidence of strong feeling in rural East Anglia. Inevitably, the bill was thrown out. The Queen had applauded its passage through the Commons as 'such a slap to the bigots';[8] in the Lords, those 'bigots' refused to be slapped into line. The Queen met Disraeli the following lunch time: 'Talked of the loss of the Bill, permitting the marriage with a sister-in-law, in favour of which Bertie presented a petition, and which we are most anxious should pass. It has passed the Commons but is thrown out in the Lords, the Bishops being so much against it. Lord Beaconsfield [Disraeli] is in favour of it, but the whole Cabinet against it!! Incredible!'[9] By the time the bill successfully became law, the Grand Duke of Hesse was dead and Beatrice a widow.

No mention is made of Beatrice in this account by the Queen of her conversation with Disraeli on 7 May 1879, but the bald ellipsis of her 'which we are most anxious should pass', with its bland, unspecific, perfunctory tone, has all the hallmarks of a Journal alteration made by Beatrice after the Queen's death. It is possible that Beatrice was not aware of the plans Bertie and the Queen were hatching for her until some time later, perhaps not even until she began her work on the Queen's Journal. The pronounced support of her family for the Deceased Wife's Sister Bill ought to have given her (as the Queen's last unmarried daughter) some indication of the way the wind was blowing. However, if Beatrice was in love with the Prince Imperial, then at this point, the last year of the Prince's life, she may have been too wrapped up in her feelings for him to spare much time for, or even take seriously, so fantastical a scheme as her mother betrothing her to Alice's widower. Whatever the explanation, it would be in keeping with Beatrice's extremely private nature had she erased from the Queen's Journal records of unfulfilled plans for her marriage – distasteful to her, hitherto unknown to her, or otherwise.

After initial irritation, the Queen appears to have renounced her plans with a degree of good grace. She found for her Hesse grandchildren a second English governess, Miss Pryde, to work alongside 'Madgie' Jackson: both women were expected to submit detailed reports on their charges to the Queen in England. In addition, the Queen chose Helena, whose daughters were of a similar age to Alice's younger children, as surrogate mother for the Grand Duke's offspring; Helena would make annual trips to Darmstadt and have the Hesse children to stay with her during holidays. Bertie remained interested in the Deceased Wife's Sister Bill, and was considered by the Archbishop of Canterbury a significant force behind its ultimate success in 1896. The Grand Duke of Hesse sincerely mourned Alice's death and, after a decent interval, embarked on a romantic liaison which, when she learnt of it, his mother-in-law moved swiftly to crush. Having spent April 1879 with the Queen at Baveno on the western shore of Lake Maggiore in northern Italy, Beatrice had resumed unruffled the life she knew so well at her mother's side. Wistfully but cheerfully she wrote to Theodore Martin, who had sent her the fourth volume of his life of the Prince Consort, 'We have returned here enchanted with our journey, but missing terribly the beautiful scenery we have just left, and I hope this will not be our only visit to Italy.'[10]

In the time the Queen spared her, when the Queen was engaged in political business (with which Leopold not Beatrice at this point helped her) or in driving with any of her ladies-in-waiting, Beatrice was at work on a book. The book was a work of design not composition. It was a birthday book, with one page for every day of the year, a lengthy index for the names of those whose birthdays were entered in the appropriate day, and an illustrated frontispiece to each month. Each of these frontispieces included a poem or poetic extract within an illustrated border. The poets chosen indicate catholic tastes on the part of the 'author', from Milton (May), Herbert (February) and Wordsworth (October), to the eighteenth-century populist Mrs Hemans (March), Longfellow, whom the Queen, Leopold and Louise had met in 1868, when Beatrice was still considered too young for such distractions (January), and Beatrice's socialist contemporary William Morris (August). The borders, painted in watercolour, all depict flowers. Like her sisters and the Queen, Beatrice had been instructed in painting by watercolourist William Leighton Leitch; she also took lessons from N. E. Green and would later be taught by Benjamin Ottewell. In the early 1880s she became an honorary member of

the Royal Institute of Painters in Watercolour, with which –
emboldened by the success of her birthday book – she exhibited
in 1883, 1884 and 1885 (unsurprisingly, given her rank and
prestige, Beatrice's paintings were illustrated in the Society's
catalogues). Later she would exhibit with the Isle of Wight Fine
Art Society, of which she was president. On 9 September 1905
the *Isle of Wight County Press* recorded that Beatrice opened the
society's twenty-sixth annual exhibition, at the School of Art,
Ryde, and herself exhibited two paintings in oils.

A Birthday Book Designed by HRH the Princess Beatrice was
published in 1881 by Smith, Elder & Co., the house which had
earlier so successfully published the Queen's *Leaves From the
Journal of Our Life in Highlands* and, more recently, had been
responsible for Theodore Martin's life of the Prince Consort, in
which the Queen took so close an interest. Like her mother's
book, Beatrice's was intended for public sale, and Smith, Elder &
Co. rewarded her handsomely for her efforts. Unlike the Queen's
compilation of illustrated journal extracts, there was to be no
cheap edition of Beatrice's *Birthday Book*. The large volume was
lavishly produced: colour lithography was undertaken in Leipzig;
several monthly frontispieces were heavily gilded; and the pages
were gilt-edged. Smith, Elder & Co. set a price of forty-two
shillings a copy, and the princess nominated the Belgrave Hospital
for Children as the recipient of all proceeds. She herself received
£500 for the copyright on 3 October 1881, one of the largest
single payments made by the publishers to any of its authors that
year. On 11 March 1882 Beatrice received a second payment of
£250. The publishers had initially decided upon two editions of
one thousand five hundred copies each, released on 15 November
1881 and 16 February 1882. A further edition of five hundred
copies was also printed in the spring of 1882, although Beatrice
did not receive additional payment. The investment Smith,
Elder & Co. made in its royal author is indicated by the large
sum the company spent on advertising the first printing – £163
13s. 11d in addition to giving forty-three copies to 'Editors and
Friends'. Beatrice herself received fifty copies of the book.

Publisher and princess both had reason to be pleased with

their first joint sortie into print. Despite its high price, the *Birthday Book* sold well, with Smith, Elder & Co. continuing to receive orders for copies as late as 1887. By then Beatrice was married with two small children and a host of new concerns. Her *Birthday Book* remains a work of considerable charm, with a strong period flavour. Brought up without the Prince Consort's deep interest in art, Beatrice nevertheless embraced current developments in art and design – she owned furniture by Collinson & Lock, for example, made in the 1880s from ebonized and gilt mahogany in a safely 'royal' diluting of current E. W. Godwin-inspired aesthetic movement ideas. The *Birthday Book*'s blend of sentimentality and Gothic aesthetics endeared it to its contemporary public, not least among them the Queen. The Queen was not only proud of her daughter's work, she had a passion for birthdays and anniversaries and also enjoyed collecting autographs. She gave a number of copies of the *Birthday Book* to favoured members of her growing family. Those that survive, annotated and autographed, provide an insight into the dramatis personae of Queen Victoria's later court.

In October 1882 the Queen and Beatrice – the latter now the author of a successful charitable work – were once more at Balmoral. They were joined by members of the Queen's extended family. Photographs record the autumn get-together, the Queen invariably seated centrally, with children and dogs at her feet, adults sitting or standing behind her. One such group shows the Queen, Arthur's wife the Duchess of Connaught holding on her knee their first baby, Margaret of Connaught, three spotted terriers, Ernest of Hesse and Alix of Hesse, the future Tsarina of Russia. To the Queen's left, implausibly kilted, sits Ernest and Alix's father, Alice's widower the Grand Duke Louis IV. Standing behind him, one hand resting on his shoulder, her fond gaze fixed upon him apparently oblivious to the camera, is Princess Beatrice.

TWELVE

'Dear Beatrice suffered much from rheumatism'

.•.

On 11 November 1882 *The Graphic*, an illustrated weekly paper, published two half-page pictures under the headline 'The Queen At Balmoral'. One showed the Queen with Beatrice in the castle drawing room, an eye-watering vision of tartan and graceless cabinetry. The other, 'The Afternoon Drive', bears the explanation: 'In the afternoon Her Majesty, in a carriage and pair with outriders, drives with the Princess and ladies-in-waiting to her favourite resorts in the neighbourhood.' The illustration is remarkable only on account of the fearsomeness of the weather. All four occupants of the open carriage – the Queen, Beatrice and two ladies-in-waiting – hold above their heads large black umbrellas. They appear calm, unruffled, even gracious in the Queen's case as she inclines her head to acknowledge the salute of a passing kilted Scotsman. Against the decorous party horizontal rain lashes with vigour. It is, we suspect, a cheerless autumn outing, horses, carriage, outriders, John Brown on the box, and all four passengers ice-cold and soaked to the skin. It was probably raining when the party set off from the castle: after fourteen years in waiting, Marie Mallet recorded, 'I can safely say I never remember a warm congenial day in the Highlands during the many months I spent there.'[1] The bracing air and vigorous Scottish climate were very much to the Queen's liking; her Highland Journals seldom deplore decidedly inclement weather except insofar as it obscures the view. But they did not suit Beatrice. By her early twenties Beatrice had developed rheumatism so acute that she was forced to take the first of a series of Continental spa cures. None yielded any permanent improvement and she would continue to suffer for the rest of her life.

In September 1873 the Royal Family was at Inverlochy Castle. The weather began ghastly, but the Queen was not to be deterred from enjoying herself and seeing as much as possible of the neighbourhood. 'As the rain did not cease, Beatrice, Jane Churchill and I walked in the grounds to the stables, which we looked at, then out at the lodge and as far as the farm.' After lunch, 'the day seemed better, but again and again the sunshine was succeeded by heavy showers; still we determined to go out ... We came home at twenty minutes to eight ... but the weather has been bad.'² It is unlikely that the 'we' who 'determined to go out' included the then fourteen-year-old Beatrice: the royal plural embraced the inclinations of only one member of the party.

If anyone was to blame for the Queen's foolhardiness in the face of cold, wet discomfort, it was her physician Sir James Clark. Clark had attended the young Princess Victoria when, in 1835, she suffered from typhoid fever at Ramsgate. Having pulled her through that crisis, he found a faithful acolyte in the future monarch. The doctrine of good health to which thereafter the Queen adhered scrupulously was Clark's youthful thesis 'De Frigoribus Effectis', in which he established the positive properties of fresh air and cold and the certain pitfalls of overheating. The Queen applied the principle indiscriminately, with all the imperturbable zeal of the convert: when pregnancy rendered one of her daughters-in-law lethargic and lassitudinous, she ordered that the house be kept without heating until the baby's birth.³ Windows in the Queen's homes were flung wide – to let in wind, as little Beatrice had explained to her German governess – and fires scarcely lit. Lord James of Hereford, a minister in attendance at Balmoral, described the castle as 'cold as death'.⁴ Bertie dismissed it as 'the place of a thousand draughts', an epithet that might easily have been applied to any of the Queen's homes.⁵

To her governess, Lady Car, Beatrice wrote from Balmoral on 21 May 1874, 'I was so sorry leaving [Windsor] thinking it would be so cold, and nothing out, but I am quite agreeably surprised, for it is very unusual to see everything out in May, in Scotland.'⁶ A hint of dread underlies this letter to one of her few confidantes of the slender seventeen-year-old who would be

'La petite Princesse Beatrice ... est si jolie,' Queen Victoria wrote to her favourite portraitist Winterhalter in 1859. The lively sketch she commissioned from the artist – of the two-year-old Beatrice in an Arab headdress, clasping an exotically costumed doll – suggests Winterhalter shared her opinion.

The Queen and Prince Consort photographed in 1857 on the terrace at Osborne with all nine of their children, Beatrice on her mother's knee. The family would exist in this form for all too short a time.

A sculpture of the young Beatrice's hands, by Sir Joseph Edgar Boehm.

This commemorative montage published in 1901 shows Beatrice from childhood to adulthood – starting with Richard Lauchert's portrait of the six-year-old princess, which Queen Victoria thought 'lovely and so like'.

H.R.H. THE PRINCESS BEATRICE.

BORN APRIL 14, 1857.
From photographs by Messrs. Hughes & Mullins, Ryde.

AT THE AGE OF SIX.
From the painting by R. Lauchert in the Royal Collection.

AT THE AGE OF TEN.

AT THE AGE OF THIRTEEN.

PRINCESS HENRY OF BATTENBERG.

AT THE AGE OF SEVENTEEN.

The five daughters of Victoria and Albert in hieratic pose surrounding the bust of their deceased father. Only Beatrice – 'a most amusing little dot' – at this stage resists complete submergence in the atmosphere of gloom.

'The happy time is when children are six to five and three years old,' wrote the Queen. In this photograph of the Queen with five-year-old Beatrice the year after the Prince Consort's death, are few intimations of happiness.

During her teenage years, Beatrice's isolation within the Queen's family grew. In 1868 – the year of this photograph – she found herself alone in the schoolroom.

Beatrice's eldest brother, Bertie, Prince of Wales, married Princess Alexandra of Denmark on 10 March 1863 at St George's Chapel, Windsor. Throughout the service the Queen's attention fastened on Beatrice: 'I could not take my eyes off precious little Baby, with her golden hair and large nosegay.'

A young woman at last: Beatrice's downcast gaze, her failure to meet the viewer's eye, were by now characteristic of the shy and hesitant princess.

A *Birthday Book* by HRH The Princess Beatrice was published in 1881 by Smith, Elder & Co. Beatrice received £750 for her work on the book. Proceeds from the sale went to the Belgrave Hospital for Children.

THE AFTERNOON DRIVE

"In the afternoon Her Majesty, in a carriage and pair with outriders, drives with the Princess and ladies-in-waiting to her favourite resorts in the neighbourhood."

Beatrice's sufferings from rheumatism began early. Daily, rain-sodden drives with the Queen at Balmoral – as depicted by *The Graphic* on 11 November 1882 – cannot have helped.

Queen Victoria was won round not simply to Beatrice marrying but to Henry himself – with his dark good looks 'the handsomest of the three handsome brothers', as she described him (in fact he was one of four brothers).

Being in love suited Beatrice – as this striking photograph of 1886 shows.

Public reaction to Beatrice's
engagement to Prince Henry of
Battenberg was muted – but
Beatrice's happiness was hard won
and she married for love. These
full-page engravings of the couple
were published in *The Graphic* on
January 10 1885.

With her 'quite simple' dress, Beatrice wore the Queen's own wedding veil of Honiton lace. Henry, known as 'Liko', wore the white uniform of the Prussian Garde du Corps. The couple were attended by ten bridesmaids (including the future Tsarina of Russia and future queens of Norway and Roumania), all Beatrice's nieces – categorized by one MP as showing a 'decided absence of beauty'.

'The scene at Osborne after the ceremony,' reported The *Illustrated London News*, 'was that of a jubilant garden party.'

expected to sit beside the Queen on her rain-lashed carriage drives and, afterwards, to wear the regulation low-cut evening gown in her Arctic dining room – a complaint reiterated by the usually mild-mannered lady-in-waiting Edith, Countess of Lytton, as late as 1897. Henry Ponsonby, the Queen's private secretary, once related a conversation between the Queen and Beatrice: if condemned to the choice, would you select residence at the Equator or the North Pole? Their respective responses did not surprise their audience. Beatrice was decided in favouring the Equator, the Queen equally certain in championing the North Pole. 'All doctors say that heat is unwholesome but cold wholesome,' she asserted with questionable veracity.[7] So pronounced was the Queen's belief in 'De Frigoribus Effectis' that, like many of her contemporaries, she endowed fresh air with moral and philosophical as well as health-giving properties. What she regarded as the reactionary spirit of the Russians arose from the 'terribly unhealthy atmosphere' in which they lived on account of sealing shut their windows from September to May.[8] Left to her own devices, the Queen chose to holiday in Switzerland, escaping the British heatwave of 1868; Beatrice's holiday destinations after her mother's death included Egypt, Algeria and Sicily.

Even when visiting what ought to have been gentler climates, the Queen embraced vagaries in the weather. Reporting on her five-week stay in the Provençal town of Grasse in 1891, the French weekly newspaper *Le Commerce* recorded: 'Despite a chilly and rather disagreeable North wind, Her Majesty Queen Victoria goes out for long drives every morning in her little donkey-chair along the approaches to the Grand Hotel and in the immediate vicinity of the town.'[9] It was nothing, of course, compared with Balmoral, or Osborne at Christmas, and happily there was no room in the donkey-chair for Beatrice, though she would regularly be expected to walk alongside it, keeping her mother company on these sedate all-weather excursions.

The Queen's second daughter Alice had been married to Louis of Hesse for ten years when, on 6 July 1872, Sir James Clark wrote to her about her health. The princess, who would die at the age of thirty-five, had complained for some time about her poor physical condition. During the Austro-Prussian war of 1866, her letters to her husband described her worsening rheumatism and neuralgia, tiredness, strain and headaches.[10] Helpfully, Clark's letter prescribed well-ventilated rooms and 'steady perseverance in the use of the cold bath every morning'.[11]

If the doctor appears to have been blind to the workings of cause and effect, it was a failing the Queen shared. She was neither unaware of nor unsympathetic to the sufferings Beatrice's rheumatism imposed, although she regarded its earliest manifestations as an inconvenience to herself rather than Beatrice – as, for example, when it threatened to cast a blight over the royal excursion to Loch Maree in September 1877: 'Dear Beatrice suffered much from rheumatism, which was very vexatious.'[12] Beatrice herself took care that her infirmity did not become a preoccupation, forewarned by the example of her haemophiliac brother Leopold, who was regularly confined to his bed by mishaps arising from his condition or, more frustratingly, by the Queen's determination to prevent such mishaps. Unlike her sister Helena, Beatrice did not mollycoddle herself. Unlike the Queen, she was not prone to hypochondria. In January 1878, despite suffering from a cold that ultimately prevented her presence at dinner, Beatrice rode out in the morning with Mademoiselle Norèle. The following New Year, Lady Waterpark's diary noted, 'A wretched day, snow and wind. Miss Phipps went to skate with Princess Beatrice.'[13]

Despite suffering from the cold and her preference for warm weather, Beatrice did not, as a young woman, allow this to curtail her activities. Partly, her pragmatic attitude arose in response to circumstances: her daily attendance on the Queen necessitated long periods outdoors regardless of the weather. Towards the end of her life the Queen suffered as much as her daughter from rheumatic pains and cramps, she had difficulty walking and her legs troubled her. But she continued to relish the cold. At Balmoral in November 1896 Marie Mallet confided to her diary, 'The Queen quite apologized yesterday for enjoying the cold weather so intensely. "I always feel so brisk," said she!

It is more than her daughters or Ladies do!'[14] As a child, Beatrice had joined her mother for tea at Frogmore on a day of such driving wind that even the doughty Queen was forced to sit under the Colonnade. As an adult, Beatrice was better able to resist her mother's whims, where resistance was compatible with the satisfaction of both. 'The Queen insisted on sitting out last night on the Terrace,' wrote Marie Mallet of an evening at Osborne in July 1898, 'but mercifully the Princesses refused to run the risk of rheumatism and kept me with them.'[15]

A stout heart and sense of duty were not enough to ease Beatrice's pain. In the summer of 1883, on the pressing advice of the Queen's doctors, she travelled to Aix-les-Bains in the South of France to take a cure. The timing was unfortunate. John Brown had been dead less than six months and the Queen herself was far from fully recovered from her fall at Windsor in the spring. She felt Beatrice's absence keenly, leaving her as it did temporarily bereft of either of her twin supports, without even Leopold to fall back on since his marriage the previous year. Her sympathy was roused for her favourite daughter, but most of the Queen's thoughts focused firmly on her return. To her old friend and occasional sparring partner Augusta of Prussia, since Prussia's defeat of Napoleon III raised to the rank of empress, the Queen wrote:

> Beatrice's absence is very grievous and unpleasant and increases my depression and the horrible ever growing feeling of emptiness and bereavement which nothing can ever really remove. But recently she had been suffering a great deal from neuritis, especially in the hand and right arm, which was a great inconvenience to her in writing and especially in playing the piano, and before that she had it in her knee and foot too. So we thought it would be advisable to try a thorough cure for three weeks.[16]

Beneath the tetchy self-pity of a woman unaccustomed to inconvenience is a genuine pang of longing for her absent daughter. The Queen was unused to being parted from Beatrice – she wrote to the Crown Princess, 'Her absence is of course a great trial to me as for twenty-two years she has only been absent for ten days once.'[17] The Queen missed Beatrice: their separation, albeit brief, brought home to her the extent of her dependence. The union the Queen described to the Crown Princess was, at twenty-two years, of longer duration than her marriage to the Prince Consort. Its temporary suspension was an unpleasant novelty. The Queen required Beatrice for emotional reasons, particularly in the wake of John Brown's death, but the demands of her unrelenting paperwork were equally exigent. Beatrice may have hoped that the thermal cure at Aix-les-Bains would lessen her aches and enable her again easily to play the piano; on the Queen's agenda was the 'writing' Beatrice undertook for her – letters, telegrams, and even copying in the case of letters she considered of special importance.

Beatrice's time away was not spent selfishly. At the end of August the Queen wrote to her eldest daughter from Osborne, 'The heat is intense since Saturday, and tires me very much. I am however getting on and I hope "Charlotte" whom Beatrice swears by will finish the rest.'[18] The Queen's 'Charlotte' was Charlotte Nautet, a masseuse from Aix-les-Bains recommended by Beatrice. In future the Queen's doctor James Reid would arrange for Charlotte and her successor Marie Angelier to spend two- and three-week periods staying with the Queen, holding at bay her own rheumatic lameness through massage. For the Queen to claim Beatrice swore by Charlotte indicates that the princess derived some benefit from her cure at Aix-les-Bains, as does the fact that the visit was repeated in 1887, although on that occasion the Queen and Beatrice travelled together.

Her summer cure at Aix-les-Bains was not Beatrice's first experience of the South of France. Her brother Leopold had travelled there repeatedly for his uncertain health and, in 1882, the Queen chose Menton as the destination for her spring holiday. During that holiday Beatrice asked to visit Nice. The gunboat *Cygnet* was placed at her disposal to transport her. A foretaste of her trip to Aix-les-Bains, she made the short journey without her mother. Afterwards, leaving France on board the royal yacht *Victoria and Albert*, Beatrice awoke on the morning of her twenty-fifth birthday to find herself being serenaded by the band of the 25th Regiment of the French Army; it dedicated to her Meyer's march 'Salut à la Princesse'.

Such courtesies, Beatrice understood, were paid to her not for herself but in recognition of her relationship to the Queen. Yet, little by little, they added to her growing sense of self. Since the Queen's lameness in the spring of 1883 she had embarked on a limited programme of public engagements deputizing for her mother. In March she presented prizes to the students of the Bloomsbury Female School of Art, and after her return from Aix-les-Bains and the court's removal to Balmoral, she visited Aberdeen to open a bazaar in aid of the Aberdeen Hospital for Sick Children and, in front of a crowd of several thousand, the Duthie Park, recently donated to the town. The ceremony took place on an early-autumn day of driving rain of a sort familiar to the illustrator of *The Graphic*. Planting a tree in the downpour, Beatrice charmed those around her with a joke that the weather would be good for the tree. Such appearances compounded the effect of her constant presence at the Queen's side and meant that Beatrice, the shyest of the Queen's children, was among the best known. She became a favourite of journals such as the *Illustrated London News*, which devoted many column inches to the Royal Family and, at the time of Beatrice's marriage, would review her recent history through the public's eyes: 'So much interest has long been felt in Princess Beatrice, the Queen's youngest daughter and the last of her children, after the marriage of all her brothers and sisters, that we believe more popular sympathy was felt upon this occasion than at any other Royal Wedding since that of the Prince and Princess of Wales.'[19]

Though she kept her counsel, in the early 1880s Beatrice was beginning to realize that, like her brothers and sisters, she too had a life beyond the Queen.

THIRTEEN

'If only she could marry now'

•-•-

*L*ouis of Battenberg was handsome and dashing, like a Raphael when he was young, like a Velázquez when he was older, according to his sister's memoirs. He was also strong-minded and intelligent. He was only fourteen when, independent of his parents, he forswore his German nationality, became an Englishman and joined the Royal Navy. He was the son of that buccaneering Alexander of Battenberg whom the Queen had invited to Windsor for the birth and christening of Victoria of Hesse. Louis had inherited his father's adventurous spirit as well as his bold good looks and winning charm.

In 1884 Louis married Victoria of Hesse. They were cousins, Victoria a favourite granddaughter of the Queen, who gave the match her qualified blessing, writing to the bride-to-be, 'I think that you have done well to choose only a Husband who is *quite* of your way of thinking and who in many respects is as English as you are – whose interests must be the same as yours and who dear Mama [the Queen's daughter Alice] liked ... One only drawback do I see – and that is "the fortune".'[1] Possibly the Queen drew a sigh of relief that the dashing naval man had succeeded in allying himself with her family only to the extent of marrying a granddaughter. Four years previously the Queen had acted with chilling ruthlessness to stamp out embryonic hopes – real or imaginary – Louis may have harboured of marrying Beatrice.

Beatrice met Louis, romantically, at a ball. Under the Queen's watchful gaze they danced together. Afterwards the Queen invited Louis to dinner at Osborne and placed him between herself and Beatrice. During the whole evening Beatrice did not utter a single word to Louis, who retired chastened and nonplussed. Years later he discovered the explanation for this extraordinary evening. The Queen had forbidden Beatrice to talk to him, and had placed them together precisely so that Beatrice, through her silence, could rebuff any thoughts of romance on Louis's part. Just to be certain, the Queen instructed the Admiralty that Louis was to be sent abroad and, for the time being, employed only on foreign stations. He departed the country on 24 August 1880, his ship the unfortunately named *Inconstant*. Scandalmongers persisted in coupling his name with Beatrice's, and far away from home Louis read in a foreign newspaper of his secret betrothal to the Queen's youngest daughter. But Beatrice had done her mother's bidding: her connection with Louis of Battenberg existed only in rumour – and the realm of might-have-beens.

The Queen's assessment of Beatrice's character at seventeen, made to her eldest daughter – 'I may truly and honestly say I never saw so amiable, gentle and thoroughly contented a child as she is. She has the sweetest temper imaginable ... and is unselfish and kind to everyone'[2] – is characteristic of her references to Beatrice in her correspondence relating to the latter's teenage years and early twenties. Repeatedly the Queen commends Beatrice's sweetness, the amiable and gentle nature she would manipulate with such steely selfishness when occasion demanded. Biographers have queried this unwavering eventemperedness, but no evidence survives to negate the Queen's appraisal or to suggest that it represents simply self-serving, the Queen salving her conscience for appropriating Beatrice's life to her own ends by interpreting the appearance of a sweet nature as complicity. Happily Beatrice made the Queen's wishes her own. This remarkable disposition may have arisen from true goodness of spirit, from fear or from a degree of self-containment. What is undoubtedly the case is that the family betrothals of the early 1880s, greeted by Beatrice with every appearance of selfless pleasure, would have tried lesser natures in a similar position.

From Balmoral in November 1881 Beatrice wrote to her brother Leopold within hours of hearing of his engagement to

Princess Helen of Waldeck-Pyrmont: 'You know too well my love and devotion to you not to believe that my good wishes come from the bottom of my heart and are no mere empty words. May her you have chosen make you as happy as you deserve to be and brighten your life which has been so sorely tried.'[3] Later she wrote to Helen, 'How thankful I am for the happiness you are giving my dear Brother.'[4] Beatrice was twenty-four. Louis of Battenberg had been banished for over a year. Beatrice's prospects of marriage appeared non-existent. The previous year, in a letter to one of Beatrice's nieces, the Queen had described her daughter as 'too young to understand many things which only a wife and Mother can'.[5] Helen was four years younger than Beatrice.

A marriage of a sibling was one thing. The marriages of Beatrice's nieces and nephews, beginning with that of Charlotte of Prussia in 1876 and escalating through the following decade until Victoria and Louis's marriage in 1884, posed different challenges for the long-suffering Beatrice. Although she had been brought up to value her mother's happiness more highly than her own, her only recourse in the face of what became increasingly frequent pinpricks of humiliation was silence. She remained attentive at her mother's side and did not share with outsiders any feelings save congratulations for those more fortunate than herself – on the brink of discovering freedom and independence in marriage.

For Leopold and his Helen, happiness was to be short-lived. The former died on 28 March 1884 in Cannes, his widow pregnant with a posthumous son. His mother's gloomy court was plunged once again into mourning. Wrestling with her own grief for the brother she loved so much more than he loved her – 'She feels it so dreadfully,' the Queen reported[6] – Beatrice had also to contend with her mother's low spirits. The Queen was still depressed by the death of John Brown the previous spring: 'It is in short the constant missing of that merry buoyant "nature" of my dearest Brown which depresses me so terribly and which makes everything so sad and joyless! – And this I carry everywhere about with me.'[7] Now she reeled from this new blow. Ever present was her anxiety over the safety of General Gordon in

Khartoum, a campaign in which she interested herself closely, in direct opposition to her detested Prime Minister, Gladstone. Fears for Gordon's safety and exasperation at Gladstone's refusal to act on those fears made the Queen frequently irritable. Added to this was her continuing infirmity. At least a light shone on the horizon: Victoria's marriage to Louis in Darmstadt in April. The wedding was postponed to the end of the month to make way for Leopold's funeral, but it was not cancelled.

As early as January, without reference to her own butterfly-wing liaison with Louis, Beatrice had made arrangements with Victoria to accommodate the Queen's special requirements – the sort of long-distance 'housekeeping' typical of the tasks the Queen allotted her. 'Auntie has sent you a Memorandum about our coming and I hope I shall not be giving much trouble,' the Queen wrote to her granddaughter with commendable disingenuousness. 'I am, however, still a very poor creature. I can hardly stand at all – and must be led down stairs, – I can go upstairs by holding on by the banisters or a rope against the wall and I must be led and helped in and out of a carriage by my own Servant.'[8] Given the feeling of claustrophobia this brief extract inspires even at a remove of more than a century, it is no surprise that, despite her grief over Leopold and unavoidable 'what-ifs?' in relation to Louis, Beatrice longed to make the journey to Darmstadt to witness the young couple's happiness (Victoria was six years younger than 'Auntie') and enjoy a brief dilution of the Queen's company in pleasant, cheerful surroundings.

Had her father the Grand Duke, Alice's widower, not determined to marry his mistress, a Russian divorcee of questionable reputation, Victoria of Hesse would have looked forward to her English grandmother's arrival in Darmstadt for her wedding. As it was, the Queen would undoubtedly oppose the Grand Duke and a degree of ill will seemed unavoidable. So certain was Victoria that her father's affairs would spoil her wedding that, when the time came, she took to her bed with an attack of highly uncharacteristic nerves.

The arrival of Auntie Beatrice, however, inspired only happy feelings for the bride-to-be. 'Auntie' was kind and gentle, essentially self-effacing and, by this stage, rapidly losing her early bloom. As the Queen called her, so she appeared – an aunt, unlikely now ever herself to be married. In November of the previous year Beatrice had given a sitting to the Queen's latest portraitist, Düsseldorf-born Carl Rudolph Sohn, for a small, full-length portrait that, on completion, must have made its subject despair. Pudding-faced and wearing an expression of stolid res-ignation, Beatrice stands at the foot of a flight of stone steps. Cylindrical of body, ungainly and without grace despite the lace-trimmed parasol she holds above her head and the spray of roses that hangs from her free hand, she presents to the viewer a dumpy, despairing figure, too overwhelmed by boredom even to look up. Her elaborate, shimmering silk dress, with its full train and pleated underskirt, and the lace shawl so artfully draped over her arm, struggle to imbue this unlovely picture with a semblance of prettiness. Vanished are the princess's bright complexion, the lustre of her hair, the aura of youth on which the Queen so determinedly insisted. In her eyes is neither light nor life; there is no light anywhere save that glinting on the folds of the dress's heavy skirt draped across barrel hips. Sohn's picture is an image of weariness, of the systematic undermining of youthful vigour; a study in lethargic acquiescence. Let us hope, for Beatrice's sake, that this is the picture that encouraged the Queen, four years later, to commission a life-size three-quarter-length portrait of her from Rudolph Swoboda – 'to replace the very ugly one Sohn did of her'.[9] It was not an image of a daughter any loving mother ought to have cherished or even displayed. Nor did it result simply from ineptness on Sohn's part. The artist produced at the same time markedly more successful images of two of the Queen's daughters-in-law, Leopold's Helen and the Duchess of Edinburgh, the latter the possessor of what she herself described as a 'pig-like face',[10] transformed by Sohn into a mask of bourgeois prosperity. Happily for Beatrice, not only her mother but her Hesse nieces recognized her many sterling qualities and essentially sweet nature. What was less certain, but did not concern the Queen, was whether any likely prince or nobleman, following in Louis of Battenberg's footsteps, would persevere beyond unpromising first impressions to find out those qualities.

The Queen's private secretary Henry Ponsonby suspected not. He and Beatrice became the Queen's right-hand 'men' at the same time – 1870. Since then Ponsonby had watched with concern Beatrice's development under her mother's iron schooling. He was fond of the princess, despite her odd manner, arising from shyness, that several courtiers found disconcerting. Lady Lytton, for example, recorded on 27 April 1897, 'Princess Beatrice gave me a little parasol from the Queen after luncheon very shyly saying, "Mama thought you would like this" and then turned away.'[11] Beatrice was forty at the time. Given the intimate nature of his relationship with the Queen, Ponsonby understood better than most the severe limitations imposed upon Beatrice. 'If only she could marry now, at once, a good, strong man who would make her do what he wished, I really think she would turn out well,' he wrote to his wife, former maid of honour Mary Bulteel.

> I think she would want a Prince, though for her sake I should like an Englishman. But it must be soon. That manner you dislike is crystallizing, and her want of interest, which I believe comes from fearing to care for anything the Queen hesitates about, will become natural to her unless a good husband stirs her up. But poor girl, what chance has she?[12]

Ponsonby did not presume to speak to the Queen about Beatrice, and his expression of concern did nothing to widen her horizons or hasten her marriage. Years passed and the oddness of Beatrice's manner – the unfocused, distant gaze of Sohn's portrait and a habit of not appearing to listen to anything addressed to her directly – did indeed crystallize.

Nina Epton, writing in 1971, quoted an unnamed 'neighbour at dinner', who painted a cruel portrait of Beatrice in her last unmarried years:

> Sitting next to a beautiful princess is a reward for bravery in fairy stories, but if the gallant man were popped down every night next

to Princess Beatrice, he would soon cease to be brave. Not that she has nothing to say, for when the subject moves her, she has a torrent, but what with subjects tabooed, the subjects she knows nothing about, and the subjects she turns to the Queen upon, there is nothing left but the weather and silence.[13]

Planting a tree at the opening of the Duthie Park in Aberdeen, Beatrice had indeed fallen back on the weather to supply her with the quip that charmed those who attended her. But charmed they were, whatever the picture painted by an exasperated dinner partner or a portraitist of middling capacity. Beatrice was a victim of the Queen's determined curtailment of experience – even her reading of that royal favourite Tennyson, we have seen, was vetted by her mother. Although this curtailment shaped her character and proscribed her social abilities, it did not overwhelm her nature completely.

Struggling to persuade his mother to allow him to go to university in Oxford, Leopold, the cleverest of the Queen's sons, had written to her,

> To meet with such companions of my own age as would be carefully selected would tend to take away that shyness of manner and general dullness of spirit in conversation and at all times indeed, of which you now so naturally and so much complain, and which must of necessity belong to one who has for so long led such a comparatively solitary life.[14]

Leopold's analysis of his social defects held true for Beatrice too – with the significant difference that, in Beatrice's case, her behaviour did not cause the Queen to complain. Leopold was a man and, as such, though she treated him as a child, the Queen expected from him a role of greater action and initiation; the role she decreed for Beatrice was entirely passive. She did not wish her last daughter to dazzle in society, as her eldest daughter had. She wanted Beatrice to remain contented at her side; the admiration of any third party would only threaten that artificial equilibrium. Dullness was the Queen's trump card – an all-pervading dullness of manner, conversation and spirit that would only finally be banished in the marriage she sought so hard and so long to prevent.

The Queen pursued her course with determination. Henry Ponsonby received a rebuke from his royal mistress, delivered by lady-in-waiting Lady Ely, after discussing a forthcoming marriage at dinner. The Queen's message requested that he refrain from bringing up the subject of marriage at table in front of Princess Beatrice.

Imagining herself all-seeing, the Queen struggled to impose on Beatrice a species of ostrich policy: if Beatrice did not hear about marriage, she would not think about it or desire it. The Queen overlooked only one factor – physical attraction. It was a surprising oversight for a woman whose own marriage had embraced such a potent element of sexual chemistry. When it happened to Beatrice, the Queen would be too preoccupied elsewhere to notice. Ironically, the culprit was once again a prince of Battenberg.

FOURTEEN

The Handsomest Family in Europe

·◆·

For the Battenbergs, the handsomest family in Europe, it was to be third time lucky. First the Queen had suspected Louis of intentions towards Beatrice and dispatched him unhesitatingly to romantic oblivion overseas. Then his brother Alexander, known as 'Sandro', chosen for the precarious distinction of becoming reigning Prince of Bulgaria, claimed that he, too, might have married Beatrice had circumstances (namely the Queen and the instability of the Bulgarian throne) been different. In April 1884 the third brother Henry fell in love with Beatrice on sight. She returned his feelings and true love carried all before it. But the path was far from smooth.

Writing to his mother in Scotland, the Queen's doctor James Reid described Darmstadt at the time of Victoria of Hesse's marriage to Louis of Battenberg as 'a dull place and none of us will be sorry to return'.[1] As so often in their polite but unsympathetic relationship – Reid privately referred to Beatrice as 'Betrave', a 'witty' corruption of the French for 'beetroot' – the doctor's opinion and that of the princess diverged widely. For Beatrice, the sleepy Rhinish town of white houses and broad chestnut avenues, wrapped about by lush country, was not Reid's 'dull place' but the bucolic Eden remembered by Meriel Buchanan in the 1890s: 'There were glorious beech woods where lilies of the valley and violets grew in profusion, there were green fields of cowslips and buttercups, there were great pine forests that were full of sandy rivers where one could gallop one's horses for miles.'[2] Darmstadt in the spring of 1884 was a romantic and special place – where Beatrice fell in love.

It lay to the south of Frankfurt, sheltered by hills, with long views towards the Rhine. The administrative capital of the Grand Duchy of Hesse and by the Rhine, it was the site of the Hesse family's two principal palaces, the Alte Schloss and the Neues Palais, the latter built by Beatrice's sister Alice with a passing nod to Osborne and Thomas Cubitt's grand London houses of the 1850s. The Grand Duchy itself was a mid-sixteenth-century creation, a collection of territories north and south of Frankfurt but excluding the city itself, and east and west of the Rhine. Poor by Prussian standards, it nevertheless furnished the Hesse family with some thirty castles and palaces.

Among those plentiful residences were the Alexander Palace in Darmstadt and Heiligenberg, ten miles south of the town, on a mountain bluff amid the wooded hillsides, a farmhouse that had spread its wings to surround a courtyard and grown into a comfortable *Schloss* with towers, stables, a ballroom, a pergola hung with wisteria, a terrace of shady lime trees and, on a clear day, views as far as France. These were respectively the winter and summer homes of Alexander of Battenberg, his commoner wife Countess Julie von Hauke, created Princess of Battenberg, and the five children of that marriage, on account of Julie's non-royal rank, semi-royal, of morganatic blood: Marie, Louis, Sandro, Henry and Franz Josef. The Battenberg children were cousins once removed of Alice's children, the Queen's Hesse grandchildren, and so by marriage connections of the British Royal Family.

Setting out for Darmstadt in the wake of Leopold's funeral, the Queen had no intention of strengthening that connection beyond welcoming Louis as the husband of a much-loved granddaughter. She did not know that, like his elder brother, Sandro too had entertained thoughts of marrying Beatrice, nor did she consider the third brother Henry, who was younger than Beatrice, though only by a year. Sandro the Queen imagined deeply in love with another of her granddaughters, the Crown Princess's second daughter Victoria of Prussia, called in the family 'Moretta'. As the Queen understood it, Sandro loved Moretta and Moretta loved Sandro, but Bismarck and the Tsar of Russia, both bugbears of the Queen's, opposed the union on political grounds. The

Queen had no idea that, having renounced Moretta, Sandro would later claim that he had sought to marry her only at the Crown Princess's instigation, and that his first choice of bride had been Beatrice. 'I might even at one time have become engaged to the friend of my childhood, Beatrice of England,' Sandro wrote to a friend, 'had not Bulgaria's remoteness, the Princess's love of her home and the Queen's reluctance to be parted from her daughter formed insuperable obstacles.'[3]

It is hard to see when Sandro imagined he had advanced any sort of suit with Beatrice sufficiently far to evaluate the factors opposing their match. A letter written by the Crown Princess to her mother refers to a visit made by Sandro to the imperial court at Berlin at the beginning of April 1881, but the suggestion of the princess's letter is that the Queen either did not know Sandro or had not seen him for some time: 'We were so much struck with Sandro Battenberg when he was here. He is grown so handsome and seemed so nice and sensible, manly and yet modest. I am sure you would have been pleased with him.'[4] It is extremely unlikely that Sandro could have paid attentions to Beatrice without encountering the Queen and becoming known to her, particularly given the evidence of the Queen's and the Crown Princess's surviving correspondence. When, three years later, Sandro reappears in the letters, it is in the guise of suitor to the Crown Princess's daughter Moretta. No reference is made by either writer to any previous interest shown by Sandro in Beatrice, a peculiar omission: though Beatrice may have seen her sister's letters to the Queen, there is no reason to assume she saw the Queen's side of the correspondence. Of the three possible explanations for a deliberate omission of this nature on the Queen's part – fear that Beatrice would see the letters; fear that any third party intercept the letters; an overwhelming aversion to the whole subject that made its very mention distasteful – all are either unlikely or uncharacteristic of the Queen. A more plausible explanation for Sandro's claim is that, elected Prince of Bulgaria, he cast about for a wife. His first choice fell on Beatrice. The Battenbergs were loosely related to the British Royal Family and marriage to the Queen of England's daughter would have brought Sandro significant political benefits, including a strong ally against Russian acquisitiveness. By marrying her previous daughter Louise to a subject the Queen had shown that she was less inflexible in the matter of purity of royal blood than the emperors of Germany or Russia were like to be, and may not have discounted his suit on the grounds of the Battenbergs' morganatic heritage.

There is, of course, the chance, however slender, that Sandro's letter is no more than a statement of fact. That being so, either Beatrice declined his offer of marriage or, as with Louis, the Queen intervened to avert what for her would have amounted to a crisis. In these circumstances the Queen could have been forgiven at this later date for congratulating herself on twice having saved her daughter from amorous Battenbergs. That Beatrice was about to fall, unobserved, at the third fence – taking the opportunity of falling in love with Henry of Battenberg in Darmstadt in April 1884 – shows the degree of the Queen's preoccupation at Louis and Victoria's wedding.

Scarcely mobile; grieving deeply for the death of 'my beloved Leopold, that bright, clever son who had so many times recovered from such fearful illnesses and from various small accidents';[5] concerned (misguidedly or otherwise) for the happiness of her granddaughter Moretta; startled into displeasure by the announcement of the engagement of the bride's sister Ella of Hesse to the Grand Duke Serge of Russia; full of maternal anxiety for the motherless bride Victoria of Hesse; and, when she learnt of it, determined to undo Louis of Hesse's secret remarriage to his Russian mistress, Alexandrine von Kolemine, the Queen found her thoughts too completely occupied to entertain the unlikely prospect of rebellion on Beatrice's part. Unwittingly, she relaxed her customary gimlet vigilance. She failed to notice the instant mutual attraction between the unprepossessing 'Auntie' of Sohn's portrait and the handsome, dark-haired army officer. It was left to Beatrice to break the news to her mother – later, when the royal party had returned to Windsor. Then the ferocity of the Queen's reaction shocked even her family. In time she would relent, but she did so only after a struggle. On Darmstadt, the scene of her fatal weakness, she never looked with the same favour again. Concerning her visit there the following year for a family christening, she wrote to the Crown Princess, 'I can't say I look forward to that visit as much as I would if the dreadful engagement of Beatrice was not in existence and if I didn't know how unwittingly I was deceived about it there.'[6] The Queen had been doubly deceived at Darmstadt: first by the Grand Duke; more significantly, since she swiftly set in motion the process of annulment of Louis's remarriage, by Beatrice. It was the site of Beatrice's liberation.

The Queen could not help the fact that for her the act of loving involved deeply possessive instincts. As early as 1870 she had written to Lord Lorne, then engaged to Louise, 'Mine is a nature which *requires* being loved, and I have lost almost all those who loved me most on earth.'[7] Her warning to Louise's fiancé was clear: though the Queen had approved their marriage, she had no intention of surrendering her daughter completely. When Louise married, the Queen still kept with her Leopold and Beatrice, in addition to John Brown. By the time Beatrice fell in love with Henry of Battenberg, Leopold and Brown were both dead; Beatrice was the last object of affection the Queen 'possessed'. That she meant not to lose her had been written in letters of steel at least as long ago as 1870.

As she watched the tapestry of fertile Hessian fields slip past the windows of the royal train carrying her home, Beatrice understood the magnitude of the task that confronted her in winning her mother's agreement to her marriage. Three years earlier, congratulating Leopold on his engagement, Beatrice had written, 'Mama is after a momentary agitation quite calm, and I only hope she will remain so.'[8] That 'momentary agitation' may have been an understatement intended to reassure Leopold, a deliberate subterfuge on his sister's part to prevent their mother's thwarted ire from spoiling his happiness. When Beatrice's turn came, the Queen's agitation would be anything but momentary. Then no mollifying sibling provided a screen for her feelings.

As early as 1860 the Queen, herself still happily married to the Prince Consort, had expressed strong reservations about the implications of marriage for women. In the years since Alice's, Helena's and Louise's weddings, that dislike had broadened. No longer did it focus specifically on the Queen's daughters and her tangible loss of their companionship. As she grew older, resisting change in many forms, the Queen opposed the marriage of anyone near to her: child, courtier or servant. Twice within a week she wrote to her eldest daughter lamenting Leopold's engagement: 'To me his marrying at all is a grief, and a shock which I can't get over';[9] 'You say you can't be enthusiastic about Leopold's bride! I never can be about any marriage ...'[10] In the case of Victoria of Hesse, the Queen's approbation rested on Victoria assuring her that her marriage would not take her away from her father – a doubtless well-intentioned claim the Queen showed surprising credulousness in believing given that Victoria was marrying an officer in the British Royal Navy while the Grand Duke her father, a German national and reigning prince, lived in landlocked Hesse. Victoria's marriage was not a match made by the Queen; in 1880 the Queen had written to the Grand Duke reminding him that Victoria's first duty was to stay with him.

Increasingly the Queen's thoughts on marriage focused on sex, and the toll it exacted on an innocent girl. For too long the Queen had deceived herself that Beatrice was a child, lily-like and pure, a stranger to sexual impulses. Any idea of Beatrice marrying was tantamount to the Queen sanctioning a massacre of the innocent. 'To me there is something so dreadful, so repulsive in that one has to give one's beloved and innocent child, whom one has watched over and guarded from the breath of anything indelicate [that she] should be given over to a man ... body and soul to do with what he likes. No experience in [life?] will ever help me over that.'[11] For so long the Queen had averted that moment in Beatrice's case. Though she rejoiced at her daughter's beauty at seventeen – its blonde innocence at her confirmation, and rosebud prettiness in Graves's portrait of the same year – she must have felt certain, looking at Sohn's picture painted only a year ago, that now finally she was safe. Her adverse reaction to the news that she was wrong was not solely the anger of a domestic tyrant thwarted in her plans for her own comfort, though this was a factor, but revulsion at the imminent despoiling of a daughter she had described as an angel and a dove, the terror of an ageing matriarch losing the child who had become her all in all, and an expression of simple incredulity. The Queen could not believe that Beatrice wanted to be married. She blamed the hapless Leopold, in death as in life an irritant to his mother; in Leopold's lifetime Beatrice had never thought of marriage. Nor could the Queen conceive that events had reached such a pass without her noticing.

The Queen's reaction took the form of silence. Beatrice's eldest son, the Marquess of Carisbrooke, told biographer David Duff that for seven months, from May to November 1884, mother and daughter continued to live side by side without the Queen addressing a single word to Beatrice. Rather she communicated by note – on those occasions, such as at the breakfast table, when she delivered the note herself, with eyes averted. The easy, intimate intercourse that had characterized the Queen and Beatrice's relationship for over twenty years, a relationship more devotedly loving on both sides than the Queen shared with any other of her children, ended overnight.

Beatrice disappeared from the Queen's letters. In June the Queen requested that the Crown Princess's daughter Moretta not communicate with Beatrice on the subject of her troubled relationship with Sandro of Battenberg. Later the same month she told her eldest daughter, 'We (Beatrice and I) are very sad! And for me pleasure has for ever died out of my life,'[12] a statement of affecting sincerity on the part of the sixty-five-year-old widow who needed a loved one on whom to rely. Not until the end of December is Beatrice's name mentioned again by the Queen to the Crown Princess: '[Helena] has told you of the pain it has caused me that my darling Beatrice should wish ... to marry, as I hate marriages, especially of my daughters.'[13] Beatrice is also absent from her mother's Journal during this period, though at such a moment the Journal, surviving only in Beatrice's own rewritten version, is an unreliable source. The Queen focused the approbation she had previously reserved for Beatrice on other members of her family, in November commending Leopold's widow Helen to the Crown Princess on account of her being 'such a good example to all ... always thinking of others and not herself'[14] – presumably in marked contrast to the currently wayward Beatrice. She also confided in Bertie's wife Alexandra. On 24 August Alexandra wrote to her mother-in-law:

> I must not close my letter without telling you, dearest Mama, how much I felt your again having placed so much confidence in me on a subject which I know has given you such pain even to mention to anyone, as you have always nursed the hope of keeping your one little ewe lamb entirely to yourself. I can therefore well understand what a terrible shock it must have been to you when you heard she had formed a new interest.[15]

Alexandra chose her words carefully. Significantly, she went on to suggest that Beatrice's marriage need not radically alter the Queen's previously happy domestic arrangements. 'We must hope ... that it will all be for the best, and that she will continue for many a long year to be the same help and comfort to you that she has always been.'[16] If the Queen could not change Beatrice's mind – and by the end of August it had become clear that she could not – she must find a way of bending her daughter's desires to her own happiness.

The solution was that the Queen allow Beatrice to marry Henry on condition that he renounce all independence, his career, his nationality and his home, and agree to live with Beatrice and the Queen as they had lived previously. Not until December did the Queen offer Beatrice this lifeline. By then Bertie, the Grand Duke (himself once intended by the Queen and her son as a husband for Beatrice) and the Crown Princess had added their voices to that of the Princess of Wales in support of Beatrice's happiness, the Crown Princess shrewdly cunning in reminding the Queen of the deep love felt for his last-born daughter by the Prince Consort. By then, as the Queen must have known, Beatrice was sufficiently worn down to accept almost any terms she cared to issue.

In the Queen's defence, it is possible that Beatrice's announcement that she wanted to marry Henry so astonished her mother that, at a loss what to do, she retreated within herself and, in silence, waited for the storm to pass. Afterwards she would tell the Crown Princess, 'You who are so fond of marriages ... cannot imagine what agonies, what despair it caused me when I first heard of her wish! It made me quite ill.'[17] But such an explanation is at odds with the evidence of inter-family consultation provided by Alexandra's letter and with the Queen's manner of dealing with her children, whom she seldom forgot were also her subjects. Instead her behaviour suggests a considered plan for ultimately forcing Beatrice's acceptance of the only conditions that could render her marriage acceptable to her mother, namely the couple's residence with her, with no independent home of their own, and Beatrice's remaining in her position of unofficial secretary and full-time companion. The Queen acted ruthlessly and cruelly. Her overriding concern was not the happiness of her favourite daughter but her own ease and comfort. After an initial shock she trusted in Beatrice's good nature, on which she had so often favourably commented, to secure the end she was determined to achieve. For twenty years her treatment of Beatrice had tended to erode the latter's sense of herself. Now the Queen learnt that her success was only partial, and that the love of a mother for a daughter cannot provide a substitute for that warmer, romantic love between a man and a woman based on physical promptings that will not bend to the whim of a refractory old woman. If the Queen considered the suffering she inflicted on Beatrice during that long summer of 1884, she did nothing to ameliorate it, sunk too deep in her own unhappiness to help the child she considered the cause of her sorrow.

By the end of the year mother and daughter were reconciled. To the outside world, even to the Queen herself, their relationship resumed its accustomed course as if there had been no breach. But something in Beatrice had changed. For the first time her dealings with the Queen betray a degree of detachment. To her sister-in-law Helen, writing on the first day of her honeymoon,

Beatrice described her parting from the Queen after her wedding: 'Mama was very kind and motherly, really not saying one word that could jar upon my feelings, and she got through the marriage very well on the whole. Of course, when I took leave of her, she got very upset, poor thing, and both [Henry] and I felt truly sorry for her.'[18] With each of her children the Queen had seen that growing up meant a loosening of the bonds of affection. In Beatrice's case the Queen had postponed that process as long as she possibly could. Her behaviour of the summer of 1884 finally catapulted Beatrice into the arena of adulthood. It was a one-way journey. Even for this most devoted of daughters there could be no turning back.

FIFTEEN

'Many daughters have acted virtuously,
but thou excelleth them all'

•◆•

The address made by 'the inhabitants of Windsor' to Princess
Beatrice on the eve of her wedding, reported in the Court
Circular on 9 July 1885, expressed a widespread popular feeling
that the daughter who had for so long considered her mother's
well-being before her own was now entering a state of deserved
happiness. 'The devotion of your Royal Highness to our beloved
Sovereign has won our warmest admiration and deepest gratitude.
May those blessings which it has hitherto been your constant
aim to confer on others now be returned in full measure to
yourself.'[1] It was as close to an admonishment of the Queen as
nineteenth-century habits of deference could hazard. On the
tray of the florid silver tea and coffee service that centenarian
philanthropist and financier Sir Moses Montefiore presented to
the couple as a wedding present, a Hebrew inscription read
simply, 'Many daughters have acted virtuously, but thou excelleth
them all.'

Two deciding factors underlay the Queen's acceptance of the
situation that she knew by the end of the summer she was
powerless to alter: Beatrice and Henry's agreement to her conditions, and Henry himself – 'as I like Liko [Henry] very much
and as they are both so very devoted to each other, and she
remains always with me, I cannot refuse my consent'.[2] There was
no question of *force majeure*. Family pressure alone could not
have persuaded the Queen to change her mind, just as it had
failed to lure her out of seclusion at the end of the 1860s. Nor
did the unhappiness of Beatrice – excluded for the first time from
her mother's confidence and approbation – supply a motivating
factor. The Queen's agreement at first was grudging – as she

explained separately to the Crown Princess, the newly married Victoria of Hesse and her correspondent the Duke of Grafton, she agreed because there were no further grounds for disagreement, a negative capitulation rather than a positive embracing of Beatrice's hopes. She did not indulge in dissimulation: the whole business had been an unpleasant surprise she could happily have done without. 'It remains a shock to me and there will be things very difficult to get over with my feelings – still as he is so amiable and prepared to do what I wish – I hope all may ... turn out well.'³ Although she gave as one of her reasons the couple's evidently sincere affection, their willingness to put her wishes before their own was the consideration that won the day. Later, the Queen would learn just how right Alexandra had been in encouraging her to hope 'that it will all be for the best': Beatrice's marriage made the Queen's domestic life happier than it had been since the death of the Prince Consort. But this came as a surprise to the Queen: assertively curmudgeonly at the outset of Beatrice's engagement, she did not dare to hope for a positive resolution. She continued to issue conditions. 'I *can't* spare Auntie, and especially at first they must *not* think of travelling or paying visits.'⁴ There were to be no public displays of affection between the couple (the Queen congratulated herself that Beatrice did not appear to like kissing anyway, a tactful modesty on Beatrice's part), and the Queen prayed earnestly that there would be no children of the marriage – happy so long as her own routine continued unchanged to deny Beatrice this blessing over which she herself had alternately rejoiced and despaired.

The Queen's only faith had been in the memory of Beatrice's lifetime of unflagging attentiveness and Henry's handsome face. To her eldest daughter she wrote that she considered Henry 'the handsomest of the three handsome brothers' (there were in fact four brothers) ⁵ The Queen had never been immune to masculine good looks. Henry was born in Milan, on 5 October 1858; as an adult his appearance whispered of that southern infancy, with his dark hair and bright, dark eyes. His Italian nurse called him 'Enrico', corrupted by the infant tongues of his brothers into 'Liko' (pronounced 'Leeko'). The moniker, with its tang of exoticism, endured lifelong and was the name by which both Beatrice and the Queen knew him. Happily, in aspiration Liko was anything but exotic. Despite his military training and the stories of his father's martial prowess that had delighted him as a boy, in 1884 he was prepared, after a struggle, to forswear such occupation in return for Beatrice's love. He renounced his commission as a first lieutenant in the Prussian Garde du Corps. With such fidelity did he accept the Queen's circumscription of his married life, that at the time of his death the *Illustrated London News* was able to claim, 'Prince Henry of Battenberg has been to the Queen, we believe, what any of her younger sons, remaining unmarried and staying with her, might possibly have been.'[6] Far from losing Beatrice, the Queen would find that (after a fashion) she had replaced Leopold.

Lady Waterpark was not in waiting at the time of Beatrice's engagement but returned to Osborne at the end of January 1885. She recorded in her diary, 'I have omitted to say that since my last waiting, the marriage [engagement] of Princess Beatrice to Prince Henry of Battenberg had been announced. The Queen seemed very happy about it.'[7] With the decision made, the Queen did her best to put a brave face on things. Mostly she succeeded. Contemplation of the wedding night, and a fear that the marriage might yet unsettle her routine in the long term (despite her best efforts to prevent it from being a marriage in anything but name) continued sporadically to haunt her. Try as she might, she could not completely overcome her initial antipathy, though she struggled to remind herself of the many reasons to be sanguine.

> I am surprised at myself [she wrote to the Crown Princess], considering the horror and dislike of the most violent kind I had for the idea of my precious Baby's marrying at all ... how I should have been so much reconciled to it now that it is settled. But it is really Liko who has so completely won my heart. He is so modest, so full of consideration for me and so is she, and both are quietly and really sensibly happy.[8]

The Queen recognized her daughter's imminent change in status by rewarding her with a second lady-in-waiting, Minna

Cochrane, known as 'Minnie'. Minnie Cochrane was a contemporary of Beatrice's and an Isle of Wight neighbour. Her
services supplemented those of Lady Biddulph, wife of Keeper of
the Privy Purse Sir Thomas Biddulph and a friend of the princess's
from childhood, who had acted as first lady-in-waiting to her for
several years. Miss Cochrane was not a stranger either to the
Royal Household or to Beatrice personally: with her sister she
had spent periods in waiting during the early 1880s and, sub-
sequently, had been received at Osborne on a more social footing,
visiting for lunch or to play duets with Beatrice. Her appointment
would prove more successful than the Queen's previous attempt
to provide her youngest daughter with her own lady attendant,
the Hon. Ethel Cadogan, whom Henry Ponsonby had hesitatingly
described on her arrival at court in 1876 as 'gushing but has
points', but who the Queen later unflinchingly dismissed as
jealous, sensitive, hot-tempered and unpopular with her colleagues.[9] The appointment of Miss Cadogan had been another
of those occasions when the Queen's treatment of Beatrice drove
a wedge between Beatrice and her siblings. Helena and Louise
reacted indignantly to the discovery; after all, they had not had
a lady-in-waiting before they were married. With the announcement of Beatrice's engagement, there could be no objections to
Miss Cochrane's appointment.

Liko spent Christmas 1884 on the Isle of Wight, the guest of his
brother Louis and heavily pregnant sister-in-law Victoria at Kent
House, on the Osborne estate. On 23 December the Battenberg
party was invited to dinner at the big house. In her manner
towards her most contentious guest the Queen made clear that,
all boxes being ticked to her satisfaction, she was now happy to
welcome him into her family. Liko did not need further prompt-
ing. As the Queen recorded in her Journal on 29 December,

> Received a letter from Liko Battenberg saying that my kind
> reception of him encouraged him to ask my consent to speaking
> to Beatrice, for whom, since they met in Darmstadt eight months
> ago, he had felt the greatest affection! I had known for some time

that she had the same feelings towards him. They seem sincerely attached to each other, of that there can be no doubt. I let Liko know, to come up after tea, and I saw him in dear Albert's room. Then I called the dear child, and gave them my blessing.[10]

With Albert's shade summoned to the party, and Beatrice once again restored to the status of 'child' through her belated compliance, the Queen smiled upon the union she had done her best to resist. To complete her volte-face, she telegraphed her old friend the Empress of Germany and her daughter the Crown Princess to share the good news. Only the latter responded as the Queen had intended.

Even the briefest pause would have allowed the Queen to anticipate the certain negative reaction to the news of the German imperial family. Although the Crown Princess's second son Henry initially wired his congratulations direct to Beatrice and Liko, he later rescinded this good opinion and joined in the family's undeviating condemnation of a marriage between a royal princess and an upstart princeling of morganatic birth. Astonished, the Queen wrote to the Crown Princess (a lone voice in Berlin in rejoicing in the match): 'I must tell you how very unamiably the Empress and even dear Fritz [the Crown Princess's husband] have written to me. I think really the Empress has no right to write to me in that tone ... Dear Fritz speaks of Liko as not being of the blood – a little like about animals.' So affronted was the Queen that she had copies made of the empress's letter. She enclosed one for the Crown Princess to digest, alongside her 'rather stern answer'. With an understated anger that would have been clear to her daughter, the Queen explained, 'I cannot swallow affronts.'[11] Unhappily, to add fuel to the fire, the Queen's letter crossed with one from the Crown Princess in which the writer detailed the disapproval of the engagement expressed by her children, Beatrice's nephews and niece by marriage. At this the Queen's fury finally erupted. William of Prussia, the Queen's first grandson, had married, in 1881, Augusta of Schleswig-Holstein-Sonderburg-Augustenburg, known as 'Dona', a portionless princess whose claims to prettiness the Queen had already previously denied. Now she denounced 'the extraordinary impertinence ... insolence and I must add, great unkindness' of the Prussian children. But she saved her parting shot for William's wife. 'As for Dona, a poor, little, insignificant Princess raised entirely by your kindness to the position she is in, I have no words.'[12] The Queen's confidence in her decision did not falter in the face of Prussian criticism. She dismissed Berlin's stuffiness, asserting, like King Cophetua, that in England if a king chose to marry a peasant girl, she would be queen as much as any princess:[13] 'If the Queen of England thinks a person good enough for her daughter, what have other people to say?'[14] To highlight the contrast with the reaction of her Prussian relatives the Queen reported the kind telegrams she had received from every other sovereign. With partial truthfulness she claimed, 'The marriage is immensely popular here and the joy unbounded that she, sweet Child, remains with poor, old shattered me!'[15]

It was true that popular opinion at home approved Beatrice's willingness to remain with her mother after marriage. A sermon preached after Liko's death commended Beatrice as 'that youngest daughter whose touching wish to remain at her mother's side, even after she became a wife, appealed to the heart of a nation'.[16] But the general public rejoiced in Beatrice's marriage only insofar as it promised happiness to the Queen's favourite daughter. Liko's foreignness and his lack of fortune went against him. A splendid position might have carried all before it, but Liko was a prince only in name, without a throne and with no close connection with any of Europe's great ruling dynasties (his brother's position as Prince of Bulgaria was rightly discounted). A 'German pauper' was not an asset to Britain's already highly Germanized Royal Family but a potential drain on the national purse. On a wave of happiness, and buoyed by the knowledge that her siblings and the Queen's Household warmly supported her engagement, Beatrice scarcely noticed public carping. Accustomed to seeing events as she wished them to appear, the Queen simply ignored the noises off, although she made plain to Gladstone's government that she had noted those of her ministers who had not written to congratulate her on the news.

Like the response of the German imperial family, the tepid, even negative national reaction to Beatrice's engagement could have been anticipated by the Queen. At the time of Louise's engagement to Lord Lorne in 1870 the Queen had supported Louise against those of her own children, chiefly Bertie and the Crown Princess, who opposed the marriage of a princess to a commoner. Correctly, the Queen had explained the two-fold nature of the popular objection, xenophobia and penny-pinching: 'Small foreign princes (without any money) are very unpopular here';[17] 'the feeling against foreign marriages has long been very strong here, especially if the Princes are poor.'[18] Fifteen years later the Queen had changed her tune. (In her defence, her previous argument had assumed the British princess would live abroad with her foreign prince, thus taking to another country the dowry and annuity provided for her from British taxes.)

Despite mutterings in the popular press, when the question of Beatrice's annuity came to be debated in Parliament in May of the following year, the vote passed with a majority of three hundred and thirty-seven to thirty-eight. The liberal republican Henry Labouchère raised the loudest protest (happily 'not in violent language' as the Queen reported afterwards[19]); yet even he failed to garner significant support. Explaining his reasons for not seconding Labouchère's opposition to Beatrice's annuity, radical MP John Bright, a potential ally of Labouchère's who had been canvassed by him as such, wrote:

> The Princess is now the only unmarried daughter of the Queen, and I cannot believe that any significant number of our people would wish her to be treated in a manner less generous than has been the case with her sisters ... I gather from the concluding words of your resolution that your objection to the grant is on the ground of economy, on which you will permit me to say a word. The annual grant of £6,000 is less than one farthing per family among the seven millions of families in the United Kingdom, and therefore cannot be regarded as a burden that can be felt ... In years past I have spoken in Parliament against the magnitude of some of the grants to the Royal family, but I could not condemn

this present grant on any grounds. I feel that in the course I am now taking ... I am acting in accordance with the general character of my countrymen, with whom whatever has a taint of unkindness and meanness is condemned.[20]

The Prince of Wales was swift to thank Bright for his words on Beatrice's behalf: 'Having read your letter ... relative to my Sister's Dowry, I cannot resist writing a few lines to express my warmest thanks to you for the kind expressions you made use of ... and I know that this will be deeply appreciated by the Queen and every member of my Family.'[21]

The Queen had not doubted that Parliament would rally to her support, and began making preparations for the wedding as soon as she announced the engagement. At Osborne, on 31 January, she formalized Minnie Cochrane's appointment as Beatrice's second lady-in-waiting; three days later, with the Dean of Windsor but without Beatrice, she went early in the morning to nearby Whippingham Church. This, the Queen had decided in a calculated break with tradition, would be the venue for Beatrice's wedding. Royal princesses did not marry in parish churches, but the Queen, with her horror of public show, was determined that Beatrice's wedding would not be a state occasion.

The use of St Mildred's restricted the number of guests who could be asked and allowed the Queen, as a face-saving exercise, not to invite the German imperial family, whom she knew, even at this stage, would refuse her invitation. She outlined preliminary plans to the Crown Princess: 'The wedding is to be here at Whippingham church – half state uniforms and evening dresses, but no trains, and Beatrice will have no train or train bearers – but eight of her nieces as at dear Alice's marriage.'[22] Later the number of bridesmaids was increased to ten, as the Queen explained to one of her favourite correspondents, the poet laureate Tennyson: 'my eldest son's three girls, Louise, Victoria and Maud of Wales, dear Alice's two motherless girls, Irene and Alice of Hesse, Princess Christian's two, Victoria and Louise of Holstein, and my son Alfred's three, Marie, Victoria and Alexandra Marie of Edinburgh'.[23] In 1866 and 1871 Helena and Louise had been attended by an octet of daughters of the aristocracy. Such pains had the Queen taken that Beatrice not make friends outside the immediate court circle, that it is unlikely Beatrice could have mustered a similar flotilla of suitable girls of her own age. Instead, her bevy of nieces included – on account of the overlap of generations – a smattering of near contemporaries (Irene of Hesse and the Wales girls), the future Tsarina of Russia and the future queens of Norway and Roumania. At least four took a close interest in the proceedings, the Duchess of Edinburgh writing to the Queen that her three daughters were 'very flattered and proud' to be asked to play such an important role in their aunt Beatrice's wedding,[24] while from Darmstadt, Irene of Hesse, Liko's cousin, wrote to the Queen shortly after the engagement, '[Liko's] letters from England have always been so full of happiness.'[25]

Beatrice did not protest as her mother seized control. After the unwonted breakdown of the summer, it must have seemed that, at last, things were returning to normal, the Queen planning and making decisions, Beatrice agreeing and falling into line. For eight months Beatrice's happiness had hung in the balance. The Queen's bossiness was a small price to pay for the realization of that joy. To Lady Waterpark, whom she had known now for twenty years, Beatrice wrote on 6 January,

> If good wishes could make me happy, I am sure I ought to be so, but I think I have every reason to look with confidence to the future. It is a great comfort to me that Mama is now thoroughly reconciled to the thought of my marrying, and that my future husband has already endeared himself to Her. Please God this event may brighten her life, and our one wish both of us is to devote our lives to her.[26]

The Queen had been correct in her assessment of Beatrice's 'amiable' nature, formed long ago; even the sufferings of the summer had not lessened her loving loyalty. Only now the princess had a soulmate to support her in her lonely task. After years of treading water, watching with kindness as life unfolded around her but never quite happened to her personally, she could 'look with confidence to the future', secure in the love of her mother and the man who would shortly become her husband. Liko had twined himself about the Queen's heart – as Beatrice's sister-in-law Marie, Duchess of Edinburgh, commented sourly, the Queen 'found in him true perfection'.[27] All that remained to trouble her complacent equilibrium were her fears for the wedding night itself.

SIXTEEN

'The fatal day approaches'

.•.

At seventy-seven Alfred, Lord Tennyson felt that he was fading fast. 'I think that, blind as I am, growing blinder, I am best away from the wedding,' he wrote to the Queen, declining her invitation to Beatrice's marriage, which had been fixed for 23 July.[1] He did, however, address a special celebratory poem to Beatrice. Later that year it was included in *Tiresias, and Other Poems* alongside 'To the Duke of Argyll' and an epitaph on General Gordon, the last an undertaking after the Queen's own heart. In advance of the general release, Tennyson printed privately one hundred copies of 'To HRH Princess Beatrice' and dispatched them to Osborne.

The Queen approved Tennyson's offering, with its tactful and ingenious reconciling of the claims of daughterly and wifely love. Beatrice herself was less enamoured, despite the Queen's claims in her letter of thanks to Tennyson written on 12 July: 'How can I sufficiently thank you for those exquisite touching, beautiful lines which I read to my beloved Child, who was equally delighted with them and with the beautiful thoughts they contain.'[2] Two lines in particular distressed Beatrice:

> The Mother weeps
> At that white funeral of the single life,
> Her maiden daughter's marriage.

Whether it was the accuracy of Tennyson's insight, his distasteful reference to sex (however politely oblique), the use of the word 'funeral' in connection with her marriage when so much of her life had already been overshadowed by death and its obsequies, or the permanent reminder in verse of something upon which she preferred not to dwell – the summer-long struggle with her mother, with all its attendant tears and sadness – Beatrice did not explain. But the lines rang truer than the vapid platitudes typical of such commemorative works, and the princess balked at so public a statement of her recent private dispute with the Queen.

For the Queen, happy as she was with her laureate's poem, the business of commemoration did not end with poetry. She commissioned commemorative medals in bronze and silver from Allan Wyon of Regent Street. Wyon not only designed but made the medals, which showed overlapping profile busts of Beatrice and Liko on one side, on the reverse their two coats of arms, hers encircled by oak leaves, his by laurel leaves, surmounted by coronets. As had been the case with all eight of Beatrice's siblings, the Queen also required a painting of the ceremony. Two years previously she had commissioned from a military painter, Richard Caton Woodville, a view of a battle in which her favourite son Arthur served. That painting having given satisfaction, twenty-nine-year-old Caton Woodville was now the surprising choice to paint Beatrice's wedding. Henry Ponsonby wrote to him on the Queen's behalf on 19 June: 'Although I have only seen War pictures by you, do you ever paint peace pictures? Such as an interior of a church and marriage ceremony.'[3] The artist accepted the round-about invitation. To help him in his task, on the day of the wedding itself all the royal guests were photographed after the service. The result is a shockingly bad painting that contains many recognizable likenesses. It must have been a source of some relief to the artistically gifted Beatrice that the picture was not destined for a wedding present. Even the Queen, a questionable judge of paintings, was not pleased, and felt herself justified in her decision to pay Caton Woodville only half the sum she had given for Linton's picture of Leopold's wedding three years earlier.

Whatever its shortcomings artistically, the picture at least furnished the Queen with happy recollections. Not only was the form of Beatrice's wedding day entirely of her devising, but all involved – from the Osborne servants, in their new blue livery ordered specially for the day, to the bride and bridegroom themselves – acquitted themselves exactly as the Queen required, enabling Henry Ponsonby to write afterwards to the Lord Chamberlain, 'The Queen commands me to ask you to convey Her Majesty's thanks to all in your Department who did their duty to the Queen's entire satisfaction.'[4]

The Queen had left little to Beatrice. The day before the wedding Beatrice, with Liko, who had arrived on the island with his family two days earlier, accompanied her on her final tour of inspection of preparations at St Mildred's. By then the temporary covered passage that led from the lychgate to the church's principal entrance, the south porch, was in place. It provided a covered corridor for the wedding procession in the event of a change in the weather and, flanked by three tiers of benches, additional seating for guests who could not be accommodated inside the church. Open at the sides, it was shady without being dark, and its rafters were garlanded with flowers and evergreens. Inside the church itself columns and arches were similarly decorated. The vicar, Canon Prothero, had finalized arrangements for decorations with the Royal Household at the end of June, writing to gentleman usher Sir Spencer Ponsonby Fane,

> I had already settled to dress up the stump of the Pulpit with ivy and ferns, but your idea of the corresponding one the other side is brilliant. Will you give orders for it. If you would order a light iron rail round each stump, the gardeners can make a pyramid of flowers in pots, which would look very well. I only hope they will send me plenty of flowers, and in good time, then we shall do very well.[5]

In the event, the lectern and the pulpit, decorated as Prothero had suggested by his wife and daughter with lilies, white roses and ferns, were moved in order to widen the aisle, and a false floor laid so that the Queen did not have to negotiate any steps; it was covered with crimson cloth overlaid with Indian and Persian carpets. The effect – in the church the Prince Consort had helped to design – won the Queen's full approval. Unhappily, St Mildred's verdant splendour was short-lived. Within an hour of the service ending locals in pursuit of souvenirs had stripped the building of every frond and flower, overcoming the attendant police through weight of numbers.

Beatrice spent the run-up to the wedding occupied as usual with the minutiae of the Queen's life, correspondence for the most part. Even on the wedding day itself, the Queen recorded, Beatrice 'was busy answering telegrams up to the last'.[6] She also accompanied her mother on engagements not connected with her wedding, such as the Queen's review of the Camel Corps from the Sudan, held at Osborne and also attended by Beatrice's soon-to-be brother- and sister-in-law, Louis and Victoria of Battenberg.

It is unlikely that mother and daughter spent cosy evenings discussing that aspect of Beatrice's marriage that now most concerned the Queen – her conjugal relations with Liko. The Queen remained agonized by the prospect of what Liko had in store for her 'Baby'. 'I count the months, weeks and days that she is still my own sweet, unspoilt, innocent lily and child,' she wrote to the Crown Princess after Beatrice's last unmarried birthday.

> That thought – that agonizing thought which I always felt, and which I often wonder any mother can bear of giving up your own child, from whom all has been so carefully kept and guarded – to a stranger to do unto her as he likes is to me the most torturing thought in the world ... I can't help saying to you what has cost me always so much, and what in poor, darling, gentle (and not very strong) Beatrice's case almost tortures me![7]

Though the Queen had doggedly subjected Beatrice to the mental and emotional harrowing of eight months' exclusion from her good graces, she felt she hardly dared risk her in bed with the man she loved enough to bring upon herself this aestival wrath. Nor would her stultifying consciousness of Beatrice's long-preserved purity allow her to discuss with her this aspect of a wife's duties, thereby potentially smoothing the path she imagined so liberally sprinkled with tears.

Instead, days before Liko's arrival, an evening at Windsor was spent with Beatrice reading to her mother from the diary of the recently decapitated General Gordon, 'which [was] painful and harrowing, as it [showed] how badly he was treated by the Government'.[8] The Queen took pleasure in these 'ordinary' evenings, with their similarity to so many evenings of the recent past to which she clung so ardently. Until the very last minute she remained, on and off, deeply unhappy about Beatrice's approaching nuptials. 'I am *very depressed*,' she wrote to Victoria of Battenberg on 11 July. 'How I dread the week after next – and how I wish it was months and years off! The nearer the fatal day approaches the more my invincible dislike to Auntie's marriage (*not* to dear Liko) – increases. Sometimes I feel as if I *never* could take her myself to the Marriage Service – and that I would wish to run away and hide myself!'[9]

For Beatrice there were no second thoughts. Her trousseau had been ordered from the London fashion house of Redfern, a favourite of her sister-in-law the Princess of Wales. It contained garments of understated luxury, simple in outline (by contemporary standards) but made from sumptuous materials of exquisite quality. Evening gowns, several with trains, were embroidered with different-coloured pearls. From Ireland came quantities of the finest linen.

Beatrice's fittings jostled for time with the reception of deputations from around the country bearing gifts. The boys of Eton College gave her a diamond-and-sapphire locket, 'the maidens of England' a Bible; members of the Royal Institute of Painters in Water Colours, of which she herself was an honorary member, presented an album of drawings; 'the tenantry of the Queen's Deeside estates of Balmoral, Abergeldie and Birkhall' offered a park phaeton and a pair of ponies in anticipation of more rain-drenched Highland drives; while a deputation from Liverpool presented an address and 'a wedding cake upon a silver plateau, ornamented with silver figures of English and German soldiers and a seaman, the whole resting upon four Liver birds'.[10] Nearer to home, on the Isle of Wight, the inhabitants of West Cowes gave the princess a large mirror in a silver frame. Mr Thomas, schoolmaster of Whippingham School, presented an opal-glass candelabrum with twelve flower glasses on behalf of the parishioners of Whippingham and children of the school. The last would be among those who stood in fields along the carriage route from Osborne to the church, cheering the last princess, whom they knew so much better than the siblings who had gone before her. All the deputations had to be welcomed and thanked; there were letters of thanks to be written to donors at home and abroad, family, friends and public bodies. The Queen's Household combined to offer a single present; courtiers close to Beatrice also gave more personal presents, such as the black-and-gold Japanese folding screen Lady Waterpark sent to Windsor in June. 'It will be most useful, reminding me of our long and pleasant intercourse, which luckily is not to be broken off by my marriage,' Beatrice wrote by way of thanks.[11] All the presents were displayed at Osborne in time for the wedding.

Only the Queen's invincible determination made a royal wedding on the Isle of Wight possible. From every practical viewpoint the scheme was unfeasible. There was not enough room in St Mildred's even for the reduced number of guests entailed by a non-state occasion. The Queen filled Osborne with her guests, then took over nearby Norris Castle and East Cowes Castle. Still there was not enough room. She dispatched guests to Osborne Cottage, Kent House and Park Villa. Two of the royal yachts, the *Victoria and Albert* and the *Osborne*, became floating hotels. Still some guests remained in London until the morning of the wedding. The choir of St George's Chapel Windsor and the organist Mr Parratt were imported for the occasion, though they received shoddy treatment for their pains, the Master of the Household asserting in advance, 'We cannot provide in any way for the choristers coming from London. They should make their own arrangements for refreshments. I suppose at East Cowes.'[12] Adding a note of confusion, the Queen – despite her earlier letter to the Crown Princess detailing the absence of trains – refused to commit herself to any definite dress code, and it was left to the Mistress of the Robes, the Duchess of Buccleuch, to provide a resolution: 'Ladies staying in the Isle of Wight to wear long dresses with demi-toilette bodies, cut down on the back and with sleeves to the elbow. Jewels to be worn on the dress and in the hair as for full dress evening party. Only those ladies who travel down to Osborne for the day are to wear bonnets and smart morning dresses.'[13] Helpfully, the Duchess made available her own dress at her dressmakers in New Bond Street, so that those who remained uncertain could see exactly what was expected.

Few of these ramifications affected Beatrice. She was accustomed to the tortuous workings of her mother's household, and the Queen's need to involve herself and make decisions at every level. Her thoughts were fixed firmly on her wedding day and what lay beyond. As she wrote to Leopold's widow, the Duchess of Albany, on the first day of her honeymoon, 'What rest and peace I feel now that all is accomplished, my heart has so long desired.'[14]

Liko arrived on 20 July with his parents, his brothers Franz Josef ('Franzjos') and Sandro, Prince of Bulgaria (the latter accompanied by his Bulgarian secretary Toptschilecheff), the Grand Duke of Hesse and his children, and the Hesse suite. At a private investiture service attended by Beatrice and Arthur, the Queen awarded Liko the Order of the Garter (she had made a similar award to all her sons-in-law except the commoner Lord Lorne), and conferred upon him the style 'Royal Highness' (as a morganatic prince he had previously been 'Serene Highness'). Liko's change in status had been an issue since the Queen announced Beatrice's engagement, the Prussians vociferously determined not to recognize or honour any escalation. So acrimonious did the debate become that the Queen had asked the Grand Duke of Hesse to try to defuse the situation, in particular by pacifying her troublesome grandson William of Prussia. The Grand Duke did not succeed, but the Queen was undeterred. In Britain, at any rate, Liko would be raised to the same level as Beatrice, even if this gave the penny press one more reason to carp. 'It is not vouchsafed to all of us to be demorganaticated, bridegrooms, Royal Highnesses, and Knights of the Garter in the twinkling of an eye,' *Vanity Fair* commented after the wedding.[15]

The wedding day itself was a perfect English summer's day, sea and cloudless sky cerulean blue. Across the island the weather provided a boon to local children. In Newport three thousand Sunday-school children marched to the home of Alderman Mew for a picnic followed by games and races; similar children's parties were held in honour of the day at Ryde and Binstead. Even the Queen resisted the temptation to lament the heat. Despite the houseful of guests, she and Beatrice breakfasted alone, outside under the trees. During the course of the morning Arthur and his wife came out to see them and, later, Liko too. The Queen gave Beatrice a special, additional wedding present, a half-hoop ruby ring that her uncle Augustus, Duke of Sussex, her father's favourite brother, had given her on her wedding day. It was the lesser of two tokens of singular esteem the Queen bestowed on her daughter that day. The other was among her most treasured possessions. It was her own wedding veil of Honiton lace, which she had additionally worn at the christening of all of her children but which no other daughter had been permitted to wear. It was a particular favouritism that signalled more eloquently than any words the Queen's drawing a line under the unhappiness of the summer and her acceptance of Beatrice's marriage. Beatrice wore it suspended from a tiara of large diamond stars.

The wheel had turned full circle. Once, it was rumoured, the Queen had wrapped Beatrice in the Prince Consort's nightshirt, a physical comfort in the painful days of longing that followed the Prince's death. Now she gave to Beatrice her own wedding veil. From the age of four Beatrice had been forced to consider the Queen not simply as her mother but as the happiest of wives dealt the cruellest blow by the one force she could not control, death. Now at last the role of wife passed symbolically from mother to daughter in the handing from one to another of the wedding veil.

The service started at one o'clock. While the Queen rested,

Beatrice began to dress, in dearest Albert's room, in order that I might be near her. I came in, whilst her veil and wreath were being fastened on. It was *my* dear wedding veil ... She wore besides, the diamond circlet with diamond stars ... Whilst my cap was being put on, Beatrice came in ready dressed. Her dress was quite simple, in ivory white satin, very long, trimmed with my wedding lace, and some small garlands and sprays of orange blossoms, myrtle and white heather. Her jewels were diamonds.[16]

In addition to the tiara of diamond stars, Beatrice wore a short necklace of large diamonds from which hung a large diamond cross, a necessary massing of bright stones if she were to avoid being eclipsed by her mother, who set off her customary black dress with a diamond necklace and the Koh-i-noor. Beatrice's dress, which the Queen described as 'quite simple', strikes the modern viewer as anything but, but beneath the lush garlanding of orange blossom and foliage the dress itself was indeed simple, a tightly laced white bodice above a long, almost straight skirt, over which was draped an overskirt of beautiful lace. On her left shoulder Beatrice wore the Victoria and Albert Order and the Imperial Order of the Crown of India, the second a present from the Queen on New Year's Day 1878 in anticipation of her twenty-first birthday. Her ten bridesmaids, whom Henry Labouchère, the MP who had voted against her annuity, described as showing a 'decided absence of beauty',[17] wore high-necked white dresses with flounced skirts and carried saucer-shaped bouquets of stephanotis. Owing to their large number, the bridesmaids travelled separately to St Mildred's. Beatrice travelled alone with the Queen in a closed carriage drawn by four greys, the last of the fourteen carriages that made up the royal procession. As they drew near to the church, their arrival was signalled by the sounding of guns and the noise of cheering from the crowds along the way.

A guard of honour of her sister Princess Louise's Argyll and Sutherland Highlanders awaited Beatrice at St Mildred's; at the entrance to the covered passage Bertie was dressed in the uniform of a field marshal. Together mother, brother and sister entered the packed church. As at any wedding, the congregation included friends and relations, childhood associates and a number of compulsory invitations. All Beatrice's siblings save the Crown Princess and her husband sat in the chancel (the absence of the

German imperial couple meant that Beatrice was married without either of her surviving godparents, just as her confirmation had been distinguished by its lack of godparents). Also in the chancel were Mademoiselle Norèle, Beatrice's French governess, and Fräulein Bauer, her German governess who was now reader to the Royal Household. Sir Henry Ponsonby, who had hoped so earnestly that Beatrice be allowed to marry, sat in the Queen's pew, as did Ethel Cadogan, Beatrice's first lady-in-waiting, who would again spend periods in attendance on the princess after her marriage. Close to the altar was Lady Waterpark, and in the Household pew the same Lord De Ros who had shown the eleven-year-old princess the Tower of London. Absent was the Queen's cousin, Princess Mary Adelaide, Duchess of Teck, in mourning for her father-in-law Duke Alexander of Württemberg; she had been the first of the Queen's correspondents for whom Beatrice became a go-between, in 1872, at the outset of Beatrice's long secretaryship. Also absent was Gladstone. Despite public disapprobation of the snub the Queen refused to relent and invite the 'half crazy and in many ways ridiculous old man' whose second ministry had recently fallen from power.[18] The Empress Eugénie declined her invitation, though there had been no breach in friendship between Napoleon III's widow and the Queen or her daughter. Eugénie kept to herself her reasons for staying away from the wedding of the girl she may once have intended as her daughter-in-law. Instead, two years later, she became the godmother of Beatrice's only daughter.

With her customary facility for embracing contradictions, the Queen had insisted that Liko wear the uniform of the Prussian Garde du Corps, though his feelings towards Prussia at this stage can have been mixed at best, and despite the Queen having made it a condition of his marriage that he renounce his military career. The effect of the dazzling white tunic, white breeches and high black boots added a note of Ruritanian whimsy to the service in a small parish church officiated at by four clergymen including the Archbishop of Canterbury, and caused the Princess of Wales to dub Liko 'Beatrice's Lohengrin'. The Queen, however, was pleased with the charming picture.

A happier-looking couple could seldom be seen kneeling at the altar together. It was very touching. I stood very close to my dear child, who looked very sweet, pure, and calm. Though I stood for the ninth time near a child and for the fifth time near a daughter, at the altar, I think I never felt more deeply than I did on this occasion, though full of confidence. When the blessing had been given, I tenderly embraced my darling 'Baby'.[19]

The bride, who had entered the church to Wagner, left to Mendelssohn's Wedding March – on the arm of her husband, Princess Henry of Battenberg at last. To the absent Tennyson the Queen wrote, 'The simple, pretty little village church, all decorated with flowers, the sweet young bride, the handsome young husband, the ten bridesmaids, six of whom quite children with flowing fair hair, the brilliant sunshine and the blue sea all made up pictures not to be forgotten.'[20]

The scene at Osborne after the ceremony [reported the *Illustrated London News*] was that of a brilliant garden party, the guests being entertained in the marquees erected out of doors. From the south entrance abutting upon the lawn was a covered way, leading to a great oblong tent, decorated with palms, ferns and flowers sent from the Royal stove-houses and gardens at Windsor. In the centre was a horse-shoe table where eighty guests lunched and dined ... On the lawns were two large tents, occupied by the band of the Marines, the other by that of the 93rd Highlanders. The music tents faced the Queen's pavilion, where fifty of the more select of the wedding party, including the inner circle and the family of the Queen, together with the bride and bridegroom, partook of luncheon.[21]

Previously the register had been signed not at St Mildred's but at Osborne, the Queen having drawn up in advance an order of precedence expressly for the purpose, to avoid family squabbles over rank. When the lunch was over, as Liko's sister Marie, Countess of Erbach-Schönberg recorded, there 'followed a march past of all the guests before the Queen and the bridal pair'.[22] It was five o'clock by the time Beatrice and Liko left – to the strains of the National Anthem, Beatrice having changed into a costume of ivory crêpe de chine trimmed with lace and wearing an ostrich-feather hat, for the six-mile drive to their honeymoon destination. Until that moment the Queen had controlled herself admirably. At the point of departure, her composure faltered. 'I bore up bravely till the departure and then fairly gave way,' she confided to her eldest daughter. 'I remained quietly upstairs and when I heard the cheering and "God Save the Queen" I stopped my ears and cried bitterly.'[23]

The unthinkable had finally happened: Beatrice had escaped from her mother. With all the cruelty of youth she reported to her sister-in-law Helen the Queen's collapse at the critical moment. She felt truly sorry for her, Beatrice admitted, as did Liko. The complicity of husband and wife in that instant, had the Queen known it, would have been the final twist of the dagger in her heart. The irony was that her behaviour of the summer arose in part from the depth of her love for her daughter and her terror at losing that love by sharing her with another. But that terrible summer had served to confirm Beatrice's love for Liko and created between mother and daughter the first tiny fissure. Once, Beatrice had refused to talk to a potential suitor because the Queen had forbidden her. Now she felt sorry for the Queen as she took her seat in the carriage beside her husband.

The couple were destined for Quarr Abbey, the home of Colonel and Lady Adela Cochrane, brother and sister-in-law of Beatrice's new lady-in-waiting. At 5.45 they passed through a triumphal arch at the foot of Wootton Bridge. 'The outrider appeared in sight, and the united bands struck up "God Save the Queen". The royal cortège passed slowly through the loyal and enthusiastic throng, the Prince and Princess graciously acknow-ledging the hearty cheers of welcome.'[24] Under the arch passed husband and wife, en route for their new life.

At Osborne, as the sun sank, fireworks erupted from the yachts in the bay. The terrace and the lawns were strung with lights; reflections of multicoloured garden lights danced in the fountain. The bands played as dinner was served in the two large tents. Among the guests was the Queen's cousin, George, Duke of Cambridge. In his diary he noted, 'The Queen was again present and seemed wonderfully cheerful and well.'[25]

Beatrice's honeymoon lasted from Thursday evening until Tuesday lunchtime. It included two visits from the Queen – on Sunday and again on Tuesday. At five days' duration, the separation, despite interruptions, was longer than the two-day break at Windsor granted to the Princess Royal when, in 1858, she had married the Crown Prince of Prussia, or the three-day honeymoon of Alice and Louis of Hesse, spent three miles outside Ryde in a house the Queen and Prince Consort had thought of buying before they found Osborne. On that occasion the Queen visited for tea on the second day.

Beatrice was grateful for the chance to spend time alone with Liko, but satisfied that they return to her mother when the five days expired. In response to a letter from Leopold's widow she wrote of her happiness, proud at last to be able to address her sister-in-law on terms of equality:

> Liko's kindness, thoughtfulness and tenderness are intensely precious to me, and I feel so safe and content in his dear hands; God grant that I may make him as happy as he deserves, and that we may be spared to each other ... We sit out nearly all day and it does me so much good, and this place is looking quite lovely. I am thankful to say we remain till Tuesday, and we are quite content with that.[26]

It was an acknowledgement that five days was not long to spend alone before returning to live with one's mother. But Beatrice was essentially a pragmatist. There had been too many times when she had doubted that this moment would arrive at all to tilt at windmills now. She would happily have married Liko with no honeymoon. Hers was neither a complaining nor a fanciful nature. She did not interpret as ominous the accident that befell their carriage on the approach to Quarr Abbey, one of the leading horses falling and taking with it its partner. The coachman detached the front two horses from the reins and the carriage continued drawn by a single pair.

SEVENTEEN

'There now burnt a bewitching
fiery passion'

•◆•

$\mathcal{F}$or Beatrice marriage changed everything and nothing. A year after her wedding she opened the annual show of the Royal Horticultural Society of Southampton and the Hampshire bee-keepers' association exhibition. The aldermen and burgesses of the town presented her with a proclamation on vellum. It expressed 'the profound respect we entertain for your personal character and our admiration of the affectionate manner in which you have comforted and assisted your widowed mother our Gracious Sovereign the Queen'.[1] In March of that year Beatrice and Liko, accompanied by Liko's sister Marie, had visited the Empress Eugénie in her house at Farnborough Hill. A member of the Empress's household described to her grandmother her impressions of the royal party: 'We kissed the Princess Beatrice's hand and curtseyed to the others, who are both very nice. The Countess is very pretty and amiable and merry, and so is Prince Henry ... Princess Beatrice is very quiet indeed and seems dull and out of spirits ... "suppressed" ... from the constant restraint of the Queen's presence she has lost all life and spirits.'[2]

Married or not, everything came back to the Queen. From long association with the Queen, Beatrice was the best known of the royal daughters, her uncomplaining attendance on her widowed mother a source of admiration for the contemporary public. Closer to home, opinions differed. 'No man can be always with the Queen,' Sir Thomas Biddulph had written in the 1870s, his immediate target John Brown, 'without being very much the worse for it.'[3] No woman either, and Beatrice's behaviour was conditioned by long years at the Queen's side, so that those who met her briefly – like 'Goodie' of the Empress's household –

considered her 'suppressed', all natural ebullition of spirits damp-
ened by the Queen's insistence on absolute subjection to her
shattered, sorrowing, widowed state. Beatrice's was a soft, quiet,
deep voice – she sang as a mezzo-soprano; its mellow hush suited
the Queen's distaste for loud and jarring noises. Her manner was
retiring and unassertive, and she had a habit of not looking her
interlocutor in the eye or even appearing to listen to what was
said to her. She resisted controversial topics of conversation and
referred anything problematic to her mother. Her clothes were
discreet, though she had a fondness for elaborate trimmings,
particularly lace, and jewels. Towards the Queen her manner
was sympathetic if unsentimental; to any third party she could
appear offhand, disinterested. She treated the Queen and the
Queen's business, however trivial, with a degree of reverence that
would increasingly become the dominant note of Victorian court
life towards the end of the Queen's reign. Marriage to Liko gave
Beatrice's life an additional focus beyond the Queen, but it did
not wholly alter her existence. What it brought her was happiness
of an active, immediate variety she had never known, save in
those first unthinking years before the Prince Consort's death.
To her husband, Liko's sister wrote during that spring visit, 'It
is nice to see how radiantly happy Liko and Beatrice are.'[4]

In her mother's eyes, those of the Royal Household and those
of the public she encountered through the increased programme
of royal engagements she undertook as a married woman, Beatrice
remained primarily the Queen's most devoted daughter, her
mother's wishes her foremost obligation. In that sense she *was*
suppressed: her perception of her duty to the Queen led her to
suppress her own desires in favour of her mother's – with the
notable exception of the question of marrying Liko. But she was
not out of spirits. Marie Erbach was correct in her assessment of
Beatrice and Liko's radiant happiness. The challenge for both
would be to sustain that happiness in a domestic environment
that required not only Beatrice but Liko too to give the Queen's
wishes preferment in every sphere. Beatrice's daughter Ena
claimed of her mother's relationship with the Queen, 'She had to
be in perpetual attendance on her formidable mother. Her devo-

tion and submission were complete.'[5] There is no question but that Beatrice was also devoted to Liko and that Liko in turn came to share her devotion to the Queen. But it was a tall order for an active twenty-seven-year-old ex-army officer to embrace the unquestioning submission to imperious caprice that in Beatrice's case had become second nature. The royal honeymoon lasted five days. On Wednesday morning, business resumed as usual. On Friday, belatedly, the House of Lords passed the bill of Liko's naturalization, overlooked amid the wedding preparations. Liko now enjoyed formally all the rights and privileges of a natural-born Englishman. He had become, by act of Parliament as well as by marriage, his mother-in-law's subject.

To her granddaughter, Beatrice's niece-cum-sister-in-law Victoria of Battenberg, the Queen wrote from Balmoral in the autumn of 1885, 'I thought you would like to hear how well all is going on – how nice and sensible dear Liko is, how happy dear Auntie is and they are together – and yet so sensibly, etc – so that I feel but little change.'[6] In emphasizing stasis over change, the Queen deluded herself. The decade of Beatrice's marriage was the Queen's happiest since the Prince Consort's death. With tact, humour and circumspection, Liko coaxed her in tiny, hesitant steps away from the shadows of the past. Within months of Beatrice and Liko's wedding, Marie Erbach wrote, 'I am glad that since Liko has been of her household, several of the Queen's lonely habits of life have gradually disappeared under his influence.'[7] The Queen danced with Liko, she even sang again – apparently unaware that these were symbolic innovations. Christmas 1885 was the most carefree the Queen had spent since 1860, when the Prince Consort had swung Beatrice in a napkin and sunlight glittered on the frost outside the windows of Windsor Castle. Like the Prince Consort and John Brown before him, Liko treated the Queen not as a figurehead inspiring awe but as a woman willing to be cajoled, susceptible to a handsome face, respectful of those who were not afraid of her. The Empress Eugénie's 'Goodie' told her grandmother, 'Prince Henry it appears keeps [Princess Beatrice] always on thorns, for he is very outspoken and not afraid of the Queen as they *all* are and he gives his opinion whenever he finds an opportunity at the risk of offending Her Majesty.'[8] Liko chose his opportunities judiciously: there are few recorded instances of the Queen taking offence.

Beatrice entered the world of publishing for the second time in 1890. Her second book differed from the *Birthday Book* of the previous decade. *The Adventures of Count Georg Albert of Erbach: A True Story* was a translation. The original – in German, by Emil Kraus – told the story of an early-seventeenth-century knight of strong religious conviction who underwent a series of adventures, involving considerable personal hardship, in defence of his faith. In her preliminary notice Beatrice offered an explanation of why she had undertaken and sought to publish the translation:

> The following translation has been made with the hope that it may prove of some little interest to those amongst our countrymen who have passed any time in the Island of Malta, as well as to those who have followed the history of the Order of St John of Jerusalem. The chief merit of the narrative lies in the fact of its having been compiled from the archives of the family to which it refers. It consequently gives an accurate picture of the times when Malta played an important part in the annals of the Order which laboured so valiantly in the defence of the Christian faith.

The princess did not return to Smith, Elder & Co. but chose for her publisher John Murray, the introduction probably made by the Dean of Windsor, Randall Davidson, who acted as go-between for author and publisher. It was Randall Davidson who submitted Beatrice's manuscript to John Murray on 9 July, and to Randall Davidson that Beatrice addressed her comments on Murray's amendments to the translation. In a statement that illustrates the way in which Beatrice's self-effacement could be mistaken for brusqueness or lack of interest, she wrote to the Dean on 5 August, 'I hasten to say that I have not the slightest objection to the corrections Mr Murray finds necessary, being made on my manuscript, which is of no value whatever to me.'[9]

For her pains, John Murray offered Beatrice less lucrative

remuneration than Smith, Elder & Co. had paid in 1881, though the arrangement – that all profits from the work be split two-thirds to the princess, the remainder to John Murray – was still generous within its terms. Murray agreed to print two thousand copies, which were released in two editions of a thousand, in December 1890 and March 1891. Although the second impression failed to sell in its entirety, with seventy-seven copies being pulped, the book made a modest profit, and Beatrice received £124.

As she grew older, 'churchiness' would become an increasingly important aspect of Beatrice's character. Count Georg Albert made greater claims on her, however, than his exemplary fidelity to his faith. The princess was doubly related to the Erbach family, through her paternal great-great-grandfather Count Georg Augustus of Erbach-Schönberg, and her sister-in-law Marie of Battenberg, who in the present generation had married Count Gustav of Erbach-Schönberg. Marie doted on her brother Liko and she and Beatrice became firm friends, corresponding regularly in German. Beatrice, like all her siblings, spoke and wrote fluent German. She also shared with her siblings an interest in their labyrinthine family history. In 1887 Helena had edited and translated *Memoirs of Wilhelmine, Margravine of Bayreuth*, while in 1892 the Queen and Crown Princess discussed an idea of the latter's for writing a memoir of the Queen's aunt Elizabeth, Landgravine of Hesse-Homburg, third daughter of George III. The Queen, in that instance, was not encouraging: 'She was very hasty and *remuante* [restless], very fond of politics, *pas facile à vivre* [not easy to live with] and a great trial to poor Aunt Adelaide [wife of William IV].'[10]

Beatrice's translation can be seen as a barometer of the degree of change and, alternatively, stasis marriage had wrought in her. It includes statements that express not only Count Georg Albert's *modus vivendi*, but that of the royal author. A knight of St John tells Erbach, 'No knight can live according to his own liking, and in all things, big or small, the one watchword is *obedience*, nothing but *obedience*.'[11] Later, playing chess with the Turkish Princess Selima, Erbach chooses the black counters. 'Thou

161

shouldst have left that to me,' Selima tells him, 'for sorrow is a woman's lot for her lifetime.'[12] As she speaks, 'a deep melancholy [overspreads] her face'. How often the Queen had uttered similar statements to Beatrice. Now, at the happiest moment of her life, Beatrice could write the words dispassionately.

The Adventures of Count Georg Albert of Erbach is not a book Beatrice could have written before her marriage. It includes passages of lush romance inappropriate from the pen of any but a married Victorian author. Erbach is Princess Selima's prisoner. Inevitably, the infidel princess falls in love with her Christian captive: 'When she looked up again, the Count found that her liquid dark Oriental eyes no longer had the same simple expression of kindliness, but that there now burnt a bewitching fiery passion within them, which caused her face to be suffused with a deep blush.'[13] This is the violet-hued titillation of the novels of Marie Corelli, an author read by both Beatrice and the Queen. It is surprisingly at odds with the image of Beatrice disliking kissing, which the Queen reported to the Crown Princess at the outset of Beatrice and Liko's engagement. But on that score the Queen had already been proved wrong. She had hoped and prayed that there might be no 'results' (children) from Beatrice's marriage. By the time she published her translation, Beatrice had three children already.

'Dear Auntie has been very unwell with the effects of a bad chill but she is nearly quite well again,' the Queen wrote to a granddaughter on 9 December 1885.[14] She omitted to point out that Beatrice's cold came hot on the heels of a more serious illness.

For the Queen's doctor James Reid 11 November 1885 was to be the first of two days of 'much anxiety'. Reid had planned a short holiday with his mother before the court's departure from Balmoral. Instead, as he noted in his diary, he remained 'at home all day with the Princess; at 6pm, removed contents of uterus.'[15] The four-months-married Beatrice had suffered a miscarriage of some seriousness. The following day, Reid reported to his mother, 'The Princess was not quite right in the afternoon and wanted me a good deal. Had I been away she and the Queen would have been a good deal anxious.'[16]

Reid had been in royal service for four years, long enough to have grown accustomed to the mild daily hypochondria that assailed so many members of the court, the Queen and her family included. Beatrice's miscarriage in the early stages of pregnancy was no such imaginary ailment. Sir William Jenner wrote to Reid, expressing the hope that the Queen – notoriously unsympathetic about other people's illnesses – would 'not press too much about the Princess going out'. Whatever pressure the Queen brought to bear, the departure from Balmoral proceeded as planned on 17 November, Beatrice making the long journey with her mother.

If on this occasion the Queen had been spared the 'result' that she so dreaded from Beatrice and Liko's marriage, she would not have long to wait for a more positive outcome. The following September she postponed the visit to Balmoral of her grand-daughter Alix of Hesse, who had contracted scarlet fever in August, in consideration of 'dear Auntie's state'.[17] By then Beatrice was six months pregnant, her due date the first week of December.

Despite her habitual inflexibility about altering her travel plans, the Queen scheduled an early departure from Balmoral to enable the birth to take place at Windsor. She jibbed at this unwonted upset to her calendar – the earliest autumn journey south for seventeen years – but took comfort from Beatrice's flourishing state: 'Thank God ... dear Auntie is so well and active and walks so well and daily.'[18] For the Queen the important word was 'active'. To the Crown Princess, in one of those letters in which she expressed her terror at Beatrice's certain martyrdom at the hands of Liko's libido, the Queen had described her youngest daughter as 'poor, darling, gentle (and not very strong) Beatrice'.[19] When it came to Beatrice's conduct of her pregnancy, one previous miscarriage notwithstanding, the Queen paid no heed to gentleness or lack of strength. A week before the birth Beatrice retired from the Queen's formal dinners, preferring to eat alone in her room. Her mother's response – like her response to Beatrice's announcement that she wished to marry Liko – strikes the modern reader as disproportionately robust. To Dr

Reid, she wrote, 'I urge [the Princess] coming to dinner, and not simply moping in her own room which is very bad for her. In my case I came regularly to dinner, except when I was really unwell (even when suffering a good deal) up to the very last day ... I (the Mother of nine children) must *know* what is right and wise and not young inexperienced people who know nothing.'[20]

It was as well the Queen had brought forward the date for travelling to Windsor. In the event, Beatrice gave birth two weeks prematurely. Happily, the monthly nurse Mrs Brotherstone had already arrived at the castle; the wet nurse by contrast was still engaged with Beatrice's newest niece, Princess Patricia of Connaught, born earlier that year and not yet weaned. 'Were you in time for the great event at Windsor?' Patricia's father Arthur wrote to Louise. 'It surely came off long before it was expected, what a fluster there must have been at the Castle.'[21]

The labour was not unduly difficult, eased by the generous administration of chloroform. It happened unexpectedly at the end of an ordinary day. The Queen described it to Victoria of Battenberg.

> [Beatrice] had walked down to the Mausoleum in the morning, been out with Liko in the afternoon, took tea with us – and was just going to dress for dinner with us ... when the water broke! ... When I came back from dinner, Auntie was already having pains which increased and became severe and continual. The Doctor (Dr Williams) arrived at twenty minutes past twelve – she went to bed at quarter to one – The pains were very severe and tedious but she was very good and brave. They feared it might go on long – but at four this suddenly changed to bearing pains and at 5.10 the Baby was born! ... Dear Liko is very happy; he was very anxious before I think, though he did not say so. He was very helpful and was there continually excepting when he took a little rest while I remained. With the exception of a short time when I laid down on the sofa, I was always with darling Auntie who you know is the apple of my eye.[22]

Beatrice slept after the birth and within hours the Queen was able to describe her as looking 'so fresh and pink'.[23] Her description of her newest grandchild – a boy, christened the week before Christmas Albert Alexander and known as 'Drino' – is less appealing: 'The Baby is not big but very vigorous and well developped [sic] with a big nose and very pretty small ears. I hope the eyes will be brown but I cannot judge yet, as I have seldom seen them open.'[24] Although no complications followed the birth, Beatrice did not hasten her return to active participation in court life, Lady Waterpark noting in her diary as late as 21 December, 'The Queen dined alone with Princess Beatrice, the latter having been confined of a son on the 23 of November.'[25]

Later Beatrice would discover that she was not particularly maternal. Like her own mother she had difficulty establishing relations of ease and intimacy with her children as infants. She did, however, like babies. To the Duchess of Teck she sent a photograph of herself with the newborn Drino. 'I think the enclosed little family group may amuse you. My little man is getting on famously and growing so quick.'[26] In the spring she commissioned from Charles Burton Barber, who ten years earlier had painted her collie Watts, a portrait of Drino asleep in his cradle, guarded by two of the Queen's dogs. By then Beatrice was pregnant again.

Her second pregnancy progressed uneventfully, despite the exhaustion she felt steering the Queen through her Golden Jubilee celebrations in June, mid-term for Beatrice. The birth would prove considerably more difficult than Drino's. In her last Journal entry for the year the Queen gave thanks for the success of the Jubilee, the apparent improvement in the condition of her son-in-law the Crown Prince of Prussia (who was in fact dying of cancer), and 'for darling Beatrice coming safely through her severe confinement'.[27] That confinement lasted almost exactly as long as Beatrice's previous labour – nine hours – except that on this occasion the Queen, if not the doctors, experienced extreme anxiety for both mother and baby. In her Journal, she recorded, 'Was up in the night with my poor Beatrice, who was very ill.'[28] Again the Queen remained at her favourite daughter's bedside. Beatrice had endured a day of severe pain before labour began in earnest at seven o'clock on the morning of 24 October. Dr Reid again administered chloroform, and the princess's gynaecologist Dr John Williams ultimately resorted to forceps – a full forty minutes of forceps. For the Queen it made painful viewing: 'After a terrible long time, the baby appeared to our great joy and relief, a very large fine girl but she was nearly stillborn.'[29] The Queen commended Williams's 'dexterity'. To Dr Reid, who remained in constant attendance on Beatrice for almost a week after the birth, the princess continuing to suffer acute uterine pains, the Queen presented a formal photograph of herself and copies of both her books of Highland Journal extracts. 'I hope you will accept this photograph and these books in recollection of the birth of my dear little Granddaughter, as well as my best thanks for all your care and attention to my beloved child.'[30] Such was the degree of the Queen's concern that as late as January she wrote to Victoria of Battenberg, 'Dear Auntie is very well and strong and looking very well ... but Auntie *must* have a very long rest.'[31]

Handing his daughter to the Queen, Liko described her as her 'little Jubilee grandchild'.[32] Of greater significance in the Queen's eyes was not the child's coincidence with her Golden Jubilee but the fact that the birth had taken place at Balmoral, the first royal birth in Scotland since that of the future Charles I almost three centuries earlier. The baptism was held in the drawing room of the Queen's Scottish home, and the baby, who was christened Victoria Eugénie Julie, after respectively the Queen, her godmother the Empress Eugénie, and her paternal grandmother the Princess of Battenberg, also received a fourth name – 'Ena (a Gaelic Highland name)', as the Queen explained to the Duchess of Connaught on 16 November.[33] In the double-page illustration published in *The Graphic* on 10 December, the Queen holds the baby while her fellow grandmother looks on; a kilted Liko stands beside his seated wife, who, apparently fully recovered, is tightly corseted and conventionally dressed.

The Queen took to heart Beatrice's suffering over Ena's birth. When, less than a year later, Beatrice discovered she was pregnant for a third time, the Queen planned ahead, clearing her diary of engagements for the weeks before and after the doctor's predicted due date. Her letter written to the Crown Princess on 15 May 1889 expresses her concern at the quick succession of Beatrice's children and a characteristic frustration at the likely disruption of her travel plans:

> I think we may expect Beatrice's (untoward) event (which happens at a most unfortunate time) any moment from the 20th, but it might be before and *now*. I am ready as all my engagements till the last day of June are over. My favourite spring visit to dear Scotland will I fear be very short. I hope for a fortnight but I would not leave Beatrice till a day or two after the fortnight when I have seen her move a little and sit in a chair.[34]

With fewer complications than Ena, Beatrice's third child, a second son, was born at 2.05 a.m. at Windsor on 21 May, in the presence of the Queen, Liko and Liko's sister Marie. The Queen described him as 'a particularly pretty child, large, fat and with darkish hair. He weighed 8lb, which is more than Ena did.'[35] Marie Mallet shared the Queen's opinion, writing on 26 May, 'Princess Beatrice is marvellously flourishing and the baby very pretty, with lots of soft brown hair and large blue eyes.'[36] The Crown Princess's daughter Victoria of Prussia, Sandro's Moretta, arrived at Windsor at the beginning of June to accompany the Queen north in Beatrice's enforced absence. To her mother she addressed her first impressions of Beatrice and her newest baby: 'Auntie is looking very well indeed and so pretty, lying on her sofa in a charming dressing gown and little white cap. The baby I have been carrying about a good deal – it's a love. You would enjoy it, and nibble it – heaps of hair on its little head and a good pair of lungs.'[37]

Beatrice called the baby Leopold. Ironically, despite his initially blooming appearance, he, too, like the deceased uncle after whom he was named, suffered from haemophilia and would die young. The Queen suspected none of this. 'The baby really is a very pretty child,' she told her daughter.[38] Beatrice's easy labour and Leopold's apparent health dissipated her earlier resignation to the disruption of her trip to Balmoral, and she began to exercise herself over what she regarded as Beatrice's self-indulgent convalescence, writing in hectoring tones to Dr Reid,

> I am very glad the Princess has been out, though I did not quite understand why she did not go out on Friday, as I thought you expected ... After the first day I always went out twice and that was earlier in the year (in April or beginning of May) – and if it rained, in the closed carriage – only always got out. And after Tuesday she should walk up and down stairs. .... I mention what my nine experiences have taught me from a most excellent nurse who always attended me and in whom the physicians had the greatest confidence.[39]

While her mother remained at Windsor, Beatrice gave in to her reiterated admonitions, Moretta reporting on 6 June, 'Auntie Beatrice has now left her sofa and tries to walk about a little.'[40] The same day the Queen departed for Balmoral, leaving Beatrice in her absence to recover as suited her best.

There would be one more child for Beatrice and Liko – to the Queen's disappointment a third son, born, like Ena, at Balmoral, on 3 October 1891. On this occasion, both pregnancy and confinement were uneventful. 'Thank God! dear Auntie seems to get better and stronger each time,' the Queen wrote to Victoria of Battenberg. She also expressed the hope that 'she will stop now for many reasons'.[41] The Queen did not elaborate on those many reasons, but was aware of criticism in the gutter press at the proliferation of the Battenberg brood. She worried, too, at the speedy arrival of Beatrice and Liko's children and the strain on Beatrice's health, which she continued to regard as fragile: 'Poor dear Auntie is well ... but it depresses me to see her carrying about this great burthen,' she had written to Victoria of Battenberg towards the end of Beatrice's last pregnancy.[42] (Increasingly, the princess herself appeared anything but fragile, her figure solidifying irrevocably with the after-effects of four pregnancies.) This baby was christened Maurice (Liko's middle name) Victor (after the Queen) Donald (a compliment to Scotland), the Prince Consort's silver-gilt font travelling north for the occasion, and handed over to the care of his wet nurse and faithful monthly nurse Mrs Brotherstone.

Four children constituted a smaller family than those of her eldest siblings, but for Beatrice, who must at times have doubted she would have any children, her three robust-seeming sons and golden-haired daughter were a source of considerable satisfaction. Despite her limited maternal sympathies, her children would bring her both pleasure and support. In the short term, with her family complete, she was free to return to the Queen's service.

EIGHTEEN

'Capital fun'

·•·

he *Colliery Guardian*, as its name suggests, was not a
publication that habitually interested itself in the Royal
Family. On 30 August 1889, however, the paper devoted a whole
page to a visit made by Beatrice and Liko to the Wynnstay
Collieries, half a mile from Ruabon in North Wales.

The couple were in Wales for the Queen's five-day visit to the
principality. On the morning of 26 August they toured the colliery
above and below ground, both cut lumps of coal from the
coalface with picks, and Beatrice 'fired a shot' (a controlled
explosion for blasting coal). The visit came as a surprise to the
miners at work that day. Beatrice had asked that her plans not
be disclosed in advance, as she wished to see for herself the
everyday workings of the colliery. Improbably, the paper attrib-
uted the visit to 'the Princess Beatrice having often expressed a
wish to descend a coalpit and see the operations there, in order
that she might know by experience and observation what life in
a colliery is'. At the end of the visit the chairman of the Wynnstay
Collieries Company expressed the thanks of all present for
Beatrice's interest and condescension: 'I am sure all your hearts
are fired with gratitude that her Royal Highness has gone through
this colliery and has seen the coal won, and has actually won
some for herself ... She has also fired a shot and brought down
the coal. I think all this shows that sympathy for the working
man of this country for which her Royal Highness and her
Majesty the Queen are so much beloved.' Further to prove that
sympathy, the paper's reporter noted that, 'Before departing, her
Royal Highness conveyed to [the chairman] her desire that the
men of the colliery might be released from their duties for the

remainder of the day, and that no portion of their wages should on that account be deducted.'[1]

The Queen was ahead of her time in foreseeing and in part applauding the inevitable future breakdown of class barriers in Britain. She insisted on rigorous standards of courtesy towards servants and frequently lamented the tendency of the Prussian royal family to bring up its children in a social vacuum, with no feeling for those below them. Part of this attitude she passed on to Beatrice. But only up to a point. During her visit to the Wynnstay Collieries Beatrice's interest in the day-to-day business of the coal mine was genuine. But what she saw that day did not change her life; she did not afterwards express a desire to improve such working conditions or the living conditions of miners' wives and families. Beatrice was not an idealist, as her sister Alice had been. Hers was a conventional royal attitude of polite interest and encouragement. It may be, as several of her contemporaries claimed, that Beatrice was simply lacking in imagination, but it is more likely that she considered such issues outside her province, the sphere of politicians not princesses, a line the Queen would have encouraged – though frequently not the attitude she adopted herself.

The visit to the Wynnstay Collieries leavened seriousness with humour.

> Although ... the royal visit was not made for amusement or to gratify mere curiosity [concluded the *Colliery Guardian*'s cor-respondent], the party appeared to derive a considerable amount of entertainment from the proceedings. It was particularly notice-able that the little discomforts inseparable from a visit to the underground workings of a colliery by persons not accustomed to them were regarded by all the members of the royal party as capital fun.

Fun was a commodity that for too long had been in short supply at court. The Queen remained aloof from fashionable society, which she regarded as frivolous, self-seeking and of questionable morals. The tone of her own homes was conspicuously higher, more earnest and less colourful. Courtiers' most frequent observations concerned their boredom, the sameness of the royal routine and the limited outlets for high spirits, which in any case were discouraged. But the Queen was not averse to pleasure or entertainment, particularly once the death of the assertively dour John Brown had removed a major obstacle to light-heartedness. In the decade of Beatrice's marriage the Queen espoused a programme of whimsical court entertainments. At the centre of this innovation was the child whose status as last princess, born too close to her father's death, had hitherto prevented her from taking part in such diversions: Beatrice.

Though the Queen had circumscribed Beatrice's pastimes before her marriage, shielding her from romantic temptation, she had sought to ensure that Beatrice was not bored by her life at her mother's side. There were trips to the theatre in London with Leopold, games of bezique after dinner and pianists invited to play at Osborne. Young women being considered for the post of maid of honour were required to answer a number of questions, including whether they were able to ride (to accompany Beatrice), play the piano and sight-read easily in order to play duets with her.[2] It was assumed that they could speak, read and write French and German, as this was essential for their work with the Queen. If this supplemented a facility for sight-reading and a well-trained voice, they could also sing after dinner, varying the pattern of in-house entertainment. Marie Mallet described to Lady Elizabeth Biddulph an evening in the New Year of 1888 when

> I was summoned to warble duets with Prince Henry, fearfully difficult sections from Gounod's operas, which *he* knew *perfectly well* and which I was expected to sing at sight. I enacted the role of Juliet, Mireille, and I do not know what else while he shouted violent sentiments such as '*ange adorable!*' at me and at one moment it was so comic that I nearly laughed outright; he has a good voice but cannot manage it and sings with very little expression. Princess Beatrice accompanied us and smiled benignly.[3]

Liko had clearly taken to heart the advice the Queen gave him through Victoria of Battenberg prior to his engagement: 'I hope that Liko will practice his Music – as you know what an essential thing that is for Auntie.'⁴ There is less evidence that he paid heed to the Queen's parting shot – 'and English also'. The Battenbergs were Germans, partly brought up in Italy; their mother spoke to them in French but employed German, Swiss and English servants; holidays were spent with Russian cousins. The Queen's admonishing suggests that, when she first encountered him, Liko spoke English only falteringly, and it is possible that, early in his marriage, his command of the language remained hesitant. This would explain his enthusiastic participation in the elaborate (mute) *tableaux vivants* that became such a feature of court life during Beatrice's marriage, while he apparently took no part in the court theatricals that ran in tandem with them. His mother had a passion for amateur dramatics and Liko was not averse to acting. He satisfied the taste in a form that required neither linguistic nor even (much) dramatic ability.

Tableaux vivants had been part of the childhood of Beatrice's elder siblings, staged by the children for their parents' entertainment, intended as an adjunct to the rigorous educational programme then obtaining and also as a means of the children showing off. When the *tableaux* were revived, in 1888, they were altogether a more adult affair, though the Queen remained the target audience: an early performance ended with 'Homage to Queen Victoria', a bust of the Queen wreathed in flowers, surrounded by her ladies, with the band playing 'Home, Sweet Home'. For the Queen, an important purpose of these revived grown-up *tableaux* was to show off to advantage her daughter's good looks.

The *tableaux* were arranged into programmes, with an emphasis on variety between scenes depicted. Each had two poses and each frozen pose was shown twice, by virtue of dropping and raising a curtain. All were elaborately costumed – when Beatrice personified 'India', she did so, the Queen recorded, 'wearing quantities of my Indian jewellery'⁵ – and accompanied by music. In May 1894 Beatrice provided the musical accompaniment single-handedly, singing and playing on the harmonium; her offerings included a song entitled 'Three Fishers', which the

Queen described as 'extremely effective'.[6] On Twelfth Night 1888 Beatrice and Liko represented Elizabeth and Raleigh ('The Princess looked so handsome as Queen Elizabeth and quite like a Holbein,' commented Marie Mallet[7]), followed by Beatrice as the Queen of Sheba opposite Sir Henry Ponsonby as Solomon, then Liko as a toreador in *Carmen*, alongside Minnie Cochrane, Harriet Phipps and Marie Mallet. A particularly ambitious programme scheduled for 5 and 6 October of the same year commemorated Liko's birthday (5 October), the first letter of the name of each scene spelling his names, 'Henry Maurice', with 'Henry' given on the first night, 'Maurice' on the second. Although Liko was the intended recipient of this elaborate compliment, he still took part, appearing as Malcolm with Beatrice as Queen Margaret in 'Malcolm Canmore' for 'M'. Perhaps on account of Beatrice's increasingly stately appearance in the years following the births of her children, a noticeable feature of the *tableaux* is the augustness of the roles she personified: Boadicea, St Elizabeth of Hungary, Henrietta Maria and Marie Antoinette. Even allegorical impersonations wore a regal aspect: in 'Twelfth Night' Beatrice appeared as the Queen of the Revels, an unlikely persona. For the most part, the Queen was enchanted. '"Fotheringay" represented the moment when poor Mary Queen of Scots, took leave of her ladies,' she recorded in her Journal on 20 January 1890. 'Louise looked lovely as the Queen standing on the steps looking up, and Beatrice as her half-sister the Duchess of Argyle, leaning against her ... Louise's expression was beautiful and sad beyond measure. Beatrice also looked sweet, with hands upraised, and looking up as in prayer. Mozart's Ave Verum was played during this scene.'[8]

Not everyone enjoyed the *tableaux*. They were rehearsed exhaustively and sometimes even photographed, which demanded in effect an additional performance. In January 1890 three of that year's five Twelfth Night *tableaux* were repeated at the end of the month, when the Empress Eugénie arrived at Osborne to stay, 'with the addition of one from "Faust" in which Beatrice looked lovely as Gretchen'.[9] Dr Reid considered them a waste of time, though for his purposes a valuable waste of time – a recognition of at least part of their purpose: 'They have given me a part to play, and I could not get out of it, though I tried to, as it takes up so much time … The tableaux begin tomorrow and will, I hope, keep the people from thinking of at least their *imaginary* ailments, which are very common among the sort of people I have to deal with.'[10]

Even more time-consuming were the theatricals – mostly short comic plays – in which Beatrice but not Liko took part. In spite of her shyness, Beatrice had an enthusiastic long-term interest in play-acting, Lady Waterpark noting as long ago as 22 January 1877, 'Princess Beatrice went with Miss Cadogan and Mlle Norèle to the rehearsals of some Theatricals at Lady Biddulph's.'[11] A question mark, however, hovers over her acting ability. While Beatrice was the more diligent in learning her lines, Louise was the more dramatically gifted of the sisters: 'Princess Louise who could act but couldn't learn her part was Miss Hardcastle; Princess Beatrice who couldn't act but could learn her part was Constantina Neville,' wrote Arthur Ponsonby of a production of Goldsmith's *She Stoops to Conquer* in 1893.[12] The twin disabilities of the sisters made them a less-than-ideal combination. Arthur's brother Frederick Ponsonby, about to join the Queen's staff as assistant private secretary, was also among the cast of the same production. He tended to greater leniency towards his royal co-players:

> Both Princess Louise and Princess Beatrice were quite good in their parts, but very sketchy with the words. I therefore learnt their parts as well as my own, so that I could either say their words or prompt them. Everyone else did the same, but there was one small bit when they were both on together and of course they stuck, each one thinking it was the other's fault. After an awkward pause the servants gave a round of applause, which I thought was a very intelligent way of helping them, but although the prompter was able to start them again, they could not get going and the stage carpenter solved the problem by letting the curtain down.[13]

Nevertheless, the Queen insisted that her daughters take the principal roles in any entertainment as the only solution befitting their rank. She also interfered with scripts to present her daughters to best advantage. *Used Up* was staged at Balmoral in October 1889. Beatrice was cast as Mrs Ironbrace, who only appears in the first act. George Rowell, in *Queen Victoria Goes to the Theatre*, claims that the Queen requested the script be rewritten to correct the oversight, leading Arthur Bigge to suggest a programme note: 'The return and reconciliation of Mrs Ironbrace is by command!' On occasion, the Queen's interference went too far and Beatrice grew irritated by her tendency to offer suggestions during performances. 'I will be good, I will be good!' the Queen replied to one stern reprimand from her daughter.[14]

In the Queen's Golden Jubilee year, 1887, a painter the Queen had once employed as a copyist embarked on an imaginary group portrait of the Queen, Helena and Beatrice. Alexander Melville was commissioned by an officer connected with the British campaign in Egypt in 1882 to paint the Queen and two of her daughters knitting the quilts that they presented to the Royal Victoria Hospital at Netley for soldiers wounded at Tel-el-Kebir. None of the royal subjects gave Melville a sitting. The large, gloomy picture of the three women knitting striped blankets is one of many bad portraits of Victoria and her family. Despite its stiffness, however, it suggests something of the easy domesticity of the Queen and her two most biddable daughters. Knitting was a favourite after-dinner occupation of the Queen and her ladies, the Queen even occasionally conducting for herself with a knitting needle at drawing-room concerts. The picture, though stagey and unconvincing, has a cosy, comfortable aspect; a fictitious scene, it is nevertheless rooted in fact.

After Beatrice's marriage, evenings of knitting more often gave way to theatricals and *tableaux vivants*, performances of operas, operettas and plays by touring companies the Queen commanded to court, adding to the life of the Queen's Household an element of worldly sophistication and amusement that had been lacking in the recent past. It was a sign of the new happiness Beatrice and Liko's marriage had brought to her life that the Queen countenanced and even embraced such changes. Undoubtedly they added to the enjoyment of life in the Queen's houses. But, happening as they did twice or three times a year, they were not enough to relieve the tedium that settled over the court as advancing age curtailed the Queen's activities and further slowed the ritualized routine of her days. 'The life here is utterly dull,' Marie Mallet wrote from Balmoral in June 1890. 'We see nothing of the Queen except at dinner on alternate nights, we have no duties to perform to occupy our minds and the weather is horribly cold and wet. At the same time it is impossible to settle to anything on account of interruptions. We just exist from meal to meal and do our best to kill time.'[15]

Marie Mallet was not alone in her assessment. No boom in amateur theatricals was enough to delude a vigorous, healthy man in the prime of life that his days were profitably occupied, and Liko was forced to look elsewhere for distraction and fulfilment. At the time of Marie Mallet's complaint, he had already temporarily escaped, cruising round the Isles of Scilly in a yacht called *Sheila* given to him by the Queen. Beatrice, of course, remained at home.

NINETEEN

'A simple life, with no great incidents'

.•.

At forty-eight Adelina Patti retained a youthful figure. The prima donna who, for twenty-five years, had been a favourite at Covent Garden, also retained for the time her extraordinary voice. Her youthfulness surprised Liko, when, on 23 August 1891, he visited Patti at Craig-y-Nos, her castle in South Wales. To mark the occasion, Patti had decided to sing the Garden Scene from *Faust* in the castle's recently completed theatre. 'For me,' Liko told a fellow guest, 'Faust never loses its freshness, besides I have never seen Mme Patti as Gretchen. How wonderful that she should still be able to sing these youthful parts.'[1] The performance took place after lunch. After tea, held to the accompaniment of an electric organ, the Orchestrion, Liko left. His visit lingered in Patti's memory. 'Poor Prince Henry,' she remarked on his death. 'What a dear, sweet man! *Et comme il etait beau, n'est-ce qu pas?*'[2]

Like the cruise to the Isles of Scilly the previous summer, Liko's visit was made without Beatrice. Again like last summer, Liko was sailing. He had anchored his yacht at the Mumbles, off the coast of South Wales near Swansea, and was staying close by at Clyne Castle. His 'bachelor' trip was a source of considerable pleasure. His sister remembered him as 'happiest of all, and most unfettered ... on board his beloved sailing yacht *Sheila*.'[3] Marie Erbach also recorded Liko as undertaking numerous voyages on *Sheila* with Beatrice beside him. But this was not always the case, and at the end of 1889 Liko embarked on a four-month trip without her.

At the time of Beatrice's engagement the Queen had been clear that she could not spare Beatrice and Liko to travel without her.

Over time she relaxed this stricture, but the journeys the couple made without the Queen, mostly to Liko's family in Germany, were of short duration. There could be no question of the Queen sparing Beatrice for as long as four months. She took a dim view of the proposal – 'Liko is soon leaving us on what *I* consider a very foolish expedition and I hope wont be very long away and come back safe'[4] – but she did not withhold her permission. It was left to Beatrice to cope without Liko as best she could. Marie Mallet described the run-up to Liko's departure:

> Prince Henry is off tomorrow on a four-month yachting trip to Corfu and next to Albania where he expects to get plenty of sport, woodcock, wild boar, etc. He is in the highest spirits just like a boy going home for the holidays but poor Princess Beatrice daily appears with red and swollen eyes and we all dread tomorrow, I think she will dissolve when she finally bids him 'Goodbye'. I am so sorry for her, she will be lonely and her children are not much to her as yet. I am sure she sometimes longs for liberty.[5]

The Prince departed on 8 November and remained away over Christmas. He had the tact to return on 10 February, the fiftieth anniversary of the Queen's wedding, in celebration of which Beatrice had organized the family present on behalf of her siblings and their spouses: a large prayer book inscribed with a short verse she had requested from Tennyson. With Liko back at court, and the status quo again established to her satisfaction, the Queen forgot her earlier irritation: she was, predictably, taken only with the changes in Liko's appearance caused by his period in the south. 'Dear Liko returned ... looking the picture of health, very brown and with a beard, which makes him look like Ludwig [his eldest brother Louis] and Sandro, but I liked him better without it.'[6] Beards and boating were not a new coupling for Liko. On 7 October 1888 Beatrice's nephew Albert Victor of Wales had written to Louis of Battenberg from Abergeldie on the Balmoral estate, 'Liko was full of his yachting trip round the west coast when he seems to have had a very good time of it. He came back looking quite the Ancient Mariner with a scrubby beard which did not suit him a bit. So we made him take it off in a day or two, and gave him no peace until he had done so.'[7] On this second, later occasion neither the Queen's opinion nor the memory of Albert Victor's distaste swayed Liko, and the beard became a fixture.

It was not in Beatrice's nature to offer recriminations, and her pleasure in Liko's return outweighed her sadness at his having gone. She recognized that the fault lay not with Liko but with the Queen. It was natural that Liko should crave vigorous activity, the masculine camaraderie of his crew members and the sense of freedom and independence sailing gave him. All were absent from his home life, hedged about as it was by the Queen's proscriptions. By having agreed to marry Liko on the Queen's terms Beatrice could not defy her mother and join him for four months away from court. Nor was it in her character to conceive as much. Instead, husband and wife reached an understanding: Liko continued to sail without Beatrice – to the Scillies and the Channel Islands in 1890; off the Welsh coast in 1891, when his handsome appearance so impressed Adelina Patti; in the Mediterranean in 1894, his cruise coinciding with a visit made by Beatrice to Cannes – but never again involving such a lengthy separation. In love with her husband as she was, Beatrice could not help longing for liberty from her mother to travel with him, as Marie Mallet saw. Perhaps she longed for liberty in the fullest sense. She recognized – as she had recognized so long ago – the impossibility of that hope, and resisted the limitations of her own life curtailing Liko's unnecessarily.

As with her response to Beatrice's wish to marry, the Queen's attitude arose partly from thoughtlessness. She adored Liko – months after Beatrice's marriage, Arthur wrote to Louise, 'The "young couple" are very flourishing and Mama more taken with him than ever'[8] – but remained determined not to lose Beatrice, that determination now compounded by her pleasure in Liko's company. She gave him his yacht, although it is doubtful that she anticipated he would make such extensive use of it, and encouraged his sporting life. In Scotland, he shot and stalked – Albert Victor described him as 'very deadly with the stags';[9] at Osborne he went out with the Isle of Wight Hunt; there was tennis at Windsor and Balmoral, the new craze for bicycling, and ice-skating in the winter. Increasingly he travelled further afield for sport, shooting with friends made at court, including Major General Sir Henry Ewart, one of the Queen's equerries. On 18 November 1890 the *Bury and Norwich Post* told its readers,

> Prince Henry of Battenberg (husband of Princess Beatrice) accompanied by Colonel Clerk, Colonel Carrington, Colonel Vivian and Captain Prettyman arrived at Kentwell Hall, Melford. The party was met by Sir Henry Ewart, on Tuesday they shot through Court Wood and Scotch Yards Wood with lunch at Court Farm, afterwards Mr Byford showed them his stud of Suffolk agricultural horses.

Shooting being an all-male preserve, it was natural that, on these occasions, Beatrice did not accompany her husband.

The sports husband and wife shared included ice-skating, riding and tennis. In February 1895 Liko put out his shoulder so badly skating at Osborne that the attack of muscle pain that followed prevented him from travelling when shortly the Queen left the island for Windsor. Moretta of Prussia, staying with her grandmother the Queen the month after Leopold's birth, records playing tennis with Liko: 'He got awfully hot – so did I.'[10] It may have been that Liko was unfit, hence the overheating and the pulled shoulder. But it is more likely that Moretta, only eight years Liko's junior, found herself pitted against a man who gave vent to the frustrations of his uneventful daily life in vigorous physical exertion, be it tennis or skating. As E. F. Benson wrote in his biography of the Queen's daughters published during Beatrice's lifetime,

> His only office was to be a family man with wife and children living with the Queen of England without any further occupations or responsibilities of his own. A few weeks intermittently of such a life would have been a most recuperative existence for a man taking a well-earned rest after a long period of hard work ... Yet the very contract of his marriage provided that he should bear the burden of perpetual leisure.[11]

Aggravating Liko's frustration was the knowledge that his petticoats existence made him a figure of ridicule. As early as November 1887 Henry Ponsonby wrote to his wife, 'One of the Society papers – the low ones – gives a sketch of Prince Henry's life here and says he tries to get through the day by playing billiards with Sir Henry Ponsonby, "no mean wielder of the cue – but an astute courtier who never permits himself to beat his opponent". I never saw Prince Henry playing billiards at all.'[12] Potentially more damaging was the fact that similar opinions were voiced by members of his wife's family. To his aunt, Beatrice's sister Louise, Prince George of Wales wrote in May 1887, 'I'm very glad you spent a pleasant time in Rome ... So Liko arrived before you left and began abusing your clothes, you certainly ought to have snubbed him and told him you had not so much money as Beatrice has to spend on your clothes, *damn* his impertinence, he has nothing else to do I suppose but look at people's clothes, poor creature.'[13]

The truth was Liko had remarkably little to occupy his time. The Queen maintained that, for any wife, 'Your first duty is to your dear ... Husband to whom you can never be kind enough,'[14] but made an exception in Beatrice's case, insisting that her first duty remain to her mother. While Beatrice's days continued to be spent at her mother's beck and call, Liko chain-smoked cigars, husband and wife meeting at meals. At the time of his death, one of the few tangible achievements with which Liko could be credited was having persuaded the Queen to relax her draconian rules on smoking at court. Even Beatrice, long after his death, wrote, 'His was but a simple life, with no great incidents.'[15] During the Queen's spring holiday in Grasse in 1891 Liko spent a day with Beatrice visiting a crystallized-fruit factory belonging to Joseph Nègre.[16] However much husband and wife enjoyed this undemanding engagement, it did not add to Liko's feeling of purpose.

In 1889 the Queen threw Liko a scrap by appointing him governor of the Isle of Wight and Honorary Colonel of the Isle of Wight Rifles, on the death of the last governor, the nonagenarian Lord Eversley. The appointment was formalized at a reception at Carisbrooke Castle in July. Liko approached the Ruritanian office with a degree of seriousness. When the SS *Eider*, with a crew of 167 and carrying 227 passengers, ran aground half a mile from the island's shore on Sunday night, 31 January 1892, Liko arrived the following afternoon to offer encouragement and assistance in what became a large-scale four-day rescue operation. Rowland Prothero remembered Liko's delight on being shown by the Keeper of Prints at the British Museum a gallery of portraits of previous governors. But his assessment of the potential of the role shows that he harboured no illusions concerning its significance: 'The duties and responsibilities of my office do not present much scope for activity,' he commented.[17]

Mostly unemployed outside the home and impotent within it, Liko turned his attention to his children, revelling in each new birth. He took control of their education, as the Prince Consort had with Beatrice's siblings a generation earlier, leaving detailed instructions about their schooling in his will.[18] Like the Prince Consort, he played games with the children, he attended lessons, and indulged them with presents brought back from his sailing trips including, prophetically, for Ena a metamorphic fan from Seville that could be made larger or smaller – Ena would grow up to become Queen of Spain. His attentions partly made up for Beatrice's detachment from her children. In 1896 the Countess of Lytton recorded a conversation with the Empress of Germany – the 'insignificant' Dona – in which 'the Empress spoke so nicely about her baby, nurse and education, fearing Princess Beatrice did not see enough of her children'.[19] Trained from infancy to consider only what was conducive to her mother's ease and well-being Beatrice put her mother before her children and sought principally to tame the latter, channelling all voluble ebullience along more gentle paths. Her efforts were mostly unnecessary. The Queen embraced her Battenberg grandchildren wholeheartedly. She took pleasure in their noise and their antics in a manner that would have been inconceivable twenty years earlier when her oldest grandchildren were of similar age, and that, ironically, the Queen had discouraged in Beatrice herself. Only one factor marred Liko's pleasure in his family: 'As his four children grew older,' his sister remembered, 'he often sighed for a home of his own.'[20] But that was not a concession the Queen was prepared to grant.

The weekly journals which recorded at the time of Beatrice's engagement that the couple would begin married life at Frogmore in Windsor Great Park, as Helena and Christian had done nineteen years earlier, were quickly disabused. The Queen gave Beatrice and Liko rooms at Windsor between the south turret and the Victoria and York towers, with adjacent rooms over-looking the Long Walk.[21] At Osborne she granted them a degree of belated autonomy with the building of the Durbar Wing in 1891, which included a self-contained suite of rooms above the large Durbar Room, with their own private entrance. This was as close as the couple got to a house of their own, and Beatrice continued to occupy these rooms after Liko's death for the remainder of the Queen's lifetime. In this situation, lacking anywhere concrete that he and Beatrice could call home, Liko found his thoughts inevitably returning to the homes of his childhood, particularly Heiligenberg, that magical house that long continued to draw Battenbergs like moths to a flame.

Flames played a dramatic part in the visit to Liko's mother at Heiligenberg Beatrice and Liko paid with five-year-old Drino in July 1892. What the Queen described as 'this dreadful fire'[22] began at midnight, as the inhabitants of the *Schloss* were retiring to bed. Beatrice was stung by gnats and, assisted by her maid, set off in pursuit of her assailants with a candle. It was a foolish escapade. Inevitably the candle caught a drapery, in this case a mosquito curtain, and the fire took hold, raging through the princess's suite. The castle was quickly evacuated, the firemen called and, in the absence of any wind, the fire contained and fully extinguished by five o'clock in the morning.[23] But Beatrice's losses had been considerable. Not only was she haunted by her folly and the knowledge of her lucky escape – 'It is too terrible for poor Auntie that it should have happened in her room! ... Really too distressing,' the Queen wrote to Beatrice's sister-in-law Victoria of Battenberg, who was also staying at the castle with her daughters Alice and Louise[24] – she had suffered material losses besides. Sophie Hahn, nanny to Victoria's daughter Alice, reported Beatrice darting about in her nightgown, wrapped in a cloak belonging to her mother-in-law, calling for help in saving her jewellery: 'It was awful hearing Princess Beatrice shouting after her pearls and jewels, but no one could save them.'[25] By the time the castle was safe to re-enter, Beatrice's jewellery was lost, alongside quantities of clothes. That the Queen should write to Victoria of Battenberg about her particular sadness at the loss of Beatrice's pearls suggests that the pearls in question were those once owned by the Duchess of Kent, the Queen's mother and Beatrice's grandmother, which the Queen had given to Beatrice as a particular mark of affection; she does not mention a parure of emeralds which was also destroyed in the conflagration. More easily replaced but giving rise to greater short-term embarrassment for Beatrice was the loss of her false fringe. A pad of tight artificial curls worn over the forehead became fashionable in the 1870s and for many years retained numerous adherents among the women of the Queen's family, chief among them the future Queens Alexandra and Mary – despite the Queen's objections ('The present fashion with a frizzle and fringe in front is *frightful*,' she wrote to the Crown Princess in 1874[26]). Beatrice began wearing a false fringe in her mid-twenties, an assertion of independent taste the Queen did not overrule. When it came to explaining her losses to the fire-insurance assessors the morning after the fire, she resorted to wearing a hat,[27] a precaution that may well have been lost on her interlocutors if, as Marie Erbach suggests, the forehead toupee was an English fashion that would not have been familiar to German insurance men. 'We must thank God!' the Queen concluded wearily, 'that you are all safe!'[28] The Princess of Battenberg took a sanguine view of events, though Marie Erbach records the repairs to Heiligenberg necessitated by the fire continuing into the autumn of 1895.

Holidays in Darmstadt, however, had a way of reminding Liko of the emasculating softness of his life. Throughout 1886 Liko, Beatrice, the Queen and, in Berlin, the Crown Princess were exercised over the fate of Sandro in Bulgaria; Liko's second brother would eventually be forced to abdicate his fragile throne. On 30 August 1885 his eldest brother Louis was promoted commander in the Royal Navy; within six years he had risen to the rank of captain and would ultimately become First Sea Lord. Measured against such tangible achievements, Liko's own purely nominal position as Honorary Colonel of the Isle of Wight Rifles was exposed for what it was – a paper honour paid to rank not ability. Contrasts are invidious and served to harden in Liko the determination to prove himself independent of his position as the Queen's son-in-law. His dissatisfaction was accelerated by the restrictions of life continually at the Queen's side, which, far from decreasing over time, grew steadily more oppressive: after Lord Guildford died as a result of a hunting accident, Liko was discouraged from the sport on the grounds of its danger. His cruise to Corsica in 1894 was abruptly curtailed when Beatrice discovered he had been 'keeping low company' at the Ajaccio carnival; she ordered a Royal Navy man-of-war to collect him, thereby forcibly removing him from damaging influences and temptation.[29] Beatrice's peremptoriness and her apparent temporary failure to trust her husband did nothing to increase his resignation to his lot. He requested and was granted permission to spend a week with the Isle of Wight Rifles at its barracks in Hampshire. As he had suspected, the environment suited him perfectly. He wrote to Beatrice, 'Altogether I feel quite in my element again among soldiers, and I am glad, even for so short a time, to take up once more my old profession. I feel like a fish in water. Everyone seems to have confidence in me.'[30] After almost a decade of obedience and charm it was relaxing to behave without constraints in an environment where every action, however small or trivial, was not dictated by an invalid septuagenarian who continued to be guided by what she interpreted as the wishes of a man who had died when Liko was three years old.

TWENTY

'Blighted happiness'

.•.

*A*ccording to the report in the *Sierra Leone Messenger* of
the consecration of Canon John Taylor Smith as seventh
Bishop of Sierra Leone, at Westminster Abbey on 27 May 1897,
first among the three hundred communicants to whom the
Eucharist was administered by the new bishop was Princess
Henry of Battenberg. The previous year Beatrice had given Taylor
Smith a pencil case of Liko's inscribed 'In memory of Prince
Henry, from Beatrice, 1896'. By the time of Taylor Smith's
consecration, Beatrice had been a widow for sixteen months.

The *London Gazette* printed a 'Letter from the Queen to the
Nation' on 15 February 1896, in which the Queen gave thanks
to her 'loyal subjects for their warm sympathy' on the occasion
of Liko's death.

> I lose a dearly loved and helpful Son, whose presence was like a
> bright sunbeam in My Home, and My dear Daughter loses a noble
> devoted Husband to whom she was united by the closest affection.
> To witness the blighted happiness of the Daughter who has never
> left Me, and has comforted and helped Me, is hard to bear ...
> My beloved Child is an example to all, in her courage, resignation
> and submission to the will of God.

The letter came from the heart, its composition the work of a
single sitting. 'Sir Arthur Bigge told me', Lord James of Hereford
noted in his diary, 'that the Queen's beautiful letter of thanks ...
was written by the Queen (notwithstanding her failing sight) by
her own hand, without making one correction. She had no
assistance in its composition.'[1] In her own Journal, the Queen
wrote simply, 'Wrote a letter to be published in the papers,

thanking my people for their kind sympathy with Beatrice and me in our great sorrow.'² The Queen's doctor reported, 'HM crying and sobbing much,' and such were the reports of her devastation on hearing the news that Liko had died, Reid told his mother, that 'there was a panic in London about the Queen, and one evening they had her "dying" and even "dead"!'³

For her part, Beatrice responded to Liko's death in a manner that blended elements of predictability and surprise. Predictably she submitted without complaint to the loss of all that had made her life happiest; she had been schooled in submission from earliest infancy. But she resisted the Queen's verdict of Liko's death as a shared tragedy, 'our great sorrow'. She comforted the Queen as she had always done, then she went away from court for a month to grieve alone, solacing her deep unhappiness that could not give place to the Queen's emotions. 'I must bear with patience the heavy crop God has seen fit to lay on me,' Beatrice wrote to the wife of the Prince Consort's biographer Sir Theodore Martin, whom she and Liko had visited on the Queen's visit to North Wales six years earlier.⁴ It is a statement of resignation, but the image of the crop is a painful one.

John Taylor Smith was three years younger than Beatrice. The Westmorland-born clergyman was a canon-missioner in Sierra Leone when he was asked to join, as chaplain, the expedition to Ashanti on the coast of West Africa, which Liko had also joined. The two men became friends. 'He gave me a message, in case anything happened, as so many deaths had taken place,' Taylor Smith told a public meeting in the year of Liko's death. 'Like a soldier, the Prince said, "I have settled my matters, everything in England, before I came out, but if anything should happen to me . . . I want you to see the Princess for me and give her the message which I have just told you."'⁵ Taylor Smith delivered that undisclosed message to Beatrice in the South of France following Liko's death on 20 January 1896. Like her husband before her, Beatrice became friends with the clergyman, and it was to Taylor Smith rather than the Queen that Beatrice looked for support in her bereavement. 'In moments of deep depression and loneliness, how often I think of your words of encouragement,' she wrote to him.[6]

On 2 February 1896 the *Illustrated London News* set forth Liko's reasons for going to war.

> It is easy to understand the manly spirit that prompted him, doubtless contrary to the wishes of the two illustrious ladies who wanted his companionship at home, to join this Ashanti Expedition for the chance of proving himself endowed with ... qualities of soldiership ... He may have been restless of late, as was suspected from his prolonged yacht voyage in the autumn, slightly impatient of the routine of the royal household, and of the lack of important work ... For his own sake we could have wished him, long ago, active professional service, like the Duke of Connaught, in the Army, or in the Navy, with the Duke of Edinburgh and his own brother Prince Louis; but then, perhaps, the married life of Princess Beatrice and the household comfort of our Queen would have missed for long intervals the genial presence of him who has cheered their feminine retirement and has aided them in the frequent reception of their relatives and friends. He has not lived in vain or unworthily as a good husband and father, a good adopted son, a prince of the royal home.

Less eloquently, in his poem 'The Funeral of the Late Prince Henry of Battenberg', the nineteenth-century's worst poet William McGonagall concluded,

> Prince Henry was a good-fearing man –
> And to deny it few people can –
> And very kind to his children dear,
> And for the loss of him they will drop a tear.

It was to avoid just such obituaries that at 5 a.m. on 8 December 1895 Liko sailed for Africa's inhospitable Gold Coast. To his sister Marie, he wrote, 'You will understand that, as a soldier, I would like to embrace the first opportunity that offers of doing something to serve my adopted country.'[7]

The Ashanti war, like so much British imperial policy, was

motivated in part by ideals, in part by commerce. Despite an earlier undertaking, the native king, Prempeh, continued to traffic in slaves and indulge in human sacrifice on a regal scale, offering up to the gods an estimated three thousand hapless subjects a year; he also neglected to keep open a two-hundred-mile-long road through densely forested country from the interior to the coast, essential for communications and trade. The British decided to install a resident to oversee belatedly Prempeh's compliance with the earlier treaty and to establish a British protectorate over the region. The ultimatum outlining these proposals having been ignored, Sir Francis Scott, Inspector of the Gold Coast Constabulary, was instructed to lead an expedition against the errant Prempeh. Liko volunteered for the post of Scott's military secretary.

The Queen refused her consent. The following day she discussed with Beatrice her objections, chief among them the dangers of the climate. But Beatrice took her husband's part. She told the Queen that Liko 'smarted under his enforced inactivity, and this was about the only occasion which presented no difficulties, as he would go as a volunteer without usurping anyone's place'.[8] Fifteen years earlier the Prince Imperial had sailed to the Cape, embarked on a similar mission, an undertaking that lived on in Beatrice's memory. On this second occasion, when she was not, as in 1879, powerless to influence events, she put her husband's wishes before her own sense of dread, assuring the Queen that Liko would soon be home, unscathed by his experiences. Against her better judgement, the Queen relented. 'Prince Henry is going to Ashantee [sic],' Marie Mallet wrote to her husband Bernard.

> Poor Princess Beatrice is inconsolable but so patient and unselfish and declares she is glad he should do some real work and that *she* will never stop him in any sort of way. I admire her more than I can say, never should I have the courage to pack you off, my darling, on such an expedition ... I have been talking to the poor Princess and comforting her as best I can. Of course he [Liko] is bursting with excitement.[9]

That excitement – so jarring to Beatrice's feelings – was not seconded by the popular press, which railed at the inconvenience to the expedition of counting a member of the Royal Family among the party, and ridiculed Liko's heroism. They were quickly disproved in the former contention. Beatrice read the Queen reports that 'the native Chiefs ... were greatly excited and surprised when Sir Francis introduced Liko, "who had married the Queen's daughter"'.[10] But the offending papers did not moderate their tone. Even after Liko's death, one society weekly, sent to the printer before the news was known, asserted, 'There is, I am assured, no truth in the report that the Poet Laureate's first "commanded" work will be an ode on Prince Henry of Battenberg's expedition to Africa.'[11]

The Queen recorded in her Journal on 6 December 1895,

> Took tea with Beatrice and Liko and directly afterwards he came to wish me good-bye, and was much upset, knelt down and kissed my hand and I embraced him. He said he went not out of a sense of adventure but because he felt it was right ... I could think of little else but this sad parting. God grant that dear Liko may be brought back safe to us![12]

Markedly less maudlin than his mother-in-law, Liko wrote to Beatrice after arriving in Africa, 'The whole thing is like a dream ... I am really happy and pleased to have received permission to see all that is going on.'[13] For Beatrice, the dream would rapidly take on the qualities of a nightmare.

By the middle of January, wife and mother-in-law knew that Liko had contracted malaria. To Bertie the Queen reported that the illness was sufficiently serious to have forced Liko to return to the coast for closer medical attention: 'It is a terrible disappointment for him, but we heard this morning that the fever is declining, so perhaps he may yet go back. It is a terrible trial for darling Beatrice.'[14] The Queen described Beatrice, understandably, as existing in a state of 'such cruel suspense'.[15]

That suspense would end with a shock. The fever did not decline. Liko's deteriorating condition ruled out a return to fighting, and a decision was made to send him home by battleship. On 22 January, as she prepared to set off to meet her husband part-way at Madeira, Beatrice received a telegram. It contained the news of Liko's death and had taken almost two days to reach her. 'All she said in a trembling voice, apparently quite stunned, was "The life is gone out of me",' the Queen confided to her Journal.[16] First Arthur and his wife Louischen, then the Queen struggled to comfort her. 'Went over to Beatrice's room and sat a little while with her. She is ... so piteous in her misery. What have we not all lost in beloved noble Liko, who has died in the wish to serve his country! He was our help, the bright sunshine of our home. My heart aches for my darling child ...'[17] In her anguish the Queen paid Liko the ultimate compliment: 'It seems as though the years '61 and '62 had returned.'[18]

In his will Liko had requested he be buried at Whippingham. With Arthur, on one of the long days between receipt of the news and the arrival of the body, Beatrice returned to the church in which she had been married to choose the spot. To the official of the Lord Chamberlain's office dispatched to Madeira to bring back Liko's remains, she gave a crucifix to be placed in his hand in the coffin, alongside sprigs of ivy, white heather and myrtle from her bouquet and a small photograph of herself attached to the symbolic posy. The partly preserved body arrived at Portsmouth on board HMS *Blenheim* on 4 February. The following day a military funeral was held at St Mildred's, with a second, more public service held simultaneously at Westminster Abbey, for which Beatrice had chosen the hymn 'Christ will gather in His own'. The day after the funeral Beatrice wrote letters of thanks to those who had sent flowers, her long training as the Queen's secretary lending discipline even to her desperate time. To Edith Lytton she wrote, 'I desire to express my most grateful thanks for the beautiful flowers which you have so kindly sent for my dear Husband's funeral and for the sympathy for me in my deep sorrow, of which I feel they are the outward sign.'[19]

On 13 February, Beatrice and all four of her children left the Isle of Wight for Cimiez in the South of France. Later she would be joined by her sister Louise and, in March, by the Queen, who wrote to her Prime Minister Lord Salisbury, 'We are well and the beloved Princess quite admirable in her courage and patient resignation.'[20] The same month, Canon Taylor Smith returned to England to deliver Liko's last message to Beatrice. The Queen requested he travel to Nice to report to her and her daughter, and there – in recognition of his services to Liko and to Beatrice – she appointed him her Honorary Chaplain. That final message, for which Beatrice had waited two months and which Taylor himself was afterwards at such pains to conceal from any third party, may have been the same message later discovered by Nina Epton and revealed in *Victoria and Her Daughters* as: 'In case I die, tell the Princess from me that I came here not to win glory, but from a sense of duty.'[21] For Beatrice, in her devastation, it must have been cold comfort.

Of greater succour to the thirty-eight-year-old widow were Taylor Smith's own words of consolation, the prayers in which he led Beatrice and the passages of religious writings he copied out for her. 'I have never half thanked you for all your helpful sympathy,' she wrote to him in May, after returning to Windsor. 'In hours of deep depression, when I feel overwhelmed by the sense of my loss and the longing for the dear "vanished hand", I recall your beautiful words of strength and hope, which indeed have done me good.'[22] Later she told him, 'I know I may count on your prayers for me, in the hours where I feel weighed down by the sense of my loss, and when for the present the joy seems to have gone out of my life.'[23] From the first Beatrice was upheld by her faith, though the battle was not an easy one. 'It is God's will,' her sister Helena wrote on 29 January in answer to a letter of condolence sent to the Queen, 'and it *must* be well, and *that it is well* is what my darling Sister feels. She is admirable beyond words. Her wonderful firm faith is sustaining and helping her in this her hour of sorest need. Her patience, gentleness, submission, her courage and unselfishness are beyond all praise. But oh! it rends one's heart to see her.'[24] Though the Queen had invoked the memory of 1861 and its aftermath, nothing in Beatrice's response to her tragedy echoed her mother's derangement of self-pity.

On 18 March the Bishop of Ripon, one of her more attentive correspondents, wrote to the Queen, 'I am sure that the quiet and restfulness of Cimiez will prove beneficial to Your Majesty;

and I hope and pray that the light which fringes all clouds may shine round about Your Majesty and the Princess ... I hope Your Majesty found the Princess well and as cheerful as can be expected.'[25] The Queen found Beatrice anything but cheerful, but was impressed by the degree of control her daughter was able to exercise over her shattered emotions; the doctor who accompanied Beatrice to Cannes had noted that she learnt to seem 'quite well' in public but broke down alone.[26] This control was not achieved without considerable effort on Beatrice's part. To her brother Arthur – to whom she admitted, 'The aching void gets worse and worse and I often feel very weary and worn out'[27] – Beatrice confided her terror at returning from France to the scenes of her vanished life with Liko: 'I dread the first return to Windsor, where the memories are still so fresh of my darling Liko's preparations for Ashanti, when he was so full of life and eagerness – I feel the strain and wearing of this constant grief is telling upon my nerves now, and I often have hardly the courage to look forward to the future.'[28] When the time came, however, Beatrice bore the trial bravely, her manner, as the Queen herself acknowledged, very different from her own thirty-five years earlier: 'But oh! the return [and] the missing our beloved Liko at every turn. His empty room and all his things *quite* overwhelmed darling Auntie, who is so good, so brave and unmurmuring and resigned – that one can but admire her and wish to do everything in the world to save her every additional trouble and worry and lessen her bitter anguish.'[29] To the Crown Princess, after Fritz's ninety-nine-day reign as emperor herself also a widow and known as the Empress Frederick, she wrote with her customary tact, 'Darling Beatrice is quite admirable, so patient, so resigned, so courageous and calm but broken-hearted. She adored him; never were two people ever happier ... It wrings my heart to see my darling child's grief. Though she is very calm [and] she can cry quite naturally.'[30]

Beatrice chose her favourite of her mother's maids of honour, Marie Mallet, to confide the extent of her unhappiness to and relate something of what had happened, including the part played by Canon Taylor Smith.

I went to Princess Beatrice and we both sat and sobbed for half an hour while she told me the whole tragic story. Prince Henry knew he was dying and sent long messages to her and all his friends by the Doctor and a chaplain with whom he had made great friends. He felt the fact of dying so far away and alone very much and this makes the poor Princess very miserable, but her grief is perfectly natural and she is extraordinarily brave and unselfish.[31]

'How terrible for you to be fetched in that way,' Beatrice wrote in the summer of 1896 to Walpurga Paget, unexpectedly summoned to the deathbed of her husband Sir Augustus Paget, 'and yet I envy you having been with your beloved husband at the last moment.'[32] She told Lady Lytton that 'she had known nothing of the Prince being worse and then all was over'.[33]

For Beatrice there was no respite from her agony. She told Canon Taylor Smith that her children helped to cheer her, but they were too young to offer her real consolation, and she was determined not to overwhelm them with her grief, as the Queen had overwhelmed her childhood: 'I try to be bright and cheerful for the dear Children's sake and not let my sorrow weigh upon their young lives, but the heart is very sore at times.'[34] As she had written to Arthur, she was tortured by the memory of Liko's last days at home with her, his cheerful preparations for what quickly became so wretched an undertaking; and additionally by the loneliness of his death.

> These are very sad days for me, so full of memories of the busy preparations of last year, when my husband was so keen and full of life, and always trying to comfort me with the thought that it would not be a very long separation, and that if God permitted it, he would come back to me in three months. But His inscrutable will decreed it otherwise, and I must seek to bow in submission, and to fulfil the work left me to do, though the present seems so dark and desolate, and the joy to have gone out of my life.[35]

Alfred's wife Marie, encountering Beatrice in November, considered her almost deranged by her sorrow: 'Poor Beatrice is very sad.' Her moods swung alarmingly, her behaviour was illogical and unpredictable: moments of tears were succeeded by raging at Liko's photograph; she immersed herself in books of piety or talked at length about the domestic economies she was making on candles; restlessly she rode her bicycle, a funereal figure in her full-length black weeds. Marie described Beatrice's mourning as not only 'bizarre' but 'incomprehensible'.[36] Christmas inevitably gave rise to further lamentations. 'Christmas could not fail to be very trying,' Beatrice wrote to Lady Martin, 'the terrible blank my beloved husband has left in the home circle seems to make itself more keenly felt. It seems so hard to begin a new year without him or at least the cheering hope of a happy meeting before very long ...'[37]

In her sitting room at Osborne, Beatrice created a secular shrine to Liko, draping a stand of three shelves with a Union Jack and placing on it four rows of photographs, crowned by a large photograph of Liko in uniform with, on the table below, his sword and helmets. If, over time, Beatrice's grief lessened, it did not disappear. He 'was the joy of my life', she wrote on 29 December 1926, 'whom I never cease to miss, however many years have passed by, since he was taken from me'.[38] From the age of four Beatrice's life had been hostage to her mother's widowhood. Her own long widow's vigil, begun so young, would exceed that of the Queen by eight years.

TWENTY-ONE

'I have taken up my life again'

•—•

*T*wenty-five committee meetings and two and a half years elapsed before the County Council of the Isle of Wight was able to invite Beatrice to unveil its memorial to Liko – the restored Memorial Rooms in the Gate House of Carisbrooke Castle, official residence of the island's governor. Beatrice's own memorial offering, a splendid sarcophagus for the side chapel of St Mildred's, was scarcely quicker. It was commissioned in white Derbyshire limestone – Hopton Wood stone – from the Hopton Wood Stone Company, which was currently enjoying a monopoly of fashionable commissions: it had supplied artefacts to the Prince of Wales and the Dukes of Devonshire, Rutland and Westminster. But the stone delivered to Alfred Gilbert for Liko's tomb turned out to be flawed, and Beatrice reported that all the work had to be redone, with the result that the chapel was not completed by the time of the first anniversary service on 20 January 1897.

The Queen acted more successfully and with greater alacrity. On 21 April 1896 she instituted the Royal Victorian Order 'as a reward for personal services to the Queen and her successors' to commemorate Liko's death.[1] She commissioned a memoir of the Prince from Rowland Prothero, son of the rector of Whippingham, and received the privately printed copies on the first anniversary of Liko's death. She also, in her customary fashion, sought to express her grief tangibly. She chose red Stirlingshire granite for the monolith thirteen and a half feet high and four feet wide she erected in Liko's memory at Craig Dyne, in the royal forest of Ballochbuie near Balmoral. Previous deaths had been commemorated by statues, granite seats and even, in the case of Sir Thomas Biddulph, a drinking fountain, but the

Queen was pleased with this latest innovation and would repeat it when, four years later, her second son Alfred predeceased her. Liko's monument was engraved with a Celtic cross and a short verse in which the Scots winds lament his passing, and liberally covered with Celtic-inspired motifs, knots for the most part. Its tangled decoration provided an unintentional metaphor for the family intrigue that had unfolded in the dark days immediately following Liko's death.

To Lady Minto, four days after the news reached Osborne, Louise wrote of Liko, 'He was almost the greatest friend I had – I, too, miss him more than I can say.'[2] The temperamental princess, at sea in her own increasingly unsuccessful marriage to the probably homosexual Lorne, was ardent in championing her deceased brother-in-law. 'How soon his efforts to prove himself useful were ended and he was brave up to the last fighting the fever!' she told Gladstone's wife.[3] Beatrice and the Queen approved the sentiment. What they did not approve – and were determined to ignore and disbelieve – was Louise's assertion that, in addition to Liko being Louise's greatest friend, she filled the same role for him, with Beatrice a mere cipher. The Duchess of Teck wrote on 9 February, 'Louise has alas! *frisséed* [Beatrice] terribly by calmly announcing, that she was Liko's *confidante* and Beatrice nothing to him, indicated by a *shrug* of the *shoulders*!'[4]

Louise's was a jealous nature. Like that of her mother the Queen, it was also probably a passionate one. Mother and daughter shared a weakness for handsome faces. But whereas the Queen had enjoyed full and satisfying sexual relations with the Prince Consort, Louise's conjugal life with Lorne was less satisfactory and may even at this stage have ceased altogether. Liko was handsome, charming, amusing; in court circles he was admired and held in affection. Louise had grown accustomed to regarding Beatrice with mingled pity and jealousy, chiefly on account of her relationship with the Queen. She did not lament Beatrice's protracted spinsterhood and, when the time came, may have regarded Liko as a more appropriate husband for herself than for her unprepossessing younger sister. Her statement that she was Liko's confidante and Beatrice nothing to him was untrue, perhaps a considered fabrication, possibly a mischief of the moment. But, in its desire to wound, it expressed truthfully Louise's jealousy of Beatrice.

It should not surprise us if Liko were physically attracted to Louise, as she was to him. Louise was the most attractive woman at court, Liko the handsomest man – in an environment in which young men were at a premium. Heinrich von Angeli's second portrait of Beatrice, undertaken in 1893, eighteen years after he first painted her, traced the passage of time and the alteration in her appearance wrought by motherhood. Middle age settled early over the plump princess, and in von Angeli's inelegant but cosy image her youthful bloom has entirely departed. Only the trace of a smile lingers to animate coarsening features. Louise by contrast remained strikingly good-looking and surprisingly youthful in appearance throughout her forties. Nevertheless, we have only Louise's word for the attraction. Statements made by the chief protagonists in this unhappy drama inevitably conflict. In June 1898, by which time the confidence could no longer wound anyone save Beatrice, Louise told Dr Reid of 'Prince Henry's attempted relations with her, which she had declined'.[5] If this is the case, Liko's criticism of Louise's clothes, when they met in Rome in 1887 – reported to George of Wales – otherwise an uncharacteristic action on his part, may be construed as a form of flirting, which Louise deliberately misrepresented to her nephew. Louise was herself a flirt and would not have been averse to stimulating such a response in others.

An awareness of an attraction between her husband and her sister is one explanation for Beatrice's determined exposure of Louise's relationship with the Queen's assistant private secretary Arthur Bigge, which had taken place shortly before Liko's departure for Africa. Beatrice described the relationship as 'a scandal'[6] and Liko – possibly exacting belated revenge on Louise for resisting his advances – claimed to have seen Bigge drinking Louise's health at dinner. Louise denied any truth in the claims, rebutting the whole affair as a concoction of Beatrice's and Helena's to undermine her position at court. The assertion should be treated cautiously: Louise not only suffered from a persecution complex, she habitually sought out grievances with the two sisters who were closest to the Queen. 'Louise is as usual much down on her sisters. Hope she won't stay long or she will do mischief!' Dr Reid wrote to his wife on a similar occasion several years later.[7] Shortly after the Louise–Bigge affair, Liko left for the Ashanti. It is unlikely that knowledge of any flirtation between Liko and Louise lay behind Beatrice's seconding of Liko's desire to fight, contrary to the Queen's wishes: her love for her husband was stronger than her jealousy of her sister. But she may have hoped that a temporary withdrawal from the hothouse atmosphere of the court, with its essentially unvarying personnel and limited number of likely candidates to divert Louise's attentions, would bring about a permanent cooling of relations between the two. In this her hope was apparently shared by Liko himself. Drino would later claim that his father had told him he went to Africa to escape the attentions of a 'lady', an unlikely confidence for a father to share with a nine-year-old son.

Whether Beatrice or Louise felt the greater remorse for the line each had taken, they quickly reached an understanding, and amicable relations – eased by their shared sorrow – were restored. It was Louise rather than the Queen who travelled first to Cimiez to be with Beatrice, and Louise who suggested she design a bronze reredos for Liko's memorial chapel at St Mildred's. The finished reredos depicts the Crucifixion with Christ supported by the Angel of the Resurrection, a composition Louise correctly surmised would comfort Beatrice in her grief. It complements the bronze screen which sculptor Alfred Gilbert designed for the chapel, and it is appropriate that work on the chapel was undertaken by artists who were both known to the Prince: Liko and Gilbert had become friends in 1892, when the latter was working at Windsor on a memorial to the Queen's grandson Albert Victor.

'All seems so different from the last waiting,' Lady Lytton confided to her diary on 11 February 1896, 'on account of the very great sorrow and the death of that good looking charming Prince Henry of Battenberg at the war.'[8] Months later, Marie

Mallet, promoted to extra woman of the bedchamber, echoed the strain: 'How all the brightness is gone, I quite fear *for ever*.'[9]

Liko's death changed the atmosphere of life at court. With him died the theatricals that had done so much to cheer the sombreness of the previous decade. The series of operatic performances staged annually at Windsor for the Queen's birthday was suspended, too, and would not be resumed until 1898. Princess Mary of Teck, now married to Beatrice's nephew George of Wales, wrote to her brother Adolphus on 28 January 1896, 'Isn't it sad about poor Liko? Poor Aunt Beatrice it is awful for her, her whole life ruined, one's heart bleeds for her in her fearful sorrow – what will the Queen and she do now, those two women quite alone, it is too sad and depressing to think of.'[10]

The problem was not Beatrice, who made a very deliberate decision that her grief, unlike that of her mother thirty-five years earlier, must not overwhelm those around her, but the Queen, to whom Liko's death and the loss of a handsome supportive male presence dealt a body blow. The Queen found herself mired in sorrow. 'My poor old birthday again came round, and it seems sadder each year ... fresh sorrow and trials still come upon me,' she wrote on her seventy-eighth birthday, in 1897, burdened by what had become a significant weight of sorrowful anniversaries.[11] Beatrice struggled to spare her mother further unhappiness. She confided her own sadness not to the Queen but to her sisters the Empress Frederick and Helena – the latter had supported her through a short preliminary service held on board HMS *Blenheim* in advance of the funeral proper – and her sister-in-law the Duchess of Albany, who had been widowed even younger than Beatrice. She drew comfort, too, from conversations with Marie Mallet (Beatrice would ask to stand as sponsor to Marie's second son Henry in 1898), and her own lady-in-waiting Minnie Cochrane, whom Lady Lytton described as devoted to her. She wrote regularly to Bishop Taylor Smith in Sierra Leone and enjoyed the sympathetic prelate's occasional visits to Windsor. It was to Taylor Smith that Beatrice commended the Duchess of Albany: 'We are very intimate together and she has been so loving and full of sympathy with me in my sorrow ... I am sure you would like my sister-in-law, she is such a good excellent woman.'[12] Added to this, Leopold and Helen's children, Alice and Charles of Albany, were close in age to Beatrice's children and provided for the latter company of the sort Beatrice herself had been denied in the years following her own father's death. Drino's relationship with Charles mirrored that of the two boys' mothers. 'He and Charles are quite inseparable and delighted to be together again,' Beatrice wrote to Drino's headmaster on Boxing Day 1899. 'Drino is nearly as tall as his cousin so one would never think there was more than two years between them.'[13]

The wider problem at court was not that Beatrice could not be roused from her mourning, but that to varying degrees both mother and daughter had lost the reason for looking forward. Their inability to anticipate pleasure in the present created an atmosphere of lassitude and stagnation that inevitably failed to rouse them and became self-perpetuating, adding to the sense of ennui that had for long lain at the centre of court life.

Nevertheless, Beatrice worked hard to rebuild her life. 'Between times when the tears do not flow, she is cheerful and her old self,' the Empress Frederick wrote in the immediate aftermath of Liko's death.[14] Over time the tears ended and, to outsiders, Beatrice quickly appeared fully herself again. This semblance of normality involved a concerted effort of self-control. In the summer of 1898 she took her daughter Ena, then aged eleven, to Germany. Mother and daughter visited a number of scenes of the past, notably Heiligenberg. 'It made me very sad for the first time to revisit my dear Husband's old home, for the first time without him,' Beatrice wrote to Bishop Taylor Smith. 'Each place is so bound up with memories of the happy past and oh! how I longed that the present might only be a dream. I have taken up my life again with all its work and interests, but there are moments where the sense of all that I have lost comes over me with overwhelming force, and I have a hard struggle.'[15]

The Queen had agreed to Beatrice's departure alone to the South of France in February 1896. Recognizing belatedly that marriage and subsequent widowhood marked Beatrice's maturity and ought to confer some degree of independence, the Queen also began, at around the same time, to consider plans for providing her with at least one separate home of her own. The Queen's choice fell on Kensington Palace, where she herself had been born and lived as a child and where, since 1875, Louise and Lord Lorne had enjoyed the use of an extremely large apartment, which would remain their principal home throughout their marriage. In March 1897 the Office of Works drew up plans for an apartment for Beatrice overlapping partly with the space once occupied by the Queen and her mother within the old state apartments. The parlous physical condition of that area of the palace and the expense involved in restoring it made the plans impractical, and Beatrice would have to wait until after the Queen's death for her permanent London base in the old palace. The Queen in the meantime did not regard either Beatrice's period of mourning alone in the South of France or her fruitless plans for a new home at Kensington Palace as preliminaries to any full-time separation from the daughter who had never left her. With the mourning obsequies over, Beatrice returned to her post at the Queen's side.

It was, of course, the only life she knew. Even marriage had scarcely altered its course. Aside from having no home of her own, Beatrice was unaccustomed to occupying her days with her children and neither her marriage nor Liko's death had diminished the belief, instilled in her from childhood, that her first duty was to her sovereign-mother. This sense of purpose helped fill the emptiness of her early widowhood. It was a role she resumed not simply through duty but prompted by compassion. The Queen, who had for so long considered herself an old woman, was now increasingly prey to the depredations of time. 'My great lameness, etc, makes me feel how age is creeping on. Seventy-eight is a good age but I pray yet to be spared a little longer for the sake of my country, and dear ones,' she wrote on her birthday.[16] Her mobility was severely impaired and her sight failing rapidly. Beatrice had become an enthusiastic amateur photographer. In 1897 she exhibited photographs – alongside pictures taken by the Princess of Wales, Princesses Louise and Victoria of Wales and the Duchess of York – at the New Gallery on Bond Street. The Queen installed a darkroom for her at Osborne. To Victoria of Battenberg the Queen wrote in 1898, 'Dear Auntie Beatrice ... photographs a great deal and most successfully.'[17] The truth was that the Queen's sight was no longer up to any reliable assessment of the success or otherwise of Beatrice's photographic efforts. As early as 1892 she had written to Dr Reid, 'My eyes are troublesome. I can get none of the spectacles to suit; they are wrongly focused, and at night reading is very trying and difficult, though I still at times find dark print not too unreadable.'[18] By mid-1895 Reid could tell his former colleague Sir William Jenner, 'The Queen's defective eyesight is now a serious hindrance to her writing letters.'[19] The following year she was diagnosed with nuclear cataracts in both eyes.

The implications for Beatrice were considerable. Despite the difficulties, the Queen had no intention of retiring from the business of government or that of managing her considerable and far-flung family. Each commitment involved extensive correspondence. Both the Queen's official and private correspondence fell increasingly within Beatrice's remit. Though Beatrice shared the task intermittently with her sister Helena and, more regularly, with Harriet Phipps, the Queen's personal as opposed to private secretary, and the cycle of women in attendance on the Queen, Beatrice was the fixed point at the centre of the circle. 'I am rather helpless about important things without Beatrice or Lenchen, Harriet Phipps also being away,' the Queen wrote to the Empress Frederick in May 1899.[20] Sir Henry Ponsonby had died in 1895. He was succeeded as private secretary by his son Frederick ('Fritz') and Arthur Bigge, whose relations with Louise – real or imaginary – had so alarmed Beatrice. To Beatrice, Fritz Ponsonby and Arthur Bigge fell the task of appraising the four bags of mail 'as big as large armchairs' that arrived daily for the Queen.[21] The task was twofold: in the first instance, the Queen had to be apprised of the contents of the day's letters; in the second, Beatrice and Harriet Phipps took dictation of the Queen's replies – to ministers and grandchildren alike. Beatrice read to the Queen from the newspapers and also the précis of official documents made daily from the contents of the Queen's red boxes by Ponsonby and Bigge.

Ponsonby, for one, considered her ill-suited to the task, writing to his mother,

> The most absurd mistakes occur ... Imagine Princess Beatrice trying to explain our policy in the East. Biggs [sic] or I may write out long précis, but they are often not read to Her Majesty as Princess Beatrice is in a hurry to develop a photograph or wants to paint a flower for a bazaar ... When her sole means of reading dispatches, précis, debates, etc, lies in Princess Beatrice, it is simply hopeless.[22]

Ponsonby's harsh assessment is that of a man struggling to carry out a job that, by virtue of the Queen's diminishing faculties, had become, in the sense that his father had understood it twenty years earlier, largely unmanageable. His frustration vented itself on Beatrice, the guardian of the gate, whose unrestricted access to the Queen and unwavering enjoyment of her fullest confidence had inspired similar responses in others. Beatrice was not stupid – her letters and two works of translation are proof of her intelligence. But hers was the mind of a dedicated amateur clerical worker rather than the naturally gifted, and she shared the political naivety of most of her siblings. The Queen relished the skirmishes of domestic policy, in which she saw no contradiction in upholding the pre-eminence of the Crown and defending the rights of the working man; and the broader picture of foreign policy, regarding herself as the embodiment and champion of British prestige across the globe. Beatrice felt no such personal interest and her attention was frequently absorbed by smaller, more immediate concerns. She was attentive and diligent up to a point, but her political acumen was limited. The Queen discouraged all her children from involving themselves in politics and guarded closely her unique access and prerogatives. Beatrice in turn did not press the Queen against the latter's will, which remained formidable, and so the royal aspect of the business of government proceeded with a growing lack of fluency through the final years of the Queen's life.

Marie Mallet suggested that the private secretaries' objections arose in part from the Princess's sex.

'Biggie' was rather cross with me yesterday because the Queen had made me read some War Office box to her and he thinks it absurd that military messages should go through the Ladies! But that is the natural result of having a sovereign of eighty! ... I am sure the tendency now will be for me and my colleagues to do more and more, and in the state of the Queen's sight and considering her age it is quite inevitable.[23]

Beatrice was foremost among those 'ladies' and more than a match for Ponsonby and Bigge. Despite her diffidence and shyness, she was not lacking in confidence and, when pressed, determination. 'She was very business-like and capable: she was extremely kind to me, but I had a feeling that I should not like to oppose her wishes,' wrote an artist who encountered Beatrice in 1900.[24] Though Bertie chafed at the confidential papers the Queen showed Beatrice and his own exclusion from the political aspects of monarchy, and Louise spoke 'with a sense of the ludicrous' about both Beatrice and Helena – 'and poor Mama so deluded by Beatrice, my dear, and by Helena'[25] – the Queen herself was quite happy with the unstinting assistance given to her by her widowed youngest daughter. In his autobiography *Recollections of Three Reigns*, published posthumously (and also after Beatrice's death), Fritz Ponsonby drew a veil over his frustrations at the Queen's working practice, simply writing of the period 1897 to 1899, 'Although I had for over two years been Assistant Private Secretary, I had never done the work of Private Secretary, nor had I ever seen the Queen about business. Occasionally after dinner she would talk to me about letters that had interested her, but all the work was done by boxes.'[26] Wisely Ponsonby – the consummate courtier – forbore to share with the Queen his reservations about Beatrice, or indeed any of the Queen's ladies. He recognized the unassailability of Beatrice's position, the Queen's favourite of her children, privy now to

On 23 November 1886, Beatrice gave birth to the first of four children, a son, Albert Alexander, known as 'Drino'.

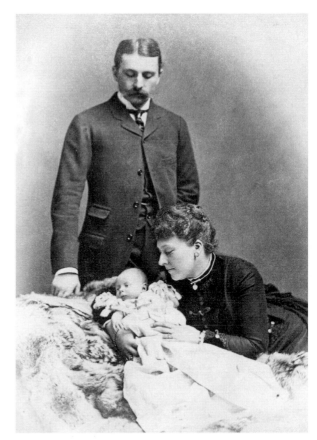

At the baptism of the Queen's 'little Jubilee grandchild', Beatrice's only daughter Ena, in December, it was the Queen who characteristically took centre stage.

FROM A SKETCH BY MR. ROBERT PRITCHETT

THE CHRISTENING AT BALMORAL OF THE INFANT DAUGHTER OF THE PRINCE AND PRINCESS HENRY OF BATTENBERG

Despite the apparent intimacy of this photograph, Beatrice found that she was not unduly maternal.

Beatrice's sons Leopold, Maurice and Alexander, photographed at Balmoral.

'A particularly pretty child', Beatrice's second son Leopold – like the uncle after whom he was named – suffered from haemophilia.

This photograph of Beatrice with Maurice was taken in the early days of her widowhood.

Despite consistently placing her mother's needs before those of her children, Beatrice would later draw comfort from her children in her widowhood. From left: Maurice, Ena, Leopold, Alexander.

The three Princes of Battenberg in uniform on the eve of the First World War: Maurice (who most closely resembled his handsome father), Alexander and Leopold.

THE GRAPHIC

AN ILLUSTRATED WEEKLY NEWSPAPER

No. 1,035—Vol. XL.
Registered as a Newspaper

SATURDAY, SEPTEMBER 14, 1889

THIRTY-TWO PAGES
AND EXTRA SUPPLEMENT

PRICE SIXPENCE
By Post 6½d.

THE PRINCESS BEATRICE DOWN A COAL MINE
THE PRINCESS PICKING COAL IN THE WYNNSTAY COLLIERY, RUABON, NORTH WALES

Among engagements under-taken by Beatrice and Liko was a visit in 1889 to the Wynnstay Collieries in North Wales, 'regarded by all members of the royal party as capital fun'.

Below: On Twelfth Night, 1888, Beatrice appeared as the Queen of Sheba along-side Sir Henry Ponsonby's King Solomon in a typically lavish tableau vivant of the sort that characterized court entertainments in the years of Beatrice's marriage.

By the time of her death, Queen Victoria's family encompassed four generations. Beatrice was ever present at family gatherings – like this group of mostly grand-children and great-grand-children pictured on the lawn at Osborne (Beatrice fourth from right).

After the birth of her children, Beatrice became a decidedly stately figure.

Although Ena's engagement to the Catholic Alfonso XIII of Spain aroused mixed emotions at home on religious grounds, this postcard was issued showing the couple with their widowed mothers.

Weeks after her fiftieth birthday, on the birth of Ena's eldest son Alfonso (called 'Alfonsito', left of picture), Beatrice became a grandmother. Alfonso XIII blamed Beatrice for Alfonsito's haemophilia and never voluntarily spoke to her again – but Beatrice remained attached to her Spanish grandchildren.

This stupendous portrait of the fifty-one-year-old princess was painted by
Spanish impressionist Joaquin Sorolla y Bastida.

In 1927, Beatrice sat for the second time for society portraitist Philip de Laszlo.
His 'winter' portrait is handsome, dignified and kindly.

every aspect of her public and private life. It was a position Beatrice shared with none of her siblings, nor any of the Queen's servants or government ministers. But for Beatrice, in her role as spectator and trusted confidante close to the centre of power, a role she had never invited and did not crave, time was running out.

TWENTY-TWO

'I ... can hardly realize what life will be like without her'

•◆•

*B*eatrice presented a pipe and a woollen cap to each of the men of the Isle of Wight Rifles she inspected at Osborne on 1 February 1900. The company was bound for South Africa and war with the Boers. Beatrice took a particular interest in its well-being. In 1885, in honour of her wedding, the battalion had been renamed after her the Fifth (Isle of Wight Princess Beatrice's) Volunteer Battalion of the Hampshire Regiment. 'I am glad to have this opportunity of bidding you farewell on the eve of your departure for South Africa on active service,' she told the company of men.

> You know how warm an interest I take in the regiment that bears my name and was, in the past, so closely associated with my dear Husband. He would have rejoiced as I do today, to see so many of you nobly coming forward to fight in defence of your Queen and Empire and I am sure you will always uphold the good name of your regiment. May God protect you all and bring you safe home again.[1]

Beatrice was doubly attached to the regiment. Not only did it bear her name, but it gathered its men from the island of which, since the death of her husband, she had been governor. The Queen made the appointment by letters patent on 8 June 1896:

> Now know ye that We ... Do by these presents give and grant unto Our dear Daughter Her Royal Highness Princess Beatrice Princess Henry of Battenberg the office of Governor and Captain of all Our Isle of Wight ... and the office of Governor of Our Castle of Carisbrooke and of all Our Castles and Fortresses

208

whatsoever in the same isle . . . and also the office of Steward of the same isle.[2]

As it had been in Liko's case, so it was with Beatrice – the office was a compliment and a crumb of independence tossed by the Queen to the daughter she knew now would never leave her. In Beatrice's case, however, the Queen took a touching degree of pride in her appointment. 'When Princess Beatrice became Governor of the Isle of Wight, a great deal was made of it, but of course it really meant nothing,' wrote the bachelor Fritz Ponsonby, with no sympathy with an ageing mother's delight in her favourite child. 'Arthur Balfour came down to stay at Osborne and during dinner the Queen said to him, "Did you see in the newspapers about the Governor of the Isle of Wight?" He replied that he had not, and added, "I never knew there was such a post, and I have not the foggiest idea who is the Governor."'[3] The Queen dropped the subject. Despite Balfour's lack of enthusiasm, Beatrice discharged the limited functions of the office with dignity and seriousness, as had Liko before her. For almost half a century she remained the island's governor. The position provided her with a fixed purpose and an enduring interest when, after the Queen's death, she found herself increasingly marginalized from the centre of royal affairs. It also formalized the bonds of affection that bound Beatrice to the Isle of Wight, effectively her home, since she felt little fondness for Balmoral, the house which, with Osborne, had formed the principal dwelling place of the widowed Queen and her youngest daughter. The governorship brought with it an official residence on the island – an apartment in Carisbrooke Castle. It would provide a note of constancy and a shelter from the storm in years to come.

'Had a shocking night and no draught could make me sleep as pain kept me awake. Felt very tired and unwell when I got up,' the Queen recorded in her Journal on 11 November 1900. 'Had again not a good night and slept on rather late. My lack of appetite worse than ever. It is very trying,' she added the following day. Six weeks later, she was still prey to 'the same unfortunate alterations of sleep and restlessness, so that I again did not get up when I wished to, which spoilt my morning and day'.[4]

With the end in sight, Beatrice's task grew daily more arduous. The Queen recognized the certain erosion of her faculties. Her frustration, added to her very real discomfort and her continuing unhappiness over the war in South Africa, made her irritable and fretful. Beatrice devoted irregular days to her comfort, writing the letters the Queen continued to dictate to her, accompanying her on the cold and cheerless drives she would shortly be forced to abandon and ministering to her physical needs in a way that, once again, suggests an inversion of the roles of mother and child. When, in November 1899, Beatrice accompanied Helena and Louise to a wedding in London, the Queen had asked, 'And who shall bring me my tea?'[5] The answer, of course, was Beatrice, who attended only the wedding, missing the reception afterwards in order that she could return to Windsor and prevent her mother from being alone. In the terrible summer of 1871 illness had incapacitated the Queen to the extent that she could not feed herself or even blow her nose. She was not so helpless now, but her feeling of dependence was the same. Once again her neediness focused on the daughter who gave her the greatest compliance. After the Queen's death, Beatrice wrote that she had been 'the centre of everything',[6] and that she missed her mother's 'daily tender care'.[7] Given no choice, in the Queen's final weeks she placed her, as she always had, at the centre of her existence. But it was the daughter not the mother who in real terms administered daily tender care. In return she received continuing reaffirmation of her *raison d'être* and her mother's love, selfish but sincere.

It was ironic that Beatrice, who had so often played the role of mother in relation to the Queen (except in any matter of control) should be prevented by this occupation from providing her children with any similar permanent loving presence. As the children grew up, problems emerged. In the years following Liko's death, when – as his father had wished and willed – Drino was dispatched to Wellington College, his academic performance was consistently mediocre, characterized by an 'extraordinary want of attention'[8] and a reluctance to take up a book in his leisure hours. Ena developed what Beatrice, apparently powerless to control it, described as a 'very difficult' nature, and Leopold was often ill. All three older children were lazy and unfocused. To Drino's headmaster, Beatrice wrote, 'He ... seems not to have quite enough self reliance, and this, odd enough to say, his brother Leopold and his sister, are also rather deficient in.'[9] Without her husband to support her, Beatrice called on Bishop Taylor Smith. Almost the same age as Liko, he appears to have got on well with the children, with a particular talent for talking to them in a manner that won their confidence and elicited good intentions: 'Anything you say', Beatrice told him, 'carries such weight with it, and the boy [Drino] has such entire confidence in you.'[10] 'Drino has disappointed me very much by telling some most unwarrantable untruths, for which I have to punish him severely,' she wrote to the Bishop on 21 September 1897.

> I am sure you will kindly say a word to him on the subject, for it naturally distresses me very much. I have such a horror of untruthfulness and it can lead to such trouble in the future. Poor Ena is still at times very troublesome and rebellious, always thinking that she is in the right and that everybody is ill using her. Leopold I am very sorry to say has had to lay up ever since we have been here, which depresses him very much and he said quite sadly 'I am sure it is God punishing me for my sins.'[11]

Only Maurice, the son who from infancy most closely resembled Liko, was too young to give trouble.

The problem was that Beatrice's absorption in the Queen prevented her from devoting to her children the attention they badly needed. As time went on, the situation became not better but worse. Beatrice refused to countenance the possibility of the Queen's death. Like everyone else at court, she experienced the strange, unsettling sensation of treading water, awaiting something too great to comprehend and living in the meantime from day to day, assuming that if she behaved as she had always done, things would continue as they had always done. Dr Reid's wife Susan wrote to her mother-in-law on 19 January, three days before the Queen died, 'Jamie is privately astonished at Princess

Beatrice not being more concerned and upset about her mother's condition. She takes it all very calmly, and was *out* yesterday when the Queen sent to say she would see her! ... She has shut her eyes willfully to the truth for so long, that now it is a shock.'[12] 'I love these darling children so, almost as much as their own parent,' the Queen had written in her Journal on 10 February 1894[13] about her Battenberg grandchildren. Sadly for the children in question, so long as she continued to minister to the Queen, their mother did not have the time or energy to love them as actively as they needed. To Bishop Taylor Smith, Beatrice wrote early in 1900,

> I have had some frightful domestic upheavals lately, which have greatly worried me, and I have to part with the governess ... There has been a great want of straightness, which has destroyed all my confidence, and I found that my children's love and trust in me, were being steadily undermined. This has been a very painful revelation to me, and I felt for their good a change must be made.[14]

Beatrice did not state – may not have arrived at – the conclusion that the children's governess could not have swayed their affections so completely had they seen more of their mother. Juggling the demands of her growing family and the mother for whom she filled the roles of daughter, mother, confidante, secretary and nurse, Beatrice, as always, gave precedence to the claims of the failing Queen.

In June 1900 Beatrice sailed to the Isles of Scilly, a voyage full of evocations of Liko, who had undertaken the same trip on board the *Sheila* a decade earlier. In December she visited her eldest sister the Empress Frederick in Germany. The Empress was dying of cancer. Mercifully she would outlive her mother, though only by seven months. Beatrice wrote the Queen's letters to the Empress and read to her mother the latter's replies, which, like the Queen's, were dictated to her youngest daughter, in the Empress's case Margaret, or 'Mossy', of Prussia. Even Beatrice's 'holidays' from the Queen were bound up with the business of dying. Her visit to Friedrichshof in December was of short duration, intended to reassure Beatrice of her sister's condition without alarming the Queen. The only assurance Beatrice drew was of the inevitability of her sister's imminent demise. Wracked with pain, the Empress scarcely clung on to life. She successfully dispatched Christmas presents to Osborne, not telling her mother her true condition. Beatrice in turn reported to her sister her determined hopes for the Queen's recovery. 'I do think she is a little better and able to take more nourishment,' she wrote on Boxing Day 1900.[15] Ten days later the Queen herself reiterated the hope, writing to the Empress that she hoped soon to improve.[16] She hoped in vain. The Queen died at 6.30 in the evening of 22 January 1901. Earlier Leopold had played his violin to soothe his grandmother's last hours, Maurice had cried so loudly that he had to be removed from the room, and Beatrice's nephew William of Prussia, Emperor since Fritz's death in 1888, dandled the twelve-year-old Ena on his knee. Beatrice sat at her mother's bedside alongside Helena and Louise, her three daughters repeating for the Queen the names of her children and grandchildren who were present.

'She was our Mother,' wrote romantic novelist Marie Corelli after news of the death was made known, a characteristic statement of sentimentality and exaggeration. Even Mary Ponsonby, who prided herself on her unrosy attitude to the Royal Family, spoke of the 'grief which is one of the greatest sorrows of my life'.[17] For Beatrice, neither verdict was an exaggeration. To Dr Story, principal of the University of Glasgow, she wrote on 15 March from her temporary retreat at the Empress Eugénie's villa at Cap Martin in the South of France, 'It is indeed a calamity that has fallen on the whole Empire, and to us her Children, you may imagine what the grief is. I, who had hardly ever been separated from my dear Mother, can hardly realize what life will be like without her, who was the centre of everything.'[18] Struggling with her overwhelming sense of loss, she fell back on the distant niceties of royal politesse, replying to Lady Elphinstone's letter of condolence, 'It is indeed a terrible blow that has fallen upon us all, and it is very soothing in our great grief, to feel that it is shared by others.'[19] To Marie Mallet – courtier, friend, near-contemporary and occasional lady-in-waiting to Beatrice – the princess expressed herself more openly. Three months after the Queen's death, her sorrow had not begun to abate: 'This first sad return of my birthday without my beloved mother! No one knows what the daily missing of that tender care and love is to me, coming as it does on top of that other overwhelming loss, so that my heart is indeed left utterly desolate. If it were not for the dear children, for whom I have alone to live now, I do not know how I should have the courage of struggling on.'[20]

Once before, writing to Bishop Taylor Smith after Liko's death, Beatrice had vowed to submerge her grief in trying 'to be bright and cheerful for the dear children's sake'.[21] In that instance, she mostly succeeded in shielding Drino, Ena, Leopold and Maurice from the full torrent of her suffering. But she did so not through the company of her children but by submergence in her mother's needs and the consolations of religion. Now there was no longer a Queen to come between Beatrice and her children, a void that for Beatrice could never be filled.

TWENTY-THREE

'I have my dear Mother's written instructions'

•◆•

*I*n the dome of the Royal Mausoleum at Frogmore, a trapped sparrow circled, fluttering. Close to the tombs of the Queen and Prince Consort, Marochetti's sepulchral effigies white as death in the pale wintry light, the Royal Family had gathered for a service of remembrance on the first anniversary of the Queen's death. An unnamed princess, distracted by the sparrow, whispered to her neighbour, 'Do you think that little bird could be Mama's spirit?' The affecting notion was passed along the row of mourners until it reached Queen Alexandra. 'No, I do not think it could be Mama's spirit,' she replied, 'or it would not have made a mess on Beatrice's bonnet.'[1] With the benefit of hindsight, the reader may choose to disagree with Alexandra's assessment.

Shadows of the past clung to Beatrice; she would never shake them free. As she had been associated with the Queen in life, so she was in death. On 28 July 1903, she travelled by train to Scarborough to open the new town hall. The seaside town was *en fête*, hung with bunting and flags. Beatrice was escorted from the train into a carriage and presented with a gold key with which to perform the ceremonial opening. Afterwards the company of local dignitaries and their guests moved into the town-hall gardens. Beatrice unveiled a statue. On its tall pedestal it towered above the watching throng; photographs and a commemorative postcard show them craning their necks to see. The statue that dwarfs them is of Queen Victoria.

The association of Beatrice and the Queen obtained not only in the minds of the public but in Beatrice's own mind too. Years passed, and the Queen's legacy faded, changed, diminished. For Beatrice her mother remained vividly part of her life. At London's

Lyric Theatre in 1937 Laurence Housman's *Victoria Regina* told the story of the Queen's life, Pamela Stanley in the principal role. A friend wrote to Beatrice, commending the production and reassuring her about the play's content. Beatrice's reply – written thirty-six years after the Queen's death – reveals the depth of her feeling. 'I am very thankful to hear from you, that you really considered it such an excellent rendering of both my dear Parents' personalities ... there was nothing in any way objectionable or too contrary to facts. But I am sure you will understand I cannot bring myself to see my dear Mother, whose memory is still so intensely vivid in my mind and heart, personified on the stage, by a stranger, however good.'[2]

For Beatrice, in whose affections she was a living presence, no one could represent the Queen. Except Beatrice herself. In 1902 she embarked on the task for which history remembers her. In itself it constitutes a significant act of representation: the editing, and where she deemed it necessary, rewriting of her mother's Journal.

Contrary to popular assumption, Beatrice is not named in Queen Victoria's will as her literary executor.[3] With her brother Arthur and Keeper of the Privy Purse Sir Fleetwood Edwards, she was a co-executor of the will. As she had during her lifetime, so after her death, the Queen placed her trust in her favourite children, regardless of the impropriety of overlooking her heir Bertie, 'for no child', she had written to Arthur's governor Sir Howard Elphinstone in 1882, '(excepting her beloved Beatrice) was ever so loved by [the Queen] as that precious Darling son ... her darling from his birth!'[4] The role of literary executor that was to provide Beatrice with employment and consolation through the next two decades was one the Queen had imposed upon the princess privately, probably without either ever having recourse to so formal-sounding a description of the task. Beatrice claimed she had her mother's 'written instructions' to assume the responsibilities synonymous with literary executorship, and since such an injunction on the Queen's part was entirely in keeping with her lifelong confidence in her youngest daughter and Beatrice's intermittent role as the Queen's amanuensis, writing on occasion both her Journal and her letters, no one doubted the claim. In the light of Beatrice's subsequent actions, it would have been an unlikely claim to have invented. Beatrice's 'editorship' extended, as we have seen, to rewriting. As the Queen's favourite child, she had least to fear from the Journal, least reason to covet the task of rewriting in order to improve her own showing in her mother's account. Given her essentially modest nature, it is also improbable that Beatrice would have fought for the job, had the Queen bequeathed it elsewhere, on the grounds that, as the Queen's most intimate confidante, she understood her best.

The importance and extent of the Queen's papers meant that Beatrice could not carry out her charge in secret. Her siblings – including the new King, whose first action in contravention of the Queen's wishes was his decision to reign not as Albert Edward but as Edward VII – knew about the bequest, as did Beatrice's co-executor Sir Fleetwood Edwards. It is possible, however, that only Beatrice understood the exact nature of the Queen's injunction. Bertie invited Lord Esher to arrange his mother's papers, an invitation that in practice extended beyond the Queen to encompass papers relating to a number of royal forebears, notably George III. Esher, *éminence grise* of the Edwardian court, became by this and similar invitations, archivist to the King. But in relation to Queen Victoria his responsibility could extend no further than official papers, given Beatrice's role and the fact that at least some of those concerned believed that the Queen had not simply intended Beatrice to exercise control over her private papers, but that the papers should, for her lifetime, fall within Beatrice's ownership. As Cynthia Colville, later a lady-in-waiting to Queen Mary, told Sir Sydney Cockerell in July 1945, 'Queen Victoria ... left the diaries and correspondence to Princess Beatrice.'[5] Beatrice herself pursued her task without subterfuge, involving Esher – whom the Queen had known and whose daughters Dorothy and Sylvia had shared dancing classes at Windsor with Beatrice's children in the 1890s – from the outset. On 13 December 1905, she wrote to him, 'I have two more volumes of the Journal to give you, for putting away at Windsor, and perhaps you could call some day for them' – an instruction that neatly encompasses the distinction of role between princess and courtier: Beatrice rewrote the Journal and destroyed the original; to Lord Esher, in his capacity as Bertie's informal archivist, she handed the copies that, though still precious, could safely be entrusted to the care of a third party.[6]

On 18 October 1902 Beatrice wrote to Esher requesting assistance: 'I feel I ought finally to go through all that remains for as I have my dear Mother's written instructions to be solely responsible for the arranging and retaining of them in the manner she would have wished, I must not leave it to others ...'[7] That Beatrice did not explain the constituents of 'them' or the extent of 'it', suggests that Esher at least understood the parameters of her authority. Sir Fleetwood Edwards recognized that authority as principally covering the Queen's Journal. He discussed the position with the Archbishop of Canterbury, the same ex-Dean of Windsor Randall Davidson who had assisted Beatrice with the publication of *The Adventures of Count Georg Albrecht of Erbach* a decade earlier. To Arthur Benson, Davidson wrote in February 1904 concerning the Journal, 'I have seen Sir Fleetwood Edwards. I find that the books in question are to the best of his belief under the unfettered and personal control of the Princess Beatrice and of her alone.'[8]

Unopposed by the King, Beatrice began her task the year after the Queen's death. Despite her letter to Esher, more than three years passed before she showed him the extent of those papers of her mother's over which she exercised control. It was not until 31 January 1906 that the latter was able to write to his son Maurice, 'Today Princess Henry [Beatrice] came down to Windsor, and we opened, for the first time, all the boxes of the Queen's private correspondence, which are in the vaults.'[9] In the interval Beatrice had made available to Esher papers she considered fell within his jurisdiction as Bertie's archivist. These included items not related to the Queen, for example, a book of letters written by George IV to his ministers in the mid-1820s, which she released in August 1905. She also discussed with Esher her working practice in relation to the Queen's Journal, but did not, before 1906, feel constrained to permit him access to any of the Journal, and did so then only at Esher's request, the latter at that point editing the first of what would become three published instalments of the Queen's letters.

Beatrice had decided before she began work not simply to retain the Queen's Journal as it existed, expunging or scoring out whatever she considered potential cause for concern, but to transcribe it in a completely new, handwritten draft, destroying the original as she proceeded, burning it page by page. (This may have been the Queen's own idea, or a plan of operation mother and daughter devised together.) She chose the firm of Parkins & Gotto, the court stationers who supplied her writing paper, to provide her with the large, blue, hardback, ruled notebooks she had decided upon, agreeing with Esher that the volumes – there would ultimately be one hundred and eleven – remain unnumbered until she had finished the task in its entirety. To Esher she wrote on 23 October 1904, 'Would you kindly order me two more books for copying my Mother's Journal into. I am working regularly at it and am really making some progress. I sent to Parkins & Gotto, but they did not seem to understand, so I must beg you to give the order. They should be without the number of any volume for as I agreed with you, those could be added later.'[10]

Beatrice's choice of the word 'copying' indicates the light in which she viewed her task. Historians have inevitably emphasized the destructive aspect of Beatrice's work, for which she is regularly vilified, and it is undoubtedly the case that much has been lost as a result of her transcription. In her own mind the undertaking was not one of destruction but preservation – preserving the Journal in a form that would preserve for posterity the Queen's memory as Beatrice considered it ought to survive. In this she acted wholly in accordance with the Queen's intention in allotting this responsibility to her. The Queen did not make such decisions lightly: she understood clearly how Beatrice regarded her, that mixture of love, veneration and deep awe. Her bequest of the role of literary executor to Beatrice signalled a green light to the work of bowdlerization, excision and revision on which Beatrice expended almost thirty years. Unlike her son Bertie and daughter-in-law Alexandra, the Queen did not leave instructions that on her death her papers were to be destroyed wholesale. She was far-sighted enough to appreciate their future historical value but recognized that they contained both incidents and expressions that reflected discredit on either the protagonists, the writer or both. Whether her motive was egotism or a proper awareness of the claims of history, the Queen's decision to sanction the preservation of her papers in revised form is a positive one; Beatrice's place as legitimized bar to any adviser to the Queen's successor who might otherwise have suggested destruction of the papers is to be celebrated. Although George V and Queen Mary would later be among the earliest protesters against Beatrice's work, the King himself had once planned that his journal suffer a more drastic fate. As Lord Esher recorded in his diary in November 1908, 'The Prince [of Wales, later George V] told me that he kept a journal, and had left instructions that it was to be destroyed at his death. We argued with him, and he fetched a volume, and made me read it. Very simply written, and quite inoffensive, but well worth preserving ...'[11]

In her conversation with Sydney Cockerell in 1945 Cynthia Colville applauded the solution the Queen had devised half a century earlier. 'She [Cynthia Colville] said that as Queen Victoria had left the diaries and correspondence to Princess Beatrice, nothing could be done – but that it might be just as well that the old Queen's good qualities would not be further hidden by the publication of her sillinesses ...'[12] – an assessment that, in different words, probably matched the Queen's own and that of her 'editor' daughter. Three months earlier, Sir Sydney had reached his own conclusion that the material Beatrice was likely to have removed would not have interested him personally:

I believe that Queen Victoria's diary ... revealed tiffs with Prince Albert, which might or might not prove of some little importance to future historians ... But I find gossip about the Royal family for the most part very small beer. They are admirable people. They do their duty as monarchs in a manner that is beyond all praise. But their private lives, so far as they have any, concern mè far less than those of men and women of character that are not under perpetual observation ...[13]

Since the only extensive surviving record of the Queen's Journal before Beatrice's transcription is the series of extracts quoted by Sir Theodore Martin in his official life of the Prince Consort, ending in 1861, it is not possible to make any but a conjectural assessment of the nature and impact of Beatrice's work. Comparisons with the Queen's written output that escaped Beatrice – notably the voluminous correspondence with the Crown Princess – suggest that the loss is as much one of tone as content: the Queen habitually expressed herself with force, vigour and complete confidence in her opinion, however extreme the viewpoint she espoused. Much of this survived Beatrice's editorship: were this not the case and the prevailing tone wholly of blandness, it is unlikely that historians would lament her excisions. Equally impossible to assess with certainty is the extent to which Beatrice's 'arrangement' and 'retention' complies with 'the manner [the Queen] would have wished'.

On 28 February 1874 the Crown Princess wrote to her mother,

Lately I have been thinking a great deal about the keeping of letters, and it is painful to see how the wishes and orders of the dead are set aside ... Such and such letters are not to be read, are to be burnt, should be carried out to the letter! But in our position it is over-ruled by the consideration 'these papers may be very useful, they may contribute remarkable facts and details to history and they had better be saved ...' I want your authorization to burn all I have except dear papa's letters! Every scrap that you have ever written – I have hoarded up, but the idea is dreadful to me that anyone else should read them or meddle with them in the event of my death.[14]

The Queen kept her daughter waiting more than a fortnight for her answer, but her reply shows both wisdom and an absolute conviction that the fate she decreed for her letters would be respected by her successors:

> Now about the letters ... I am not for burning them except any
> of a nature which affect any of the family painfully and which
> were of no real importance, and they should be destroyed at once
> ... Your letters are quite safe and would be returned to you in
> case of my death ... I would however destroy any of a nature to
> cause mischief ... I am much against destroying important letters
> and I every day see the necessity of reference.[15]

If the Queen intended the same criteria to be applied to her
Journal, only passages '[affecting] any of the family painfully ...
of no real importance', that is, concerning domestic rather than
political issues, should have been destroyed by Beatrice. But
Beatrice was not privy to her mother's correspondence with her
eldest sister, even though she would later have access to the
Crown Princess's letters; and views expressed in 1874 by Queen
Victoria in rude good health, with no thought of death, may
have been significantly at variance with those expressed almost
thirty years later by the same Queen in her dotage, to a daughter
of very different character.

Beatrice treated the Queen's commission with seriousness.
'Could you call on me at Kensington,' she wrote to Lord Esher
in November 1904. 'I would give you the key of the box, so that
you could get some volumes of the Journals out for me. Having
finished the last book I had for writing into, I am anxious to
lose no time in looking through some more. It is such a tre-
mendous work, that I do not like to waste any time.'[16] That she
adopted such a line is not surprising. Her whole life had tended
towards the promotion of the Queen's well-being. For forty years
she had loved and attended to her mother devotedly. Now she
devoted herself to fulfilling this last charge. She did so with a
sense of application absent from much of her ordinary life –
ladies-in-waiting record her beginning paintings then handing
them over to be finished, for example – demonstrating what
Marie Mallet, one of her chief supporters, characterized as
Teutonic rigour: 'She is very German in the way she concentrates
her mind on a given line of thought or action.'[17] Her one further
published work, undertaken once her transcription of the Queen's

Journal was complete, again involved diaries and was again inspired by the Queen: a translation of extracts of the diary of her maternal great-grandmother, Duchess Augusta of Saxe-Coburg-Saalfeld, in 1941. But by then Beatrice was an old woman, condemned by ill health to such sedentary occupations as reading and writing. In the short term, despite the responsibilities of the Queen's literary executorship, she was a member of the Royal Family, with her own children all still unmarried and, for the first time in her life, her own home and a life to call her own.

TWENTY-FOUR

'Osborne ... is like the grave of
somebody's happiness'

•◆•

*I*n February 1909 Beatrice travelled from Gibraltar to Tangiers aboard HMS *Antrim*, making use, as was the Royal
Family's custom, of a ship of the Royal Navy to transport her.
'February 18 HRH Princess Henry of Battenberg came aboard
and passage to Tangiers and landed until Saturday. Ship left and
we carried out Night Firing Practice and then anchored at Gib,'
wrote crew member Owen Budd in his diary. His entry for 20
February recorded, 'Went to Tangiers to fetch HRH Princess
Henry of Battenberg and took her to Algercerias [*sic*, Algeciras
in south-west Spain] and then anchored at Gib.'[1] Two years later,
Beatrice returned to North Africa, on this occasion her destination
Algiers.

Her purpose on both trips was her health, her continuing
battle against rheumatism that made her crave the sun and warm
climates. The spas of Continental Europe that, with their 'healing'
waters and programme of massage, had brought Beatrice such
relief in her twenties, failed to effect any discernible improvement
two decades later. In 1905 Beatrice opened the Spa Baths at
Ripon in North Yorkshire; she did not add the northern watering
hole to her annual itinerary. But in the sunshine of North Africa –
even briefly sampled – she found relief at last. To an Isle of
Wight neighbour, Beatrice's lady-in-waiting Bessie Bulteel wrote
on 17 May 1911, 'The Princess is wonderfully better since being
in Algiers and is able to walk quite well now.'[2] The letter offers
an insight into the severity of Beatrice's condition; it would
continue to cause her suffering for the next thirty years.

Travel satisfied Beatrice's curiosity about exotic, distant countries. Such was her enjoyment of her five-month trip to Egypt

during the winter of 1903–4 that, on her return, she accepted the position of patron of the new Institute of Archaeology at the University of Liverpool. In the immediate aftermath of the Queen's death travel offered an escape from the scenes of the past, with their still painful memories of the Queen and Liko. Describing Beatrice as 'terribly unhappy' during an extended visit to Germany in the summer of 1901, Marie Mallet wrote, 'She never grumbles or repines or regrets the luxurious advantages of the past ... she only dreads returning to the familiar haunts where all is now so fearfully changed.'[3] But more than health, diversion or distraction, in the years before the First World War travel provided Beatrice with a refuge – as it has generations of the dispossessed. With the death of the Queen, the princess who had remained constantly at her side lost not only her mother and closest confidante – the emotional centre of her life – but her home – a physical as well as a spiritual dislocation.

Beatrice was unique among her siblings in having no independent home of her own during her mother's lifetime. Newspapers such as *The Graphic* may have suggested at the time of Beatrice's engagement that the newly married couple would live at Frogmore, but the Queen had other ideas. On 1 August 1885 the *Illustrated London News* dispelled any illusions its readers may have harboured: 'At Windsor Castle a suite of apartments is being prepared for the use of Prince and Princess Henry of Battenberg, when residing at the Palace with the Queen. Apartments will likewise be prepared for the Prince and Princess at Balmoral when the Court is in Scotland.' As we have seen, plans made in 1897 for an apartment at Kensington Palace, in the short term, came to nothing.

At the Queen's death her homes became Bertie's homes, Beatrice welcome only by invitation. Windsor Castle and Buckingham Palace were maintained by the State; Balmoral and Osborne had been the Queen's private property. In addition, Sandringham in Norfolk had been Bertie and Alexandra's home in the country for almost forty years. The Queen had firmly intended that both Balmoral and Osborne henceforth be considered official residences of the British Crown, and to that end her will bequeathed a share in Osborne – the house most closely associated with the childhood of the nine royal offspring – to each of her surviving children. Perhaps it was this very connection with his childhood – marred, as it would remain in his mind, by a succession of unsympathetic tutors and the troubled nature of his relationship with his parents, who compared him unfavourably with his more precocious elder sister Vicky – that set Bertie on his course of resistance to the Queen's wishes. He neither needed nor wanted Osborne, and determined to rid himself of it. Its associations were negative. He did not feel, as Beatrice did, Osborne's near sanctity: it was not for him, as it was for her, the scene of any great happiness. Beatrice had spent so much of her life at Osborne and on the Isle of Wight. There she had married Liko and there Liko was buried. She was governor of the island, as Liko had been before her. The regiment that bore her name drew its numbers from the island's men and several of her patronages and presidencies were Isle of Wight organizations. She recognized Osborne as the tenth child of her parents' love and cherished it accordingly.

Beatrice had lost her home at Windsor, her rooms at Buckingham Palace and at Balmoral. In August 1901 she was summoned, with Helena and Louise, to meet Bertie at Osborne to discuss with him his plans for the house. Their discussion was conducted in German, to prevent the siblings' respective attendants overhearing a debate that grew increasingly heated. Beatrice had so much to lose. But Bertie's mind was made up: he would brook no gainsaying. So swiftly did Beatrice lose this home too.

The Queen had left both Beatrice and Louise houses on the Osborne estate, Osborne Cottage to Beatrice and Kent House to Louise. Although Beatrice had used the cottage – a substantial mock-Tudor villa – since the death of its previous full-time resident, Sir Henry Ponsonby, in 1895, and in 1899 had built Albert Cottages close by for the use of her children, connecting the two buildings by a covered passageway, she had not anticipated it becoming her principal home, detached from life at the Big

House. But Bertie had no plans to live in the Big House: on the contrary, he had already decided to present it to the nation. His decision caused Beatrice consternation. The reaction of the youngest sister with whom he felt no intimacy had two effects on the King. In the first instance, Bertie increased the size of Osborne Cottage's garden as a guarantee of Beatrice's privacy once the main house was no longer a royal residence; in the second, he made a last-ditch effort to keep the house within the family at no inconvenience to himself. He offered it to his heir, Beatrice's nephew George. The offer was made in December, four months after Bertie's 'discussion' with his sisters, with a degree of insistence that James Pope-Hennessy, in his biography of George's wife Queen Mary, claimed distressed the King's son and daughter-in-law, who had no use for Osborne and, like Beatrice, could not have afforded to maintain it. On 12 December Mary wrote to her husband, 'Just returned from tea with Mother-dear [Queen Alexandra], she spoke to me about Osborne ... she says that of course if we cannot take it the old place will have to go to rack and ruin. I told her we were going to talk it over and see what could be done.'[4]

What could be done, of course, was nothing – the result the King must have anticipated – and Bertie moved quickly to settle Osborne's fate. On 22 February 1902 Lord Esher wrote to his son,

> I had an 'audience' of the King yesterday, and settled a lot of small coronation details. Also, a really important thing if he sticks to it, that he will give Osborne to the nation – on the day of his coronation. He wants me to go down there next week and report on the place generally. I shall do this. I shall stay with Princess Henry at her house. Just for one night. He wants me particularly to look at the things which can be brought away. There are *tons* of rubbish! Of course the part of the house in which the Queen died will be kept as a shrine. It is in fact the scheme which I originally proposed to the King.[5]

In the face of Bertie's determination and Esher's characteristic self-satisfaction with the scheme he claimed as his own, Beatrice was powerless. She did, however, succeed in influencing Esher's perception of Osborne and its importance, so that the disposal of the house was accomplished not with the gung-ho abandon of a new broom sweeping clean old cobwebs but with an appropriate degree of regret. Esher's follow-up letter to his son, written after he had stayed with Beatrice at Osborne Cottage, shows the extent to which her thoughts about Osborne had shaped his: ' . . . I have been all over Osborne, and the property. There is a sadness hovering over the whole place. It is like the grave of somebody's happiness. I suppose it is because one realizes that it was everything to the Queen, and is nothing to those who come after her.'[6] But Beatrice's persuasiveness – her unique perception of the extent to which the house *was* everything to the Queen – was not sufficient to make Esher abandon the scheme he had settled on with the King. 'Still, I don't think it *can* be given up,' he concluded, 'and I must tell the King so.'[7]

Preparations began to transform Osborne into a college for Royal Naval cadets, replacing the old Dartmouth-based training ship *Britannia*, and a convalescent home for officers. The central portion of the house was sealed off with iron grilles, with no unauthorized admittance, looked after by a caretaker and the house governor. For the remainder of her life Beatrice retained a protective interest in this preserved core of her parents' home, replying to a request from Lady Mottistone on 2 July 1936, 'In answer to your letter, I shall be very pleased to authorize you to request the Governor of Osborne to let you take the Duke and Duchess of Brunswick over the Private Apartments at Osborne during their visit to you at Mottistone, for naturally it must be of great interest to them.'[8] In the meantime Bertie cleared the house of many of its contents. He dispatched to Beatrice at Osborne Cottage Barber's portraits of her collie Oswald, and Drino in his cradle watched by the dogs Spot and Basco; a painting by Rudolph Swoboda of baby Ena with one of the Queen's Indian servants; a small portrait by Tuxen of Beatrice and Liko with Drino at the time of the Queen's Golden Jubilee; and Sohn's horrible portrait of Beatrice, the last hardly a welcome gift even to one, like Beatrice, without vanity. Objects and paintings made their way to Windsor and Buckingham Palace. Other sitters, like Beatrice, found themselves recipients of their own portraits. To Balfour, his Prime Minister, Bertie wrote on the morning of his coronation, 'The King feels that he is unable to make adequate use of Osborne as a Royal Residence, and accordingly he has determined to offer the property on the Isle of Wight as a gift to the nation.'[9] By August 1903 the college was almost finished and ready to accept its first intake of cadets. Beatrice did not linger to witness their arrival. At the beginning of December a member of her staff wrote to a friend, 'The Princess will be away from the Island about eight months.'[10] Egypt was calling.

Accompanied by two of her children, Ena and the invalid Leopold, along with the children's cousin and Beatrice's goddaughter, nineteen-year-old Beatrice of Coburg, Beatrice arrived in Cairo for Christmas. The depleted family – Drino and Maurice remained at home, Drino having begun training with the Royal Navy the previous year, Maurice still at school – spent Christmas as guests of the Khedive at the Jhezireh Palace. Warmed by the African sun and released by distance and the strangeness of all around her from the anxieties that had oppressed her since her mother's death, Beatrice rode camels, visited the bazaar, ancient temples and the Sphinx. The Khedive loaned the royal party his yacht, the *Ferouz*, in which they travelled up the Nile, stopping to visit recent excavations. They viewed the digs at the Plain of Thebes and there met Howard Carter, who with Lord Caernarvon would later discover Tutankhamen's tomb. At the beginning of February they travelled into Sudan and to Khartoum, where Beatrice met the Inspector General of the Sudan, the Austrian-born Slatin Pasha, who had dedicated his book *Fire and Sword in the Sudan* to Queen Victoria and visited the Queen at Balmoral. Maurice wrote to his ex-tutor, Mr Theobold, 'I had a letter from Mama, saying that they had enjoyed themselves very much at Khartoum; they saw Slatin Pasha there.'[11] Ever her mother's daughter, in Khartoum Beatrice visited the site of the death of General Gordon, that hero in whose exploits the Queen had interested herself so closely and whose journal Beatrice had read to her mother only nights before her wedding; and she laid the foundation stone of the Anglican cathedral, All Saints. The royal party visited Aswan, where Beatrice's brother Arthur had officially opened the famous dam two years earlier. They crossed the desert on camels, pitching camp at an oasis; they visited Wadi Hammamat, famous for its wells and hieroglyphic tablets scored with pharaonic graffiti. Both Beatrice and Ena took photographs by the dozen. It was not a trip Beatrice could have made while the Queen was alive. It was the most adventurous holiday she would take.

Eight months after her departure, having book-ended her voyage with sojourns in France and Germany, she returned to England, to Osborne Cottage on the Isle of Wight, and her new London home, an apartment at Kensington Palace. This was not the apartment that had first been discussed during the Queen's lifetime and abandoned on the grounds of expense, but a smaller though still substantial apartment close to that of her sister Louise in Clock Court. For the next forty years Apartment Two, Kensington Palace would constitute Beatrice's principal home. But for Osborne Cottage the clock was ticking.

In the summer of 1903 Beatrice had carried out a programme of improvements to the cottage and its adjoining Albert Cottages. To Mr Theobold she wrote in June, 'The houses are in a complete state of dismantlement, and there will be many little repairs needed, following on the putting in of the electric light.'[12] The work complete, Beatrice continued to spend part of each year on the island, happy in the short term with her new home. On 12 December 1906, *The Bystander* confidently but erroneously reported that she would shortly be bringing out a book on the Isle of Wight, the mantle of association passed firmly from mother to daughter. The following year, her great-nephew Edward of York, the future Edward VIII, arrived at Osborne College as a cadet; he was shortly joined by his younger brother Bertie, later George VI. Both were entertained to Sunday tea by Beatrice at Osborne Cottage. But in 1912 Beatrice sold the cottage. With her mother no longer at the Big House, Osborne was a changed place, its soul departed. Maintaining a house on the estate that she used only part-time was expensive and inconvenient for Beatrice. As governor of the Isle of Wight, she had a second, official home on the island, a suite of rooms at Carisbrooke Castle. Restoration work at the castle had been under way ever since Liko's death, when a series of rooms had been repaired in his memory. It was to Carisbrooke Castle that Beatrice moved, flying her standard from the flagpole when she was in residence to denote the official nature of her occupancy. Henceforth her connection with the island would be just such an official one and one that she held in her own right. She had taken a step away from her mother's life on the Isle of Wight. It was a partly regretful, partly necessary move.

TWENTY-FIVE

'Please God the young couple
may be very happy'

·•·

On 22 December 1888 Ada Leslie, a member of the nursery
staff of the Emperor of Germany, wrote from Osborne to
her cousin Pollie, 'One of my greatest pleasures at Windsor was,
and here is, visiting the Nurseries, the little Prince Alexander
and the Princess Victoria of Battenberg are the sweetest little
things you can imagine. The little Prince is two and the little
Princess rather more than a year. If I possibly can I will get you
a photograph of them.'[1] It was an opinion Beatrice had shared
wholeheartedly, delighting in her babies. As they put babyhood
behind them, however, she made a faltering connection with her
children, regarding them with a degree of detachment evident, as
we have seen, in her letter to Drino's headmaster in which coolly
she analysed the shared failure of self-reliance of Drino, Ena and
Leopold; and consistently accorded greater import to the needs
of her mother than those of her children. Accompanying Beatrice
to Germany the summer after the Queen's death, Marie Mallet
was astonished when, rather than alter her plans to look after
the haemophiliac Leopold, who had fallen ill, Beatrice left him
behind at the hotel and proceeded as planned to the next stage
of her journey: 'The Princess tries to cultivate the maternal
instinct – she loses so much. Leopold is an angel child, so sweet
and attractive. He pines for someone to cling to – he wants
petting and spoiling.'[2] 'Petting and spoiling' were not in Beatrice's
nature: she had been attentive and, as an adult, undemonstratively
loving towards her mother, but she had never petted her. Nor
would she her own children. She abandoned Leopold to hasten
to her sister, the Empress Frederick, then only weeks from death.
It was a mission the Queen would have applauded. For Beatrice,

family piety and duty remained a one-way street: the Queen's family came first, her own a belated second.

There were positive implications of this detachment on Beatrice's part. It never occurred to her that her own daughter Ena should forsake marriage and remain at home with her. She eschewed the plan the Queen had devised for her and the fate Beatrice's sister-in-law Alexandra decreed for her middle daughter Victoria, although, like the Queen, Beatrice increasingly undertook engagements with Ena at her side: on 7 October 1905, the *Isle of Wight County Press* recorded, 'Princess Henry of Battenberg and her daughter, Princess Ena, presented prizes at the 1st Royal Fusiliers' annual regimental sports day at Parkhurst Barracks.' As a child, Beatrice considered Ena a girl of 'very difficult' character; as an adult, Ena showed a preternatural reserve in all matters of affection. She offered cold comfort as a long-term companion. What she did possess was good looks entirely in line with contemporary taste that ultimately won her a crown. When it happened, her dazzling marriage would be regarded by some as Beatrice's crowning achievement. By others Beatrice was almost eliminated from the equation. Ena married Alfonso XIII of Spain on 31 May 1906. Two days later, in its special royal wedding number, *The Sphere* told its readers, 'It is very noticeable that in the lives of both the royal lovers women of strong character have played an important part. To his mother ... Alfonso owes much, while his Queen has had the benefit of being brought up under the eye of her grandmother Queen Victoria, and her godmother the Empress Eugénie ...'[3] In thrall to her mother, Beatrice had forfeited authority or influence over her pretty daughter.

If relations between Beatrice and Bertie were strained by Bertie's decision over Osborne, they did not break down completely. Brother and sister were not close. The Queen's confidence in Beatrice and, for a time, Liko, in marked contrast to her behaviour towards her heir, erected for Bertie an insuperable barrier of long standing, and Beatrice would never be admitted to the King's inner circle (unlike her sister Louise). But throughout Bertie's reign, despite the fiasco of the coronation when, at one of the most solemn moments in the service, Beatrice noisily dropped her service book from the princesses' balcony on to a table of gold plate below, Beatrice remained a presence at court (although from the moment of the Queen's death, her position descended further in the royal order of precedence). When Lord Esher visited the King at Windsor to discuss illustrations for his edition of the first series of Queen Victoria's letters, he found in the library not only Bertie but 'the Queen, the King and Queen of Norway [the latter the King's youngest daughter Maud], Princess Henry and Princess Louise.'[4] Beatrice joined the King and Queen for yachting trips in the Royal Yacht *Victoria and Albert*, and on the yacht belonging to the Portuguese ambassador and court favourite the Marquês de Soveral. When the King died in May 1910, he was alone with his wife and doctors; in an adjoining room waited his daughters Louise and Victoria, his son and daughter-in-law the Prince and Princess of Wales, his sister and brother-in-law Helena and Christian – and Beatrice.[5] Bertie's avuncular kindness, which played such an important role in Ena's marriage, was in part a product of the relationship that, though built on uncertain foundations, he enjoyed with Beatrice.

Ena came out in London, in November 1904, at a court at Buckingham Palace, at Bertie's invitation, 'a charming gesture,' she afterwards remembered, '[which] touched my mother greatly'.[6] In February of the same year, as a gesture of rapprochement, Bertie invested Beatrice with the King Edward VII Royal Family Order (Second Class). Mother and daughter were henceforth jointly included in the official life of Bertie's court. The highlight of the following season was the state visit to Britain of the King of Spain in June 1905.

Alfonso XIII, the posthumous son of a short-lived father, was nineteen: he had been king since birth of one of Europe's most unstable thrones. He was eager to marry a member of the British Royal Family, his choice having fallen on Beatrice's niece, Arthur's daughter Patricia of Connaught. His visit to London lasted a week, characterized by glittering parties and appalling weather. Over the course of that rain-drenched week, Alfonso lost Patricia of Connaught and won the affections of her cousin Ena of

Battenberg. Nine months later, on 7 March 1906, their engagement was announced.

The course of true love had run relatively smoothly, Alfonso
declaring himself in an eight-month barrage of postcards, Ena
receiving his ardour with placid good humour. Beatrice, for one,
did not doubt their love. 'Please God the young couple may be
very happy,' she wrote to Louisa Antrim on 16 February 1906,
'as they are absolutely devoted to one another, and I have every
confidence in the King making her the best of husbands. He has
such a charming nature, that to know him is to love him.'[7]
Thanking Lady Bathurst for her wedding present for Ena, Beatrice
wrote in May, 'Many thanks for all your good wishes for her
future happiness, which I hope is assured, as she and the young
King are so devoted to one another.'[8] The exchange of mutual
affection, however, was the only simple element in a tortuous and
controversial wedding contract involving religious conversion.

It was inconceivable that a king styled 'His Most Catholic
Majesty' should marry a non-Catholic. For Ena, conversion to
Catholicism was a *sine qua non* of her marriage. Beatrice began
making enquiries into the delicate matter as soon as Ena told her
of Alfonso's transferral of affections from Patricia of Connaught.
On 30 July 1905 she received a reply from the Archbishop of
Canterbury Randall Davidson that did not mince words:

> To marry a Roman Catholic would in any case be an extraordinary
> breach with all the teaching of our Church ... But the mere phrase
> 'Roman Catholicism' conveys ... comparatively little of what is
> meant by the sort of Roman Catholicism which characterizes the
> Spanish Court. It is the most blind and bigoted form of unintelligent
> ultramontanism ... The circle is honeycombed with corruption
> and bigotry of a sort hardly to be found elsewhere in Europe ...
> It is of course possible for a pure and high-minded lady ... to
> preserve a high tone of faith and life even in such a hotbed of ...
> corruption. But for a young Princess, or Queen to do so, after an
> upbringing so entirely different in every respect, would seem ...
> to be almost an impossibility.[9]

If this unflinching assessment were not enough, the prospect of

Ena's conversion – distant from the throne though she was in the line of succession – provoked an outcry at home and in Spain, disaffected parties in both countries vocal in their determined anti-ecumenicalism. The Bishop of London appealed directly to Beatrice, begging that as a devout churchwoman she reconsider her daughter's alliance. Even the usually effusive *Sphere* recorded after the marriage, 'When the project of an English alliance ... was first mooted it was received in this country with doubt and then with dislike, and some leaders of the Church of England even dared to enter a public protest.'[10] Conversion could not be avoided, however – the Spanish would not formally announce or indeed countenance the engagement without it – and the challenge for Beatrice and Ena was to accomplish it as unobtrusively as possible.

To Bertie, Beatrice telegraphed in cipher in February, 'What do you think of asking the Empress Eugénie to have us quietly at Cap Martin for the change'[11], but the King rejected the idea, possibly mindful that, with emotions running high, this was not the moment to remind people that Ena's godmother was herself Catholic. Instead Ena received instruction on neutral territory, at Versailles, from the Catholic Bishop of Nottingham, Monsignor Robert Brindle. She was received into the Church on 7 March at a service in the private chapel of her soon-to-be mother-in-law Queen Maria Christina. The service itself, though described as private, was attended by the Spanish royal family, twenty-three leading courtiers, and the Prime Minister and his family, with only Ena's own family not represented. Beatrice rejoined the couple once the service was over. Later she telegraphed again to Bertie for his guidance on how to proceed with the announcement of the engagement, which could now, at last, formally be made. Her message reveals not only the delicacy of the situation but Beatrice's sense of indebtedness to her brother for supporting her in an increasingly unpopular match at home. 'Alphonso [*sic*] wishes to know if he should make official announcement tomorrow whilst we are still here or await your coming on Saturday. Wish to do what seems to you best.'[12] Spanish and British authorities complied with Bertie's reply – 'It would be better if King made announcement at once' – and Ena and Alfonso's engagement was made public the day of her reception into the Catholic Church. The nature of the response to the news in Britain can be judged from a letter written by the Prince of Wales to his wife Mary: 'Beatrice is advised on her return to England to keep Ena quiet somewhere, at Osborne, and not to bring her to London as the feeling is so strong.'[13]

For Beatrice, however, the deed was accomplished, as she had not doubted it would be. Her concern was less for public reaction to Ena's change of religion – two decades earlier, she had not allowed negative public reaction to spoil her own engagement – than with the prospect of losing her only daughter to married life abroad. In her letter to Louisa Antrim written during Ena's period of religious instruction, she had confessed, 'Though the thought of my child going so far from me, is a real trial, I feel I have really gained a son, who does everything to make things easy.'[14] In the carefree days of Ena and Alfonso's engagement, that 'everything' included fitting up an Anglican chapel for Beatrice in the palace in Madrid.

On the Spanish side, two further objections remained, both questions of blood, both insuperable: Ena's partly morganatic status, inherited from Liko; and the possibility that she was a carrier of haemophilia, inherited from her mother and grand-mother. 'So Ena is to become Spanish Queen! a Battenberg, good gracious!' Queen Victoria's reactionary cousin Augusta, Grand Duchess of Mecklenburg-Strelitz, wrote to her niece, the Princess of Wales.[15] Her dismissal echoed the opinion of prominent Spanish courtiers – a feeling Bertie tried to quash by raising Ena from the style of 'Highness' to 'Royal Highness'. Concerning the potentially more serious issue of haemophilia, Bertie, his foreign secretary Lord Lansdowne, Beatrice and Ena herself all spoke to Alfonso. He made light of their warnings. Although he dismissed their fears, they would be realized in full, the afflictions of Ena and Alfonso's children later becoming a significant factor in the long-term failure of their marriage.

Ena's wedding to Alfonso is remembered chiefly for the bomb thrown at the royal couple's carriage. The culprit was an anarchist, Mateo Morral. He had stationed himself on the fourth-floor balcony of a house on the Calle Mayor, a street close to the end of the long processional route, and spent the morning of the wedding throwing oranges into the street, practising his timing. This highly questionable behaviour having failed to arouse police suspicion, Morral was free to throw his bomb – disguised as a bouquet of flowers – at the royal coach. Narrowly, it missed. It killed horses, decapitated an outrider, blew away the legs of one of the coachmen. The King and Queen, though shaken, were unhurt. Ena's dress was dark with blood. Back in the palace, numb but dignified, she repeated over and over, 'I saw a man without any legs.' The newlyweds' was the last carriage in the procession. When they returned to the palace, few ahead of them suspected what had happened, the sound of the bomb having been mistaken for the firing of a salute. Only when Beatrice arrived, minutes earlier in the penultimate carriage with Alfonso's mother, was the truth known. Her sister-in-law Marie of Erbach-Schönberg rushed to congratulate her on Ena's great day. Beatrice 'looked agitated', the latter remembered afterwards, 'and said in a level tone: "Someone threw a bomb, but they are both alive."'[16]

This 'diabolical act'[17] distracted Beatrice's attention from the lesser slights of what should have been a mother's day of triumph. So often had the princess, who was first in her mother's affections but the last of nine in the strict royal order of precedence, been banished to a subsidiary position in the great royal pageants of the previous reign. In both the Golden and the Diamond Jubilees it was Beatrice who watched over and upheld the Queen, but Beatrice who rode in a distant carriage, sat at a remove in church or banqueting hall. So, too, at Ena's wedding. Beatrice followed Ena into the narrow Gothic Church of San Jeronimo, but while Ena advanced towards the altar, Beatrice sat, as Marie of Erbach-Schönberg remembered, 'half-way down the aisle',[18] separated from her daughter by the rows of princes attending the wedding as representatives of Europe's crowned heads (no sovereigns had been invited to the wedding in order that no one distract attention from Alfonso and Ena). Behind them sat their wives and princesses. Behind them Beatrice. She did not complain.

Writing to the Bishop of Ripon afterwards, her thoughts were all of Ena and Alfonso:

> It does seem so sad, that a day which had begun so bright for the young couple, and where they were just returning with such thankful happiness, at belonging at last entirely to one another, should have been overclouded by such a fearful disaster. God has indeed [been] merciful to have preserved them so miraculously, and this has only if possible deepened their love for one another, and rendered the devotion of their people still more marked.[19]

Within less than a year Beatrice would rejoin her daughter and son-in-law in Madrid for an extended visit. Ena was expecting a baby. Still unable to speak Spanish fluently – no one at the Spanish court had considered it necessary to provide her with a tutor – she felt isolated and afraid in Alfonso's vast palace. Beatrice travelled to Spain for the last tremester of Ena's pregnancy, which ended on 10 May 1907 in an event that provoked nationwide rejoicing among Spaniards: the birth of a male heir to the throne. Nine pounds in weight and blond like his mother, baby Alfonso (called 'Alfonsito') appeared strong and robust. 'No words can say the intense joy that this happy event causes the dear young Parents, and all classes in the country here,' wrote Beatrice, a grandmother for the first time within weeks of her fiftieth birthday. 'My dear daughter passed through her hours of great suffering most bravely and is a very tender mother, hardly liking to have the child out of her arms. He is a splendid strong boy and thank God both he and my daughter are doing as well as possible. I shall find it hard to tear myself away from them ... I have had such a delightfully undisturbed three months, with my dear child ...'[20] On 14 September the *Illustrated London News* published a formal photograph of Ena, Alfonso and Alfonsito. 'The Prince', it claimed, 'is making great progress and is reported to be a particularly fine child.'

But Ena and Alfonso knew differently. Alfonsito was haemophiliac. In his deep disappointment, Alfonso denied the strength and frequency of the warnings he had received of such a possible outcome. Later the Spanish would claim he had been deceived by Ena and her mother, so eager were they for the marriage to take place. Perhaps Alfonso himself came to believe it. From the time of the terrible discovery, except when absolutely necessary, he never spoke to Beatrice again and avoided spending time with her. In July 1908 Drino wrote to his cousin's wife Onor, Grand Duchess of Hesse, about an impending visit of Ena to Beatrice and her sons at Osborne Cottage without Alfonso and without her babies: 'Ena arrives here on the 15th and Alfonso comes for a week on the 25th to take her home. I think it rather a sore subject that the children can't come as well.'[21]

For her part, Beatrice remained loyal to her son-in-law. She was holidaying in Vernet in the South of France in March 1913 when an Isle of Wight neighbour, Colonel Seely, then Secretary of State for War, wrote to tell her about his visit to the King and Queen in Madrid. 'I was sure you would be interested by your interview with the King,' she replied. '[He] certainly is extraordinarily clever and knows so much. He works so hard for his country, and it is wonderful what improvements and impetus he gives to everything.'[22]

Whatever the truth of Beatrice's feelings concerning Alfonso and his changed behaviour towards her following the revelation of Alfonsito's condition, she would soon have weightier matters to concern her. The year after her letter to Colonel Seely war broke out. Although Spain remained neutral, hostilities enforced a separation between Beatrice and Ena – and her brood of Spanish grandchildren had by then grown to six in number.

TWENTY-SIX

'Days of overwhelming anxiety'

••−••

On 22 June 1911 several thousand commemorative medals were distributed to the children of the Isle of Wight in the name of the Royal Governor. Accompanying the medals was a letter from Beatrice explaining their significance: 'Children, I am today sending to each of you a Medal to commemorate the solemn occasion of the Coronation of my dear Nephew King George V. That the effigy which these medals bear may be a constant reminder to you of your loyalty and devotion to your Sovereign and Country is my fervent hope.'[1] Nine years earlier, at the time of Bertie's coronation, she had presented similar medals.

Beatrice bore a German title. Her husband, her father and three of her four grandparents were German. She spoke German fluently and, like her mother – but unlike Bertie – took a pro-German view of Continental politics. Both her published works – *The Adventures of Count Georg Albert of Erbach* (1890) and *In Napoleonic Days* (1941) – were translations from the German. In the aftermath of the Queen's death Marie Mallet went so far as to suggest, 'I am ... sure Princess Beatrice would far rather live in Germany, but for the sake of her children that would not be wise.'[2] But she defined herself as fiercely English. In a letter to a friend, written in September 1924, she distanced herself from the land of her fathers: 'The German frame of mind is a very difficult force to fathom.'[3] When, on 4 August 1914, Britain found itself at war with Germany, Beatrice was not wanting in patriotism.

Like the war itself, her war work operated on a number of fronts. In relation to the Isle of Wight she saw her role as one of commendation and encouragement. She wrote to Tennyson's son shortly after the outbreak of hostilities, about island volunteers:

> It is one of the most critical moments of our Empire's history, when its very existence is at stake. All should gladly prove their love for their country, their homes, and their determination to defend them to the last, as well as to help our friends and allies in their dire hour of need ... In these days of overwhelming anxiety, surely none can hear the call to arms in vain, and I feel convinced that the men of the Isle of Wight will not be behindhand in volunteering to take their part in this great struggle.[4]

Though her letter reveals much of the spirit of the times, it was not mere empty sabre-rattling. Beatrice had three sons: all would serve in France, even the haemophiliac Leopold, whose condition, had he wished it, would have disqualified him from active service. To Colonel Seely, Regimental Commandant of the Isle of Wight Volunteer Regiment, Leopold wrote from barracks in Aldershot on 16 March 1914, 'I wanted to thank you so very much for your kindness in getting me my regular commission. I am more than grateful, as I have always wanted to be able to soldier seriously and never thought I should be able to do so.'[5] In fact Leopold's serious soldiering was of an extremely circumscribed nature: he entered the war as a lieutenant in the King's Royal Rifle Corps, his activities restricted to a staff appointment. Nevertheless he embraced voluntarily a patriotic duty from which he might easily have been excused. His service consolidated that of Drino, in the Grenadier Guards, and Maurice, who in 1910 fulfilled his own childhood promise of following his cousin Christian Victor of Schleswig-Holstein into the 60th King's Royal Fusiliers. When, early in the war, Beatrice received a letter from a member of the public asking in peremptory tones what part she was playing in the effort to win the war, she replied that she had already lost her husband on active service, and that all three of her sons had left for the front on 12 August.[6]

The willingness of Drino, Leopold and Maurice to expose themselves to the dangers of the arena of war was not, of course, purely altruistic. For the third generation of Princes of Battenberg the armed forces provided a career and a purpose. Beatrice's position as the youngest of the nine royal children effectively prevented her sons from inheriting any royal role as we understand it today; Liko's lack of fortune meant that they inherited little else besides. As early as 1901, when Maurice was only ten, Marie Mallet claimed that Beatrice was 'anxious now about the future of the three boys, who must work their own way; they are handicapped rather than helped by rank'.[7] Significantly, all had embarked on military careers before war was declared. After six years in the navy, from 1902 to 1908, Drino joined the army. To Alice's son Ernie, Grand Duke of Hesse, Beatrice wrote on 30 September 1909, 'Drino is ... hard at work now in his military duties. I had a very satisfactory report of him from his Colonel.'[8] In the same letter she asked her nephew to entertain Maurice for a Sunday at Darmstadt, as he was shortly 'going to Germany for a couple of months, to work up his German before going to the Military Academy at Sandhurst'.[9]

Beatrice was at Carisbrooke Castle in the summer of 1914. She had been expecting a visit from her niece, Helena's daughter Marie Louise of Schleswig-Holstein but, under pressure from her brother-in-law Louis of Battenberg, altered her plans. She telephoned Marie Louise early on the morning of 4 August, the day war was declared, to announce her immediate return to London. On a bank holiday, with no supplies save a solitary chicken in the larder, Marie Louise found herself not, as she had anticipated, embarking on a pleasant holiday in the Isle of Wight, but entertaining to lunch her mother, her aunt Beatrice and their respective ladies-in-waiting. Drino and Maurice, Beatrice told her, were already under orders. She did not relish the prospect of their departure but told her niece, 'You must come and stay with me as I cannot face being alone.'[10]

The destination for that 'stay' was Kensington Palace, to which Beatrice had moved at speed for the duration of the war. Marie Louise had been divorced by her husband, Aribert of Anhalt. She and Beatrice were both alone and the arrangement suited each equally. Marie Louise moved into Apartment Two, Kensington Palace and remained there for the next three years.

Although aunt and niece pursued separate public lives, Marie Louise's presence helped stave off Beatrice's loneliness during the long period when the war prevented her from visiting Ena in Spain. Marie Louise was an ideal companion. Like Beatrice she had been among the small number of the Queen's intimates at the end of her life, all quiet, devoted acolytes who treated the Queen with reverence and awe. The two princesses shared a similar outlook and similar interests, although not, sadly, music: Marie Louise's piano playing was so bad that to listen to it gave Beatrice hiccups. The war work undertaken by both focused on the wounded, Marie Louise having inherited her mother Helena's interest in nursing, Beatrice being assiduous in her hospital visiting – as she wrote to Sir Frederick Milner at the beginning of 1915, 'It is intensely interesting is it not, visiting all the poor wounded. They are so brave and uncomplaining, one feels, one cannot do enough for them.'[11]

In Hill Street, in Mayfair, Jeanne, Lady Coats, widow of the J. & P. Coats cotton sewing thread magnate, owned a small private hospital. At the outbreak of war, the hospital became the centre of Beatrice's activities and was named, in her honour, the Princess Henry of Battenberg Hospital for Officers. Beatrice took more than a nominal interest in it, and it was due to her enthusiasm that, only weeks into the war, the hospital received a visit from the King and Queen. They talked to patients, admired the operating theatre with its X-ray equipment, met Dr Rice-Oxley and his staff. Their visit was dutifully recorded in the *Illustrated War News* of 23 September, which announced that Beatrice's 'interest in the hospital is such that she visits it daily'. Closer to home, Louise would go on to convert several rooms in her apartment at Kensington Palace to a temporary hospital.

That interest did not, however, make Beatrice forgetful of the claims made on her by her position as governor of the Isle of Wight. From a distance she continued to involve herself administratively with those aspects of island life that fell within her jurisdiction. On 18 March 1916, she appointed Lieutenant Colonel Augustus Macdonald Moreton Sub-Commandant of the Isle of Wight County Volunteers; on 4 June 1918 she wrote to her deputy governor General Seely about a recent memorandum issued by the Central Land Association concerning agricultural landowners evolving a scheme to express their gratitude to the men of their estates who had gone to fight. At the same time she continued intermittently to be called upon in her role of executor of the Queen's will. When, in May 1917, publisher John Murray wrote to the King's private secretary Lord Stamfordham requesting permission to pulp ten thousand unsold copies of the Queen's *Leaves from the Journal of Our Life in the Highlands* (Murray having bought out Smith, Elder & Co.), Stamfordham referred the request to Beatrice. Her unsentimental response – whatever she may privately have felt about the Queen's evidently declining stock among the reading public – allowed Stamfordham to give Murray a prompt reply to his request: 'I have heard from Princess Henry of Battenberg who entirely appreciates the position with regard to the 10,000 copies ... and gives you authority to deal with them as you think best.'[12] Like her mother, Beatrice had become an assiduous desk worker. She immersed herself in paperwork, a diligent correspondent; steeped herself in the escapism of her public role. By the time of Murray's letter she had suffered her own war tragedy that put into perspective the degree of her sadness at the destruction of the Queen's book written long ago. Her heart was not in the Queen's beloved Scotland of fifty years earlier, nor in the peaceful fields of the Isle of Wight, but in bloodier, muddier pastures – Flanders fields near Ypres.

Beatrice's youngest and almost certainly favourite son Maurice died on 27 October 1914. He was twenty-three. He died at Zonnebeke near Ypres, leading an attack on the front line, killed instantly by an exploding shell. The news devastated Beatrice. She felt keenly the irony of the death so young of this the liveliest, most handsome and dashing of her sons. Inevitably her thoughts returned to Liko's death. 'You can imagine,' she wrote to a friend, 'how this fresh great sorrow has reopened the old wound. But I try to think of Father and Son reunited, having both left such a bright example behind them.'[13] Newspaper reports echoed her comparison of father and son, the *Sketch* reporting on 4

November, 'Prince Henry of Battenberg, father of the deceased Prince, a Colonel in the British Army, gave his life, as Prince Maurice has done, for England.'[14] Months later Ena wrote to Queen Mary of Beatrice's continuing sorrow and her pain at their separation: 'It is very hard to be away from my old home at such a time as this and especially so since Maurice's death, when I know that Mama is so sad and needs me so much. I would give anything to be able to go to her.'[15]

Beatrice received morsels of consolation from the many letters written to her in the weeks after Maurice's death. Her replies reiterate the same story, a sentiment shared by those bereft in war since time immemorial: she struggles to assuage her grief with the knowledge that her son died valiantly in a noble cause. To Lady Elphinstone Beatrice wrote on 13 November,

> Sympathy such as yours is very helpful in this awful trial, and to know how much my darling Boy was appreciated. It is one of those losses one can never get over, and it is so terribly hard to sit quietly and resignedly realizing that one's dear child, who was like a ray of sunshine in the house, will never be amongst us again in this world. In the midst of all I have much to be thankful for, in that he died a noble soldier's death and without, as I am assured, suffering, and I have two dear sons still spared to me, when so many poor mothers have lost their one and only one.[16]

To Lord Knutsford, at whose invitation she had visited war wounded in the London Hospital, Beatrice wrote, 'Nothing could touch and help me more to bear this great trial, than to know that others feel for me. To lose a beloved promising young son is a terrible trial, but I can look back with pride on him, and on his work nobly fulfilled, and life willingly given for his King and Country.'[17] 'My aunt', wrote Marie Louise forty years later, 'was wonderfully brave when the terrible news came that Maurice ... had died of wounds. Her courage never failed, and she looked on herself as one of the thousands of mothers who had given their sons for the safety of England.'[18]

Despite her sadness Beatrice went through the motions of royal life, duty before inclination, others before self. On 18

November she telegraphed her condolences to Lord Cadogan – 'I feel so deeply for you in the loss of your dear son'[19] – a simple, even commonplace message, its poignancy derived from the shared experience of sender and recipient. She also steeled herself to reject Lord Kitchener's exceptional offer to have Maurice's body brought back to England for burial at home. Instead the Prince was buried with his comrades in the town cemetery at Ypres. Although Beatrice did not doubt that she had made the right, indeed the only possible, decision, it was not one she found easy and it affected significantly her sorrow at her son's loss. To exacerbate her disquiet, Ypres would shortly be subjected to extensive shelling. Colonel Seely wrote to reassure her. 'I can assure you [you] have greatly ... relieved my mind,' she replied, 'for I was indeed anxious lest all the shell fire there has been might have disturbed and damaged my dear son's last resting place. I am most thankful to hear from you that this is not the case nor likely to happen in the future, for this apprehension was such an aggravation to my distress.'[20] It was not, however, an easy Christmas. Beatrice wrote to Sir Frederick Milner in the New Year, 'All these festive days have been peculiarly trying ... one cannot help one's thoughts going back to that lonely little soldier's grave in a foreign country, and to that bright young life, cut off so early.'[21]

On 28 September 1920 the Ypres League was founded. It provided an association for those who had survived the battle-fields around the Belgian town, and a focus for remembrance of the 250,000 men, Maurice of Battenberg among them, who had not survived. Its patron-in-chief was George V, its patrons the Prince of Wales and Beatrice. In her capacity as patron of the Ypres League she would lay a wreath at the Remembrance Day celebrations long into the thirties, though by then she walked with difficulty and the effort cost her sorely.

To commemorate Maurice more visibly Beatrice commissioned from Philip de Laszlo a posthumous portrait undertaken from photographs in 1916. Although de Laszlo disliked working in this way, he made an exception in Beatrice's case. Six years earlier she had supplied him with a letter of introduction to the

Queen Mother of Spain, which resulted in a number of lucrative and highly publicized commissions from the Spanish Royal Family, including a portrait of Ena. Beatrice herself had also sat for de Laszlo and, in June 1913, allowed her portrait to hang among an exhibition of his work held at Agnew's.[22] In St Mildred's, Whippingham, she hung a painting by Lavery, *The Supreme Sacrifice*, in Maurice's memory, and for the Church of St Nicholas-in-Castro she commissioned an altar painting to mark his death. The church stood within the precincts of Carisbrooke Castle. In 1897 its chancel had been restored in Liko's memory. During her summers on the Isle of Wight, Beatrice attended Sunday evensong there and would later be accused of treating the church as a royal peculiar.

Beatrice would soon have reason to feel relief that she had taken pains to commemorate both Maurice and Liko in so concrete a form. In the summer of 1917 George V asked those of his relations with German titles to relinquish them and, where necessary, assume 'translated' English versions of their names. The request was in effect a command, as Louis of Battenberg wrote to his daughter Louise on 6 June: 'It has been suggested that we should turn our name into English, viz: Battenhill or Mountbatten. We incline to the latter as a better sound ... of course we are at his mercy. We are only allowed to use our German title as the Sovereign has always recognized it, but he can refuse this recognition any moment.'[23] At a stroke the name Battenberg disappeared in Britain. Beatrice reverted to her premarital style of HRH The Princess Beatrice, dropping the additional 'Princess Henry of Battenberg'. On 11 September Leopold became by royal warrant Lord Leopold Mountbatten and, on 7 November, Drino was created by letters patent Marquess of Carisbrooke, Earl of Berkhamsted and Viscount Launceston. Responses to this process of forcible 'adjustment' were mixed. Victoria of Battenberg, Alice's daughter Victoria of Hesse, now Marchioness of Milford Haven, wrote to her lady-in-waiting that she regretted her relocation to the peerage: 'I am unduly influenced by the recollection of brewers, lawyers, bankers Peers';[24] while Drino, whose hauteur and self-importance made him a figure of fun for many in his family, was predictably resentful of the demotion. 'I shriek with laughter when I think of Drino,' wrote his cousin Louise of Battenberg on 13 June.[25] The following month, deprived of his princely rank, Drino married Lady Irene Denison, daughter of the second Earl of Londesborough, at the Chapel Royal, St James's. In due course, on 13 January 1920, their marriage would provide Beatrice with her only British grandchild, Lady Iris Mountbatten – added to a daughter-in-law, whose relations with Beatrice were considerably easier than those Beatrice enjoyed with the increasingly disaffected Alfonso of Spain. Iris's childish antics offered Beatrice an antidote to the sadness of the decade that lay ahead. Like her own mother, she embraced her status as grandmother. 'I spent a very peaceful, quiet Christmas,' she wrote on 29 December 1926, 'and had the pleasure of seeing my dear little granddaughter's joy over her tree and toys.'[26] It was for Beatrice a timely reminder. So much had happened that was far from joyful.

TWENTY-SEVEN

'The older one gets the more one
lives in the past'

•◆•

*I*t was so much easier to look not forwards but back. In
her Christmas card to Louisa Antrim, in December 1943,
Beatrice wrote, 'The older one gets the more one lives in the
past.'[1] In truth she had done so for decades. Portraits, photographs, letters, journals, and memories happy and sad continually
drew her back. 'To me alas! the war is always a very present
memory and anything connected with it is of supreme interest,'
she wrote from Carisbrooke Castle in September 1924.[2] Maurice
had been dead for almost a decade. Two years earlier, suddenly
and unexpectedly, while Beatrice was on holiday in Sicily,
Leopold, too, had died.

Leopold did not die as a result of the war. His haemophilia
restricted his 'active' service to an aide-de-camp's role and, at the
cessation of hostilities, he returned to London to live with Beatrice
at Kensington Palace. Though the timing of his death shocked
Beatrice, the fact of its happening did not. Leopold's health had
always been precarious, and there had been a number of scares
in the past. In December 1909 he was reported to be seriously
ill in a nursing home in Manchester Square in London. Ena made
a special journey from Spain to visit him. The *Tatler*, clearly
anticipating the worst, printed a full-page photograph of all four
of Beatrice's children taken the previous year at Osborne Cottage,
with the caption: 'A reminiscence of a visit under happier circumstances'; ominously the photograph was surrounded by a
broken black border.[3] Leopold rallied on that occasion – only to
die alone on Sunday morning, 23 April 1922. The previous day
he had undergone an emergency operation at Kensington Palace.
His apparently normal recovery was followed swiftly by an

unexpected relapse. Too late Beatrice cut short her holiday.

Death would provide for her the keynote of the twenties. As the decade began, she continued to work at her mother's Journal. Slowly, certainly, she witnessed the final demise of its lengthy cast list. It had begun during the war, with the death of Louise's husband Lord Lorne in 1914. Arthur's wife Louischen died in March 1917, then, in October, Helena's husband Christian. In July 1920 the Empress Eugénie died in Madrid. Louis of Battenberg, restyled after 1917 Marquess of Milford Haven, Beatrice's brother-in-law, died in September 1921; months later followed Leopold's widow Helen. With the death of Helena in May 1923 only three of the Queen's children remained: Beatrice, Arthur and Louise. Marie Erbach also died in 1923, joined in 1924 by Franzjos, the last of the Battenberg brothers. In November 1925 Beatrice's sister-in-law Alexandra died, Beatrice briefly forewarned in a telegram explaining that, though conscious, Alexandra was not expected to survive the night.[4] At the same time, Beatrice's own health began its slow descent: the rheumatism that had plagued her for forty years escalated in severity and she suffered increasingly from bronchial complaints. 'Poor Aunt Beatrice has had a bad time while we have been away,' the Prince of Wales wrote to his great-aunt Louise in October 1925, thanking her for her present of throat lozenges; letters do not record if Louise sent Beatrice a similar parcel.[5]

So much of Beatrice's life and work was connected with death. In addition to the Ypres League, she involved herself closely with the League of Remembrance – one of its tasks was providing hospitals with medical supplies in peacetime – writing to Lady Bathurst on 16 May 1920, 'How too kind of you, besides becoming a Patron of the League of Remembrance, saying you wish to give it a donation of £50. I am indeed grateful to you.'[6] The same year, Beatrice saw a picture in the *Illustrated London News* of a shrine in a Russian Orthodox chapel in Peking. Within the shrine were two coffins containing the remains of the Grand Duchess Elizabeth of Russia (Beatrice's niece and Liko's cousin, formerly Ella of Hesse) and her companion Sister Barbara.[7] Beatrice passed on the cutting to her sister-in-law Victoria Milford

Haven, Ella's sister; Louis and Victoria Milford Haven had the coffins removed to the Mount of Olives in Jerusalem, and Louis sent Beatrice a detailed description of the service of re-interment.

Bertie's death in 1910 and the accession of George V transformed Beatrice from sister of the King to aunt of the King, thereby further downgrading her status within the Royal Family as well as adding to the toll of her sadness. Her relationship with her nephew was, however, cordial and positive. In January 1919 the King created Beatrice a Dame Grand Cross of the Most Excellent Order of the British Empire, in recognition of her wartime services as president of the Isle of Wight branch of the British Red Cross. In December 1931, when Beatrice issued an appeal in aid of the Isle of Wight County Hospital, Frederick Ponsonby responded on the King's behalf, enclosing a cheque for £100: 'While of course it would be impossible for His Majesty to subscribe to all the hospitals in the United Kingdom, the King has decided to make a special exception in this case, in view of the fact that Princess Beatrice is issuing the appeal.'[8] Privately, in an off-the-record note, he confided, 'There was . . . the sentimental reason of Osborne which made a difference.'[9] The King's fondness for his aunt did not prevent him from overruling her objections, in 1928, to Frederick Ponsonby's publication of a selection of letters of the Empress Frederick. John van der Kiste attributes Beatrice's reservations to her unwillingness to bring before the public the controversy surrounding her marriage to the morganatic Liko, in which the Prussian imperial family had entered so forcefully.[10] It may be, more simply, that, busy 'editing' her mother's Journal, Beatrice's guiding principles in such matters had become blanket concealment and withdrawal from the public arena of anything potentially inflammatory. Ponsonby himself, never Beatrice's greatest admirer, later recorded, 'Princess Beatrice, who had not read the book but only the extracts in the newspapers, said it was a dreadful book.'[11]

Prey to worsening health, marginalized within a large and much younger family, Beatrice embarked on her protracted 'twilight' period, increasingly forgotten by the public, busy with small-scale duties and private concerns, chief among them her ongoing work on her mother's Journal. Publicly her stock was boosted by her position as mother of the Queen of Spain. Despite Spanish political instability and Ena and Alfonso's unhappiness – Alfonso was openly unfaithful to Ena and, at some point during the twenties, probably considered requesting from the Pope an annulment of their marriage – Ena's life had settled into a pattern. From October until the end of May she lived in Madrid, before travelling to England in June or July, returning to the royal seaside palace at San Sebastián in time for Alfonso's mother's birthday on 20 July. Beatrice looked forward to Ena's yearly summer visits, invariably without Alfonso but with one or more of her six children. In 1924 Ena's holiday coincided with the British Empire Exhibition at Wembley. She and Beatrice visited twice. Unsurprisingly, since both were fond of precious stones – in Ena's case the predilection amounted to a passion – their visits were characterized by a curiosity about the displays of jewels and they lingered in the areas devoted to Ceylon, Burma (with its famous rubies) and India. In the Indian quarter they also admired a display of Madras lace, Beatrice still loyal to one of her earliest loves. When finally they tore themselves away to inspect the Canadian pavilion, they received an escort of Canadian Mounties.

Beatrice withdrew gradually from public life. In June 1926, she was created Dame Grand Cross of the Order of St John of Jerusalem, an appropriate decoration for the author of *The Adventures of Count Georg Albert of Erbach*, which partly traces the history of the order. The following year she sat for the last time for Philip de Laszlo. His 'winter' portrait is a handsome image showing her in profile, her face thinner with age; not crushed by the years but wise and kindly, staring into the distance, as always in Beatrice's case avoiding eye contact with the viewer.

Not until the following decade would her rheumatism significantly affect her mobility. In the meantime she was troubled by cataracts, and rheumatism in her hands and fingers effectively curtailed her piano-playing. One of the last formal photographs for which she sat, taken in 1930, shows her at her desk in her apartment in Kensington Palace, writing in a large notebook like those into which she transcribed her mother's Journal, a task she would not complete for another year. Beside the notebook, close to hand, is a magnifying glass. The compass of her interests contracted. With work on the Journal complete, she devoted herself to her responsibilities on the Isle of Wight. On 2 November 1934, she wrote to Lady Mottistone,

> I am much interested at what you tell me about a Branch of the Personal Service League being started in the Isle of Wight, and I shall be very pleased to become its Patroness. You can say in the letter you intend publishing in the County Press that I am very glad to hear of and much approve the effort to organize a Branch of the League in the Island, as it is a movement that is doing so much good all over the country, and I wish it every success. I am already Patroness, as President, of the Hampshire Branch.[12]

Two years later, her lady-in-waiting Bessie Bulteel wrote again to Lady Mottistone to tell her how interested Beatrice had been to hear of the fledgling branch's success, 'which she thinks is wonderful!'[13] In August 1935, at Northwood Park, Cowes, she presented medals for long service and efficiency to the men of the Isle of Wight Rifles. Two years later, following the death of George V, she became at last Honorary Colonel of the regiment – fifty-two years after it was renamed in her honour in the summer of her wedding.

Increasingly, bouts of activity sandwiched protracted periods of unwellness, the winter proving particularly hazardous. 'I unfortunately have been laid up for a long time with a bad attack of septic Bronchitis,' Beatrice wrote in February 1930. '[It] has left me very frail, but I am getting better at last, and in time trust to be able to get away to the south, to get a change, and pick up again.'[14] She suffered almost continuously from respiratory problems, eventually finding relief in a Coltixone inhaler, which she used daily to positive effect and thereafter recommended enthusiastically to friends and fellow sufferers. In January 1931 she slipped at Kensington Palace. Falling heavily, she broke two bones in her left arm. In the aftermath of the accident she developed bronchitis again – so severely on this occasion that her doctors feared the worst and Ena hurried from Spain to be at her mother's bedside. Happily, Beatrice rallied. On 16 February Ena returned to Madrid and Beatrice made plans to remove to Torquay to recuperate.

The Spanish capital was in a state of fermenting political turmoil. On 10 January the Queen of Greece, Beatrice's niece Sophie of Prussia, had written, 'Poor Aunt Beatrice must be anxious about her daughter – Fortunately it looks quieter in Spain just now.'[15] The Queen was wrong in her second contention. Elections held on 12 April returned an overwhelming republican majority in Spanish cities and on 14 April, Beatrice's seventy-fourth birthday, Alfonso suspended his power (he refused to abdicate) and left the country. The morning after, Ena followed him into exile, accompanied by her children, her sister-in-law Irene Carisbrooke and a handful of courtiers; she took with her her jewels. Though understandably afraid, Ena accomplished her flight unharmed. But the collapse of Alfonso's throne did nothing to speed Beatrice's recovery.

Recover she did, however, and in 1932 she was well enough to journey south again, this time to San Remo, close to the French Riviera, with Ena, who had settled temporarily in Paris. In 1935 Ena took the lease of a house at 34 Porchester Terrace in London, which placed her close to her mother in the event of an emergency. Beatrice for her part continued to spend part of each summer at Carisbrooke Castle in the Isle of Wight. She also undertook a limited number of engagements on the mainland, including, on 27 October 1935, laying a wreath at the Cenotaph in Whitehall to mark the fifteenth anniversary of the Ypres League. The date was significant. It was exactly twenty-one years since Maurice's death. Her health remained fragile and she received close regular medical supervision. In March 1936 lady-in-waiting Bessie Bulteel wrote to Lady Mottistone with a degree of uncertainty on seeing Beatrice again after a short interval, 'I think the Princess seems well ...'[16] She did not attend the coronation of her great-nephew Bertie as George VI on 12 May 1937, although her granddaughter Iris Mountbatten was a train-bearer to the Queen, but remained in London and was at Buckingham Palace to greet the new King and Queen on their return from Westminster Abbey. In April of the same year she had spent her eightieth birthday quietly at Kensington Palace, dining with her sister and neighbour Louise.

The islanders of the Isle of Wight had different ideas, however, and decided to offer Beatrice a special token to celebrate not only her birthday but also her long period as governor. Friends elicited from Beatrice that she coveted an organ said to have been played by Charles I's daughter Princess Elizabeth when she was a prisoner at Carisbrooke Castle. The organ, dated 1602, belonged to Lady Maud Warrender, who let it be known that she was willing to sell the instrument for £400. Mrs Pearson Crozier and Mrs Wilson Heathcote initiated an island-wide subscription to raise the sum, explaining in the *Isle of Wight County Press* on 9 September 1937 that each subscriber would be entitled 'to sign a commemorative book, which is to be presented to the Princess'. The subscription list was closed on 25 September, the instrument bought, and the presentation of what was referred to as the 'All-Island Gift' made at a special ceremony at Carisbrooke Castle on Sunday, 3 October. Alfred Noyes had composed a sonnet in Beatrice's honour; his son Hugh, a future parliamentary correspondent of *The Times*, presented her with the book containing the signatures of the subscribers. Beatrice, according to the local newspaper 'obviously delighted', made a speech of acceptance in which, simultaneously, she donated the organ to the castle. 'The pleasing ceremony', reported the *County Press*, 'will remain in the memory of all who were privileged to witness it as a remarkable demonstration of the Island's affection for the gracious lady who has spent her life here, never sparing herself in promoting its welfare and that of all worthy works.'[17]

If those who had conceived the idea were motivated in part by the fear that, though she had served as governor for forty-one years, Beatrice was unlikely to make it to her fiftieth anniversary, their fears were well founded: the service, which was followed by a reception in her lodgings in the castle, proved to be her swansong on the Isle of Wight. Within less than two years Britain was again at war, and Beatrice was prevented from travelling to the island. 'It is very kind of you to say that you miss seeing my flag fly at Carisbrooke Castle and I am truly sorry to be kept away from there for such a long time but it is impossible under the circumstances to go there,' she wrote to her old friend Lord Mottistone on 28 July 1940. 'I cannot help rather worrying about all my nice things which I left there, and their being possibly destroyed should bombs fall on the Castle.'[18] Some time previously Beatrice had injured her knee. The injury failed fully to heal and, with her mobility definitely impaired, she had taken to using a wheelchair, which made travel difficult even without the added complication of the war. 'An injury to her knee which nothing could cure, caused her intense pain both day and night, as she herself once confessed to me,' Lord Mottistone told his audience in his obituary address to the House of Lords.[19] Before the war had ended, Beatrice was dead. Carisbrooke Castle, Osborne and St Mildred's all happily escaped enemy bombing. Late in 1945 Beatrice did return to the Isle of Wight, her body escorted by a naval guard of honour to its final resting place alongside that of her adored Liko. She had been his widow for forty-eight years.

But before then she had one last task to accomplish.

TWENTY-EIGHT

'She struggled so hard to
"carry on"'

•◆•

*E*ighty-two is an unusual age at which to begin building
follies. If local legend is true, Beatrice's first and only
exercise in folly-building occurred during the eleven months,
from late September 1939 to mid-August 1940, she spent at a
house called Ravenswood near Sharpthorne in West Sussex.
Her health had deteriorated since the happy eightieth birthday
presentation at Carisbrooke Castle in October 1937. By the
spring of 1939 she was too unwell even to visit her sister Louise,
close by at Kensington Palace.

> I can assure you I am [thinking] of you morning noon and night
> [she wrote to Louise on 9 March], and felt it terribly not being
> able to go over and see you, if you cared for me to come. But my
> tiresome bronchial asthma has been very troublesome of late, I
> suppose owing to the cold winds, and I am at times so breathless
> I can hardly talk, and the least exertion brings it on. I am so
> grieved that your foot and ankle cause you so much pain and can
> thoroughly sympathise with you as mine are much the same.[1]

By September, with war declared and the prospect of worsening
weather through the course of the London winter, Beatrice
decided to leave Kensington Palace for Sussex. 'I must send you
a little note to say that I am off to the country as it has been
thought better for me to go away for a little while, my bronchial
asthma having been so very troublesome of late,' she wrote again
to Louise. She was still not well enough to make her farewell to
her only remaining sister by any other means and had for the
first time this summer not made her annual journey to the Isle

258

of Wight. 'I hate not being able to wish you goodbye, but my breathlessness is so bad every exertion and agitation brings on an attack which makes me speechless and choky, so I could not dare venture to come for fear of upsetting you.'[2]

With her ladies-in-waiting Minnie Cochrane and Bessie Bulteel, both of whom had been with her now for almost a lifetime (Minnie Cochrane's appointment coinciding with Beatrice's engagement in January 1885), and a secretary Mrs Norah Thomas, Beatrice left London for Sharpthorne. Ravenswood is a part-sixteenth-century house with later, mock-Tudor, half-timbered additions. Beatrice's contribution — a narrow tower with a spire and half-timbered upper storey, set just off centre of the irregular rear façade and distinctly German in appearance — represents an eccentric act of beautification and a surprising undertaking for a woman of her age and state of health at a time of international crisis. But Beatrice, whom Marie Mallet had once dismissed as lacking in imagination, had, like her mother, a strong romantic streak, as well as a love of the past. She also loved the German landscape and its buildings, writing to a friend as recently as 1936, 'Of course the whole Valley of the Rhine is beautiful.'[3] Germany occupied her thoughts during her stay at Ravenswood, and not solely on account of the war.

Beatrice had embarked on her second and last work of translation, half a century after the publication of *The Adventures of Count Georg Albert of Erbach*. This time the material was a diary, that of Queen Victoria's maternal grandmother, Augusta, Duchess of Saxe-Coburg-Saalfeld. It covered the period from 1806 to 1821, including the marriage of the Duchess's daughter Victoire to Edward, Duke of Kent, Queen Victoria's father. There was a further topicality, in addition to the family connection, which Beatrice explained in her proposed introduction to the translation: 'The curious similarity between the days of the Napoleonic wars and our own times has led me to think that this Diary might appeal to some readers, interested in that period.'[4] It was a thought shared by her eventual publisher, and one on which he pinned many of his hopes for the book's sales: 'The references to Napoleon and his marshals and to matters of general European importance are very interesting indeed. It is curious how if Hitler and Nazis be substituted for Napoleon and France, extremely suitable and apt many of the criticisms are to the present day.'[5]

Beatrice's choice of publisher fell on John Murray. The company had published her previous translation and more recently, in September 1938, John Murray himself had sent Beatrice a present of its edition of the letters of the Prince Consort, edited by Dr Kurt Jagow. Beatrice did not approach Murray, however, until the work was complete, indicating that to a large extent the translation had been undertaken not in order to write a book, but for her own enjoyment, interest and occupation. Bessie Bulteel's letter to Louise on 3 October 1939 suggests there was little else to do at Ravenswood: 'We are leading a very quiet life here, and have seen nobody, so there is nothing to tell you.'[6] What's more, despite their recent exchange of letters, when the time came, the letter of approach was written not by Beatrice but by Minnie Cochrane – on 28 October 1940. 'Princess Beatrice has asked me to write and say that as you once very kindly published a book for Her Royal Highness, The Princess wonders if you would do so again. Her Royal Highness has translated from German the diary of the ... maternal grandmother of the late Queen Victoria. The original is in the archives of Windsor Castle. The King has given his permission for it to be published.'[7]

By this time Beatrice had left Ravenswood. The house had offered limited respite from the winter cold, January 1940 bringing deep snow and hard frosts, both of which prevented Beatrice from getting outside and served to exacerbate her ongoing struggle with bronchial asthma. Added to this, despite its remoteness, Ravenswood was in a defence area: extensive troop movements threatened the prevailing tranquillity. On one occasion in July 1940 the troops in question were Canadian. Beatrice invited them into the garden, where she joined them in her wheelchair, a gesture that marked her clearly as her mother's daughter.

We have masses of troops all round us, and I saw some Canadians a few days ago, who were resting near the gate. I had them told to come into the grounds and go round the garden. After they had been given a little refreshment, I went out in my chair to speak to them, which seemed to please them very much, and one asked leave to photograph me. They were very fine looking young men, in the Artillery, and showed me their guns, with great pride.[8]

Beatrice was much struck by the coincidence of the soldiers being Canadian. She had recently settled to move from Ravenswood to nearby Brantridge Park near Balcombe. The house belonged to her niece, Leopold's daughter Alice, and Alice's husband Alge, Earl of Athlone, Queen Mary's brother. Before the outbreak of war Lord Athlone had been appointed Governor-General of Canada. During their absence on the other side of the Atlantic, the Athlones had decided to let Brantridge Park. The house offered an ideal solution for Beatrice. Princess Louise had died at Kensington Palace in December 1939 and Ena was spending the duration of the war in neutral Switzerland: there were no longer any ties for Beatrice in London. Brantridge, a handsome, mid-eighteenth-century house in an extensive park, was both larger and quieter than Ravenswood. Despite its proximity to the latter, it stood outside the defence area; its size allowed Beatrice to have living with her, in addition to her attendants, her remaining son Drino and his wife Irene. On 28 July 1940 she wrote to Lord Mottistone of her plans: 'I am going to move in the middle of next month to Brantridge Park, which Alge and Alice are letting, so as to be able to have my son and daughter-in-law living with me, and am thankful not to have to face another winter here all alone and so isolated.'[9]

Within weeks of settling in to what would be her final home, Beatrice completed her translation of her great-grandmother's diary. On 1 November Minnie Cochrane wrote from Brantridge to John Murray, who had agreed in principle to accept the work for publication but asked that he be allowed to see it to estimate the likely costs involved. 'Her Royal Highness wishes me to say she always meant to send you the typed translation, and will do so directly she gets it back. At present the King is reading it, and it then goes to Queen Mary – but as soon as the Princess has it back, it will go to you.'[10] It 'went' on 26 November, Beatrice taking the opportunity to write to Murray herself for the first time. 'I am at last sending you my typewritten manuscript which I received from Queen Mary this morning, who seems most interested and impressed with it, thinking it would be sure to be appreciated (by the public) and all the more so being a private Diary ... I should like the book to be published very simply and inexpensively, and shall naturally await your verdict with anxiety!'[11]

Happily, Beatrice's anxiety was without foundation. John Murray delivered his verdict on 6 December:

> I have been reading the Diary with much pleasure and interest and should like if I may to congratulate Your Royal Highness on the very skilful way in which the work is done so as to avoid an impression of being a translation at all ... The Diary well deserves publication and it will be a pleasure and honour to me to bring it out. I shall be willing to bear all the cost of production and publication and pay Your Royal Highness a royalty of twelve-and-a-half per cent on all copies sold after the first 500 and fifteen per cent if or when 1,500 copies have been sold ... The book, including a moderate amount of advertisement, will cost over £200.[12]

Beatrice accepted Murray's terms by return of post.

The book was published on 12 June 1941. Over the course of the intervening seven months, publisher and author – referred to by John Murray privately as 'the Royal translator'[13] – enjoyed a regular, polite correspondence concerning such matters as the index, illustrations for the book, and its title, Murray making the suggestion that was ultimately accepted of *In Napoleonic Days*. Together they devised the unavoidably cumbersome sub-title: 'Extracts from the private diary of Augusta, Duchess of Saxe-Coburg-Saalfeld, Queen Victoria's maternal grandmother, 1806 to 1821'. Due to the cleanness of the manuscript, Murray decided to save time and expense 'by having only one stage of proof',[14] and Beatrice – as she had in 1890 over the publication of *The Adventures of Count Georg Albert of Erbach* – deferred to her publisher's knowledge and experience: 'If you should wish to make any further small alterations,' she wrote to him on 15 December, 'please do so without referring back to me.' Beatrice chose 'a dull green binding'[15] and, ever modest, found herself 'agreeably surprised at how pleasantly it reads' after receiving through the post the first proof.[16] Although publication was slowed down by the Ministry of Aircraft Production, which briefly took over the printing works – with the result that 'all work was thrown into confusion with consequent weeks of delay', as Murray explained to Beatrice – and despite John Murray's publicity material advertising the book's price as eighteen shillings rather than the correct 7s. 6d, 230 advance copies had been sold to booksellers by the eve of sale. 'It has been a great pleasure to me to be associated with Your Royal Highness over the publication of this book and I do indeed hope that the results will be really satisfactory to reward the care and thought which you have given to the work,' Murray wrote to Beatrice on that occasion, adding that at least a thousand copies needed to be sold in order to cover expenses.

Both John Murray and Beatrice herself placed their trust in the magnetism of the royal name. Murray printed 1514 copies and offered seventy-seven to members of the press. *In Napoleonic Days* was favourably reviewed in the *Spectator*, *The Times*, the *Daily Telegraph* and the *Times Literary Supplement*. By August almost a thousand copies had been sold, that figure rising to 1300 by early October. At regular intervals Norah Thomas wrote on Beatrice's behalf enquiring after the progress of sales and offering, at one point, Beatrice to autograph copies in order to speed up the process (an offer Murray refused as unnecessary, though he did ask Beatrice to sign his own copy). On 10 February 1943 John Murray wrote to Beatrice announcing the sale of the last eighteen copies of the edition.

As had her work on her mother's Journal, *In Napoleonic Days* provided Beatrice not only with employment but with a continuing interest, as she followed the progress of its production and eventual sale. Not for a moment now did the pain in her knee leave her, her fingers and her limbs ached with constant rheumatic pains and no glasses properly corrected her worsening sight. Unable to walk, continually troubled by her breathing, her life had become that of an invalid. When first she moved to Brantridge Park there had been visits to and from her brother Arthur, the last survivor of her eight siblings. But Arthur died in January 1942. More than a century after the birth of the Queen and Prince Consort's eldest daughter, Beatrice found herself indisputably the last princess. Her parents, her siblings, her husband, two of her children and six of the ten nieces who had been her bridesmaids were all dead. Tired and suffering, she remained, the last gently flickering candle of Britain's dazzling Victorian age. 'She struggled so hard to "carry on" in spite of all her sufferings with supreme courage but it was very painful for those who loved her,' Irene Carisbrooke wrote after her death.[17] To the small group living together at Brantridge Park, it was obvious that it was only a question of time and that, when it came, the end would be a blessing.

But for Beatrice herself there was no question of giving up. Both the Isle of Wight and the progress of the war continued to absorb her attention. One of her last letters to Lord Mottistone, a friend for fifty years, written on 11 November 1943, reveals the scope of her interests:

> I think your suggestion of submitting the name of General Aspinall-Oglander as a Deputy Lieutenant [of the Isle of Wight] a most excellent one, for he certainly has rendered great services ... How thankful one is for all the splendid war news, but I fear the end of this ghastly war is not yet in sight and that there are still very serious hard times to face ... I am keeping fairly well but continue to be much troubled with my bronchial asthma, which is so fatiguing. But this time of year is very bad for that sort of thing.[18]

That bronchial asthma troubled Beatrice throughout the winter of 1943–4. Though the following summer witnessed a temporary lessening of pain, the autumn saw the return of her old sparring partner with renewed vigour. By October she was seriously ill and, on 25 October, summoned by telegram, Ena left Geneva to return for the last time to her mother's side. She travelled by converted bomber sent by the British government, but still arrived only just in time. At ten past five on the morning of 26 October, in a house deep in the English countryside belonging to a granddaughter of Queen Victoria, the last princess died peacefully in her sleep. Close beside her, adding colour and flesh to the ghosts of the past that had cloaked her through most of her eighty-seven years, were her son and daughter and her only daughter-in-law. Beyond the rolling fields and the steel-grey sea that wrapped the shores of her mother's kingdom, world war would continue for a further eight months. Among its casualties was a pretty, insignificant little town near Frankfurt, seat of a grand duchy and a dynasty that, except as a memory, had disappeared. That town was Darmstadt. Four months after Beatrice's death, flattened by bombs, it too disappeared. On 26 February 1945 Queen Mary wrote to her brother in Canada, 'Poor Darmstadt has ceased to exist, everything gone. This was done by Americans, rather sad.'[19] It was the town where Beatrice had fallen in love, the agent of her liberation, the X factor that gave to the last princess a love and life of her own.

NOTES

CHAPTER ONE: 'It is a fine child'

1 Longford, Elizabeth, *Victoria RI* (Weidenfeld & Nicolson, London, 1964), p. 261.
2 Hibbert, Christopher, *George III: A Personal History* (Viking, London, 1998).
3 Weintraub, Stanley, *Victoria: Biography of a Queen* (Unwin, London, 1987), p. 225.
4 Hibbert, Christopher, *Queen Victoria: A Personal History* (HarperCollins, London, 2000), p. 219.
5 Steuart Erskine, Mrs (ed.), *Twenty Years at Court: From the Correspondence of the Hon. Eleanor Stanley, 1842–62* (Nisbet & Co., London, 1916), p. 325.
6 Longford, *Victoria RI*, p. 151.
7 Hough, Richard, *Advice to a Grand-daughter: Letters from Queen Victoria to Princess Victoria of Hesse* (Heineman, London, 1975), p. 126.
8 Longford, *Victoria RI*, p. 234.
9 Ellis, Richard (ed.,) *The Case Books of Dr John Snow, Medical History Supplement No. 14* (Wellcome Institute for the History of Medicine,

London, 1994), p. 271.
10 *The Lancet*, 14 May 1853.
11 Ellis, Richard (ed.), op. cit., p. 471.
12 Ibid.
13 Ibid.
14 Longford, *Victoria RI*, p. 266.
15 Jagow, Dr Kurt, *Letters of the Prince Consort 1831–1861* (John Murray, London, 1938), p. 272.
16 Ellis, Richard (ed.), op. cit., p. 471.
17 Longford, *Victoria RI*, p. 266.
18 Fraser, Flora, *Princesses: the Daughters of George III* (John Murray, London, 2004), p. 398.
19 Stuart, D. M., *George III's Daughters* (John Murray, London, 1939), p. 256.
20 Benson, A. C. (ed.), *Letters of Queen Victoria* (John Murray, London, 1908), vol. III, p. 234.
21 Ibid.
22 Fulford, Roger (ed.), *Darling Child: Private Correspondence of Queen Victoria and the Crown Princess of Prussia 1871–1878* (Evans Brothers, London, 1976), p. 41.
23 Stoney, Benita and Weltzein,

Heinrich C., *My Mistress the Queen: the Letters of Frieda Arnold, Dresser to Queen Victoria, 1854–9,* trans. by Sheila de Bellaigue (Weidenfeld & Nicolson, London, 1994), p. 20.
24 Longford, *Victoria RI,* p. 283.
25 Queen Victoria to 'Minnie', 21 December 1859, collection of Science Museum, London, MS 1191.

CHAPTER TWO: 'The most amusing baby we have had'

1 Van der Kiste, John, *Childhood at Court 1819–1914* (Sutton, Stroud, 1995), p. 50.
2 Longford, Elizabeth (ed.), *Darling Loosy: Letters to Princess Louise 1856–1939* (Weidenfeld & Nicolson, London, 1991), p. 155: Queen Victoria to Princess Louise, 11 November 1871.
3 Tisdall, E. E. P, *Queen Victoria's Private Life* (Jarrolds, London, 1961), p. 43.
4 Weintraub, *Victoria,* p. 323.
5 Ibid., p. 226.
6 Windsor, Dean of, & Bolitho, Hector (eds.), *Letters of Lady Augusta Stanley* (Gerald Howe, London, 1927), p. 145.
7 Hough, *Advice,* p. 104: Queen Victoria to Victoria of Hesse, 12 October 1889.
8 Van der Kiste, *Childhood at Court,* p. 50.
9 Queen Victoria to the Crown Princess of Prussia, 6 March 1870.

10 Warner, Marina, *Queen Victoria's Sketchbook* (Macmillan, London, 1979), p. 121.
11 Duff, David, *The Shy Princess* (Evans Brothers, London, 1958), p. 22.
12 Bennett, Daphne, *Queen Victoria's Children* (Gollancz, London, 1980), p. 130.
13 Millar, Oliver, *The Victorian Paintings in the Collection of Her Majesty the Queen* (Cambridge University Press, Cambridge, 1992), vol. ii, p. 280: Charles Grey to Henrietta Ward, 29 October 1857.
14 Ibid., p. 315.
15 Zeepvat, Charlotte, *Prince Leopold: the untold story of Queen Victoria's youngest son* (Sutton, Stroud, 1988), p. 10, 3 June 1858.
16 Jagow, op. cit., p. 298, 14 March 1858.
17 Epton, Nina, *Victoria and her Daughters* (Weidenfeld & Nicolson, 1971), p. 81.
18 Van der Kiste, *Childhood at Court,* p. 69.
19 Ponsonby, Magdalen (ed.), *Mary Ponsonby: A Memoir, Some Letters and a Journal* (John Murray, London, 1927), pp. 3–5.
20 Steuart Erskine, Mrs (ed.), op. cit., p. 329.
21 Howard McClintock, Mary, *The Queen Thanks Sir Howard* (John Murray, London, 1945), p. 44.
22 Noel, Gerard, *Princess Alice:*

Queen Victoria's Forgotten Daughter (Constable, London, 1974), p. 29.

23 Longford, Elizabeth, *Victoria RI*, p. 278.

24 Epton, op. cit., p. 126.

25 Van der Kiste, John, *Childhood at Court*, p. 41.

26 Duff, *Shy Princess*, p. 26.

27 Windsor, Dean of Bolitho, Hector (eds.), *Later Letters of Lady Augusta Stanley* (Jonathan Cape, London, 1929), p. 46.

28 Princess Beatrice to Prince Consort, undated, RA VIC/M 19/70.

29 Millar, op. cit., p. 206, 18 September 1860.

30 Ibid., p. 203.

31 Windsor, Dean of etc., *Letters*, p. 130, 15 August 1859

32 Ramm, Agatha (ed.), *Beloved and Darling Child: last letters between Queen Victoria and her eldest daughter, 1886 – 1901* (Sutton, Stroud, 1990), p. 193, 19 August 1896.

33 Dyson, Hope & Tennyson, Charles (eds.), *Dear & Honoured Lady: The Correspondence between Queen Victoria and Alfred Tennyson* (Macmillan, London, 1969), p. 77.

34 Windsor, Dean of etc., *Letters*, p. 131, 15 August 1859.

35 Zeepvat, op. cit., p. 26.

36 Steuart Erskine, Mrs (ed.), op. cit., p. 371.

37 Windsor, Dean of etc., *Letters*, p. 146, 18 July 1860.

38 Ibid., p. 170, 15 January 1861.

39 Steuart Erskine, Mrs (ed.), op. cit., p. 371, 14 July 1860.

40 Ibid.

CHAPTER THREE: 'Paroxysms of despair'

1 Longford, *Victoria RI*, p. 293.

2 Bullock, Rev. Charles, *The Queen's Resolve: A Jubilee Memorial* (Home Words Publishing, London, 1887), p. 102.

3 Ibid.

4 Fulford, Roger (ed.), *Your Dear Letter: Private Correspondence of Queen Victoria and the Crown Princess of Prussia, 1865–1871* (Evans Brothers, London, 1971), p. 90.

5 Millar, op. cit., p. xli.

6 Benson, E.F., *Daughters of Queen Victoria* (Cassell & Co., London, 1939), p. 72

7 Noel, *Princess Alice*, p. 73.

8 Ibid., p. 75.

9 Watson, Vera, *A Queen at Home: an intimate account of the social and domestic life of Queen Victoria's court* (W. H. Allen, London, 1952), p. 142.

10 Epton, op. cit., p. 92.

11 Van der Kiste, *Childhood at Court*, p. 80.

12 Epton, op. cit., p. 96.

13 Ponsonby, Magdalen (ed.), op. cit., p. 13.

14 Ibid., p. 40.

15 Steuart Erskine, Mrs (ed.), op. cit., p. 396.

16 Tisdall, op. cit., p. 50.

17 Duff, *Shy Princess*, p. 10.

18 Ibid., p. 26.

19 Hibbert, Christopher, *Queen Victoria*, p. 281.
20 Ibid., p. 290.
21 Fulford, Roger (ed.), *Dearest Mama: letters between Queen Victoria and the Crown Princess of Prussia 1861–1864* (Evans Brothers, London, 1968), p. 23.
22 Clark, Ronald W., *Balmoral: Queen Victoria's Highland Home* (Thames & Hudson, London, 1981), p. 78.
23 Hough, *Advice*, p. 116.
24 Fulford, Roger (ed.), *Dearest Mama*, p. 74.
25 Weintraub, op. cit., p. 311.
26 Tisdall, op. cit., p. 60.
27 Weintraub, op. cit., p. 308.

CHAPTER FOUR: 'The bright spot in this dead home'

1 Longford, *Victoria RI*, p. 367.
2 Fulford, (ed.), *Your Dear Letter*, p. 23.
3 Zeepvat, op. cit., p. 6.
4 Duff, *Shy Princess*, p. 23.
5 Dyson & Tennyson (eds.), op. cit., p. 105.
6 Fulford (ed.), *Dearest Mama*, p. 62.
7 Hibbert, *Queen Victoria*, p. 291.
8 Ibid., p. 266.
9 Fulford (ed.), *Dearest Mama*, p. 74.
10 Ibid., p. 280.
11 Windsor, Dean of etc., *Letters*, p. 255.
12 Fulford (ed.), *Dearest Mama*, p. 73.
13 Duff, David, *Hessian Tapestry* (Frederick Muller, London,

1967), p. 49
14 Clark, op. cit., p. 78.
15 Noel, op. cit., p. 108.
16 Epton, op. cit., p. 109.
17 Ibid., p. 122.
18 Clark, op. cit., p. 78.
19 Ibid.
20 Noel, *Princess Alice*, p. 24.
21 Watson, op. cit., p. 160.
22 Ibid., p. 162.
23 Windsor, Dean of etc., *Letters*, p. 285, 12 March 1863.
24 Ibid, p. 308, 14 March 1863.
25 Ibid.
26 Wake, Jehanne, *Princess Louise: Queen Victoria's unconventional daughter* (Collins, London, 1988), p. 54.
27 Epton, op. cit., p. 108.

CHAPTER FIVE: 'Beatrice is quite well'

1 Duff, David, *Victoria Travels: journeys of Queen Victoria between 1830 and 1900, with extracts from her journal* (Muller, London, 1970), p. 85.
2 Fulford (ed.), *Dearest Mama*, p. 281.
3 Wake, op. cit., p. 20.
4 Ibid., p. 29.
5 Princess Beatrice to Lord De Ros, 14 May 1868, private collection.
6 Windsor, Dean of etc., *Later Letters*, p. 32.
7 Windsor, Dean of etc., *Letters*, p. 271, 4 October 1862.
8 Longford Elizabeth (ed.), *Darling Loosy*, p. 88.
9 Steuart Erskine, Mrs (ed.), op. cit., p. 401.

10 Epton, op. cit., p. 98.

11 Windsor, Dean of etc., *Letters*, p. 206.

12 RA VIC/Add A 15/304A, Princess Beatrice to Prince Arthur, 21 June 1863.

13 Windsor, Dean of etc., *Later Letters*, p. 48.

14 Hough, *Advice*, p. 9.

15 Weintraub, op. cit., p. 328.

16 Noel, *Princess Alice*, p. 88.

17 RA VIC/T4/65, Princess Beatrice to the Prince of Wales, 8 November 1865.

18 Zeepvat, op. cit., p. 34.

19 RA VIC/Add A15/607, Princess Beatrice to Prince Arthur, 11 December 1864.

20 Wake, op. cit., p. 63.

21 Fulford (ed.), *Dearest Mama*, p. 198.

CHAPTER SIX: 'A nervous way of speaking and laughing'

1 Hough, Richard, *Louis and Victoria: The Family History of the Mountbattens* (Weidenfeld & Nicolson, London, 1974), p. 18.

2 Ibid., p. 17.

3 Rowell, George, *Queen Victoria Goes to the Theatre* (Paul Elek, London, 1978), p. 84; Queen Victoria's Journal, 2 October 1865.

4 Matson, John, *Dear Osborne* (Hamish Hamilton, London, 1978), p. 75.

5 Fulford (ed.), *Your Dear Letter*, p. 121.

6 Zeepvat, op. cit., p. 57.

7 Lady Waterpark's Diary 1865–91, British Library Add 60750, 21 November 1865.

8 Ibid., 7 April 1868.

9 RA VIC/Add C26/142, Princess Beatrice to Lady Caroline Barrington, undated, 1868.

10 Tisdall, op. cit., p. 164.

11 Fulford (ed.), *Your Dear Letter*, p. 217.

12 Wake, op. cit., p. 78.

13 Hough, *Advice*, p. 29.

14 Zeepvat, op. cit., p. 114.

15 Lady Waterpark's Diary, 29 January 1877; 19 January 1878.

16 Arengo-Jones, Peter, *Queen Victoria in Switzerland* (Robert Hale, London, 1995), p. 98.

17 RA VIC/Add A17/677, Princess Beatrice to Princess Louise, 19 January 1875.

18 Fulford (ed.), *Your Dear Letter*, p. 259.

19 Victoria, Queen, *More Leaves from the Journal of a Life in the Highlands: from 1862 to 1882* (Smith, Elder & Co., London, 1884), 10 September 1873.

20 Lady Waterpark's Diary, 14 August 1874.

21 Ibid., 14 April, 1881.

CHAPTER SEVEN: 'Auntie Beatrice sends you many loves'

1 Princess Alice to Princess Charlotte of Prussia, 1 March 1877, previously with Sophie Dupré.

2 Van der Kiste, John, *Edward VII's Children* (Sutton, Stroud, 1989), p. 21.

3 Windsor, Dean of etc., *Letters*, p. 218, 9 June 1861.

4 Pakula, Hannah, *An Uncommon Woman: The Empress Frederick* (Phoenix paperback, London, 1997), p. 371.

5 Fulford (ed.), *Your Dear Letter*, p. 114.

6 Fulford (ed.), *Dearest Mama*, p. 168.

7 Hough, *Advice*, p. 9.

8 Ibid., p. 11.

9 Ibid., p. 12.

10 Ibid., p. 25.

11 Fulford (ed.), *Dearest Mama*, p. 311.

12 Hibbert, *Queen Victoria*, p. 411.

13 Duff, *Hessian Tapestry*, p. 158.

14 RA VIC/Add C26/146, Princess Beatrice to Lady Caroline Barrington, 21 July 1870.

15 Marie Louise, Princess, *My Memories of Six Reigns* (Evans Brothers, London, 1956), p. 153.

16 Hibbert, *Queen Victoria*, p. 332.

17 Fulford, Roger (ed.), *Beloved Mama: private correspondence of Queen Victoria and the German Crown Princess, 1878–1885* (Evans Brothers, London, 1981), p. 87.

18 Victoria, Queen, *Our Life n the Highlands* (Victorian & Modern History Book Club, Newton Abbot, 1972), p. 127.

CHAPTER EIGHT: 'Youngest daughters have a duty ...'

1 Bennett, op. cit., p. 129.

2 Hibbert, *Queen Victoria*, p. 340

3 Bennett, op. cit., p. 136.

4 Longford, *Victoria RI*, p. 368.

5 Bennett, op. cit., p. 129.

6 Windsor, Dean of etc., *Later Letters*, p. 160, late 1872.

7 Ibid.

8 RA VIC/Add C26/145, Princess Beatrice to Lady Caroline Barrington, 8 June 1870.

9 Wake, op. cit., p. 65.

10 Fulford (ed.), *Your Dear Letter*, p. 20.

11 Fulford (ed.), *Darling Child*, p. 188.

12 Lutyens, Mary (ed.), *Lady Lytton's Diary* (Rupert Hart-Davis, London, 1961), p. 109.

13 Plunkett, John, *Queen Victoria, First Media Monarch* (Oxford University Press, Oxford, 2003), p. 140.

14 Ponsonby, Magdalen (ed.), op. cit., p. 63.

15 Fulford (ed.), *Your Dear Letter*, p. 314.

16 RA VIC/ S31/99, Princess Beatrice to Disraeli, 5 February 1881.

17 Longford (ed.), *Darling Loosy*, p. 105.

18 Pakula, op. cit., p. 293.

19 St-John Nevill, Barry, *Life at the Court of Queen Victoria 1861–1901* (Webb & Bower, Exeter, 1984), p. 72.

20 Fulford (ed.), *Darling Child*, p. 86.

21 Noel, *Princess Alice*, p. 169.
22 Hibbert, *Queen Victoria*, p. 340.
23 Fulford (ed.), *Darling Child*, p. 18.
24 St-John Nevill, op. cit., p. 73.
25 Ibid.
26 Ibid., p. 74.
27 Lady Waterpark's Diary, 25 December 1871.
28 Lant, Jeffrey L., *Insubstantial Pageant: Ceremony and Confusion at Queen Victoria's Court* (Hamish Hamilton, London, 1979), p. 33.
29 St John Nevill, op. cit., p. 80.
30 Lant, op. cit., p. 26.
31 St-John Nevill, op. cit., p. 76.
32 St Aubyn, Giles, *Edward VII Prince and King* (Collins, London, 1979), p. 217.

CHAPTER NINE: 'The flower of the flock'

1 Longford (ed.), *Darling Loosy*, p. 177.
2 Fulford (ed.), *Darling Child*, p. 124.
3 Ibid., p. 34.
4 Fulford (ed.), *Your Dear Letter*, p. 142.
5 Pakula, op. cit., p. 71.
6 Fulford (ed.), *Darling Child*, p. 124.
7 RA VIC/Add C26/153, Princess Beatrice to Lady Caroline Barrington, 20 January 1874.
8 Millar, op. cit., p. 88.
9 Ibid.
10 Ibid.
11 Victoria, Queen, *Our Life*, 14 September 1873.
12 Epton, op. cit., pp. 224–5.
13 Ibid., p. 146.
14 Aronson, Theo, *Queen Victoria and the Bonapartes* (London, Cassell, 1972), p. 151.
15 Ibid.
16 Fulford (ed.), *Your Dear Letter*, p. 311.
17 Stothard, Jane T., *The Life of the Empress Eugénie* (Hodder & Stoughton, London, 1906), p. 296.
18 Lady Waterpark's Diary, 9 August 1876.
19 Stothard, op. cit., p. 290.
20 Aronson, op. cit., p. 169.
21 Wade, Alf, The South African Military History Society, *Military History Journal*, vol. 3, no. 2, 'The Prince Imperial', 1974.
22 Stothard, op. cit., p. 273.
23 Weintraub, op. cit., p. 436.
24 St-John Nevill, op. cit., p. 102.

CHAPTER TEN: 'A good, handy, thoughtful servant'

1 St-John Nevill, op. cit., p. 95.
2 Epton, op. cit., p. 146.
3 Fulford (ed.), *Beloved Mama*, p. 3.
4 Lady Waterpark's Diary, 10 August 1876.
5 Noel, *Princess Alice*, p. 237.
6 Longford, *Victoria RI*, p. 457
7 Longford, *Darling Loosy*, p. 224.
8 Reid, Michaela, *Ask Sir James* (Hodder & Stoughton, London, 1987), p. 57.

9 Ibid., p. 55.
10 Queen Victoria to Mrs William Brown and Mrs Hugh Brown, Windsor Castle, April 3 1883; qu. Lamont-Brown, Raymond, *John Brown, Queen Victoria's Highland Servant* (Sutton, Stroud, 2000), p. 142.
11 Hibbert, *Queen Victoria*, p. 323.
12 Cullen, Tom, *The Empress Brown* (The Bodley Head, London, 1969), p. 82.
13 St Aubyn, op. cit., p. 141.
14 Hibbert, *Queen Victoria*, p. 399.
15 Fulford (ed.), *Your Dear Letter*, p. 23.
16 Ibid., p. 90.
17 Auchincloss, Louis, *Persons of Consequence: Queen Victoria and her Circle* (Weidenfeld & Nicolson, London, 1979), p. 154.
18 Victoria, Queen, *Our Life*, 13 November 1872.
19 Ibid., 6 September 1872.
20 Ibid., 12 September 1877.
21 Hough, *Advice*, p. 24.
22 Stoney and Weltzein, p. 25.
23 Epton, op. cit., p. 164.

CHAPTER ELEVEN: 'She is my constant companion'

1 Duff, *Shy Princess* p. 89.
2 Hibbert, *Queen Victoria*, p. 411.
3 Reid, op. cit., p. 207.
4 Hough, *Advice*, p. 10.
5 RA VIC/Add A8/2362, Princess Beatrice to Princess Mary Adelaide, Duchess of Teck, 22 January 1879.
6 RA VIC/Add A8/2369, as above, 2 March 1879.
7 Bennett, op. cit., p. 135.
8 Longford, *Victoria RI*, p. 436.
9 Duff, *Shy Princess*, p. 92.
10 RA VIC/2 506/56, Princess Beatrice to Theodore Martin, 29 April 1879.

CHAPTER TWELVE: 'Dear Beatrice suffered much ...'

1 Mallet, Victor (ed.), *Life with Queen Victoria: Marie Mallet's letters from court, 1887–1901* (John Murray, London, 1968), p. 5.
2 Victoria, Queen, *Our Life*, pp. 168–9, 10 September 1873.
3 Zeepvat, op. cit., p. 175.
4 Lutyens, op. cit., p. 16.
5 Clark, op. cit., p. 124.
6 RA Vic Add C26 154, Princess Beatrice to Lady Caroline Barrington, 21 May 1874.
7 Mallet, op. cit., p. xix.
8 Longford, *Victoria RI*, p. 205.
9 Grihangne, Roger (trans. David Lockie), *Queen Victoria in Grasse* (Imprimerie Magenta, 1991), p. 14.
10 Noel, op. cit., p. 136.
11 Ibid., p. 99.
12 Victoria, Queen, *Our Life*, p. 226, 17 September 1877.
13 Lady Waterpark's Diary, 10 January 1879.
14 Mallet, op. cit., p. 94.
15 Ibid., p. 130.
16 Epton, op. cit., p. 163.
17 Fulford (ed.), *Beloved Mama*, p. 144.

18 Ibid., p. 146.
19 The *Illustrated London News*, 1 August 1885.

CHAPTER THIRTEEN: 'If only she could marry now'

1 Hough, *Advice*, p. 48.
2 Hibbert, Christopher, *Queen Victoria in her Letters & Journals* (Viking, London, 1985), p. 234.
3 RA VIC/Add A 30/432, Princess Beatrice to Prince Leopold, 18 November 1881.
4 RA VIC/Add A 30/433, Princess Beatrice to Princess Helen of Waldeck-Pyrmont, 23 November 1881.
5 Hough, *Advice*, p. 29.
6 Ibid., p. 60.
7 Ibid., p. 48.
8 Ibid., p. 58.
9 Millar, op. cit., p. 241.
10 Ibid., p. 233.
11 Lutyens, op. cit., p. 106.
12 Epton, op. cit., p. 150.
13 Ibid., p. 152.
14 Zeepvat, op. cit., p. 77.

CHAPTER FOURTEEN: The Handsomest Family in Europe

1 Reid, op. cit., p. 62.
2 Vickers, Hugo, *Alice, Princess Andrew of Greece* (Viking, London, 2000), p. 17.
3 Pakula, op. cit., p. 416.
4 Fulford (ed.), *Beloved Mama*, p. 98.
5 St-John Nevill, op. cit., p. 133.

6 Fulford (ed.), *Beloved Mama*, p. 187.
7 Longford, *Darling Loosy*, p. 139.
8 Zeepvat, op. cit., p. 169.
9 Fulford (ed.), *Beloved Mama*, p. 111.
10 Ibid., p. 111.
11 Gelardi, Julia, *Born to Rule* (St Martin's Press, New York, 2004), p. 37.
12 Fulford (ed.), *Beloved Mama*, p. 168.
13 Hibbert, *Letters & Journals*, p. 287.
14 Ibid.
15 Battiscombe, Georgina, *Queen Alexandra* (Constable, London, 1969), p. 151.
16 Ibid.
17 Hibbert, *Letters & Journals*, p. 287.
18 RA VIC/Add A 30/1357, Princess Beatrice to the Duchess of Albany, 24 July 1885.

CHAPTER FIFTEEN: 'Many daughters ...'

1 *The Times*, 9 July 1885.
2 Fulford (ed.), *Beloved Mama*, p. 176.
3 Hough, *Louis and Victoria*, p. 129.
4 Ibid.
5 Fulford (ed.), *Beloved Mama*, p. 178.
6 *The Illustrated London News*, 1 February 1896.
7 Lady Waterpark's Diary, 30 January 1885.
8 Hibbert, *Letters & Journals*, p. 287.

9 Millar, op. cit., p. 350.

10 Duff, *Victoria Travels*, p. 115.

11 Hibbert, *Letters & Journals*, p. 287.

12 Fulford (ed.), *Beloved Mama*, p. 178.

13 Duff, *Hessian Tapestry*, p. 207.

14 Fulford (ed.), *Beloved Mama*, p. 178.

15 Longford, *Victoria RI*. p. 478.

16 Meres, the Rev. H. J., 'A Sermon Preached in the Stowell Memorial Church, Salford, 9, February 1896, the Sunday after the Funeral of His Royal Highness Prince Henry Maurice of Battenberg', p. 18.

17 Fulford (ed.), *Your Dear Letter*, p. 303.

18 Ibid., p. 309.

19 Hough, *Advice*, p. 74.

20 'Mr Bright on The Princess Beatrice's Dowry', 16 May 1885, collection Rochdale Metropolitan Borough Council.

21 The Prince of Wales to John Bright, MP, Marlborough House, 19 May 1885, collection Rochdale Metropolitan Borough Council.

22 Fulford (ed.), *Beloved Mama*, p. 178.

23 Tisdall, op. cit., p. 153.

24 Gelardi, op. cit., p. 17.

25 RA VIC/Z 88/67, Princess Irene of Hesse to Queen Victoria, 10 January 1885.

26 Princess Beatrice to Lady Waterpark (Lady Waterpark's Diary), 6 January 1885.

27 Gelardi, op. cit., p. 17.

CHAPTER SIXTEEN: 'The fatal day approaches'

1 Tisdall, op. cit., p. 152.

2 Dyson & Tennyson (eds.), op. cit., p. 120.

3 Millar, op. cit., p. 338.

4 Watson, op. cit., p. 256.

5 Ibid., p. 251.

6 St-John Nevill, op. cit., p. 117.

7 Fulford (ed.), *Beloved Mama*, p. 185.

8 St-John Nevill, op. cit., p. 116.

9 Hough, *Advice*, p. 75.

10 *The Times*, Court Circular, 17 July 1885.

11 Princess Beatrice to Lady Waterpark, 18 June 1885.

12 Watson, op. cit., p. 251.

13 Ibid., p. 252.

14 RA VIC/Add A30/1357, Princess Beatrice to the Duchess of Albany, 24 July 1885.

15 Hough, *Louis and Victoria*, p. 132.

16 St-John Nevill, op. cit., p. 117.

17 Weintraub, op. cit., p. 475.

18 Hibbert, *Queen Victoria*, p. 373.

19 Hibbert, *Letters & Journals*, p. 294.

20 Epton, op. cit., p. 174.

21 The *Illustrated London News*, 1 August 1885.

22 Erbach-Schönberg, Princess Marie zu, Princess of Battenberg, *Reminiscences* (Royalty Digest reprint, Ticehurst, 1996), p. 218.

23 Hibbert, *Letters & Journals*, p. 294.

24 Ednay, Peter, *Princess Beatrice: Island Governor* (Vectis, 1994), p. 17.

25 Reid, op. cit., p. 65.
26 RA VIC/Add A 30/1357, Princess Beatrice to the Duchess of Albany, 24 July 1885.

CHAPTER SEVENTEEN: 'There now burnt a ... fiery passion'

1 'To HRH Beatrice Mary Victoria Feodore, Princess of Battenberg', from 'the Aldermen and Burgesses of the ancient and loyal borough of Southampton in Council', 31 July 1886.
2 'Goodie' to 'Darling Granny', Bloomsbury Book Auctions, sale 504 (5 November 2004), lot 176, letters 16 February to 6 November 1886.
3 Cullen, op. cit., p. 181.
4 Erbach-Schönberg, op. cit., p. 231.
5 Gelardi, op. cit., p. 17.
6 Hough, Advice, p. 77.
7 Erbach-Schönberg, op. cit., p. 231.
8 'Goodie', op. cit.
9 Princess Beatrice to 'Dear Dean', 5 August 1890, John Murray Archives.
10 Ramm, Agatha (ed.), Beloved and Darling Child: last letters between Queen Victoria and her eldest daughter, 1886–1901 (Sutton, Stroud, 1990), p. 141.
11 Battenberg, Princess Henry of, The Adventures of Count Georg Albert of Erbach (John Murray, London, 1890), p. 101.
12 Ibid., p. 237.
13 Ibid., p. 235.
14 Hough, Advice, p. 79.

15 Reid, op. cit., p. 68.
16 Ibid.
17 Hough, Advice, p. 82.
18 Ibid., p. 83.
19 Fulford (ed.), Beloved Mama, p. 185.
20 Reid, op. cit., p. 68.
21 Longford, Darling Loosy, p. 228.
22 Hough, Advice, pp. 84–5.
23 Ibid.
24 Ibid.
25 Lady Waterpark's Diary, 21 December 1886.
26 RA VIC/Add A 8/2657, Princess Beatrice to Princess Mary Adelaide, Duchess of Teck, 18 February 1887.
27 St-John Nevill, op. cit., p. 136.
28 Noel, Gerard, Ena: Spain's English Queen (Constable, London, 1984), p. 2.
29 Ibid.
30 Reid, op. cit., p. 69.
31 Hough, Advice, p. 93.
32 Noel, Ena, p. 3.
33 Ibid., p. 4.
34 Ramm (ed.), op. cit., p. 87.
35 Reid, op. cit., p. 70.
36 Mallet, op. cit., p. 27.
37 Pope-Hennessy, James (ed.), Queen Victoria at Windsor and Balmoral: Letters from her Granddaughter Princess Victoria of Prussia June 1889 (George Allen & Unwin, London, 1959), p. 29.
38 Ramm (ed.), op. cit., p. 88.
39 Reid, op. cit., p. 71.
40 Pope-Hennessy, op. cit., p. 48.

41 Hough, *Advice*, p. 113.
42 Ibid., p. 111.

CHAPTER EIGHTEEN: 'Capital fun'

1 The *Colliery Guardian*, 30 August 1889, reproduced, collection Staffordshire Record Office, File D4466/H/3/1, 1889.
2 Mallet, op. cit., p. 4.
3 Ibid., p. 15.
4 Hough, *Advice*, p. 70.
5 Rowell, op. cit., p. 90.
6 Ramm (ed.), op. cit., p. 167.
7 Mallet, op. cit., p. 151.
8 St-John Nevill, op. cit., p. 143.
9 Ramm (ed.), op. cit., p. 103.
10 Reid, op. cit., p. 117.
11 Lady Waterpark's Diary, 22 January 1877.
12 Osborne House guidebook, p. 39.
13 Ponsonby, Frederick, *Recollections of Three Reigns* (Eyre & Spottiswoode, London, 1951), p. 51.
14 Epton, op. cit., p. 201.
15 Mallet, op. cit., p. 37.

CHAPTER NINETEEN: 'A simple life ...'

1 Klein, Herman, *The Reign of Patti* (The Century Company, New York, 1920), p. 299.
2 Ibid., p. 300.
3 Erbach-Schönberg, op. cit., p. 273.
4 Hough, *Advice*, p. 105.
5 Mallet, op. cit., p. 34.
6 Ramm (ed.), op. cit., p. 104.

7 Cook, Andrew, *Prince Eddy: The King Britain Never Had* (Tempus, Stroud, 2006), pp. 141–2.
8 Longford, *Darling Loosy*, p. 227.
9 Cook, op. cit., p. 142.
10 Pope-Hennessy, op. cit., p. 89.
11 Benson, E. F., op. cit., p. 255.
12 Lutyens, op. cit., p. 46.
13 Longford, *Darling Loosy*, p. 231.
14 Vickers, op. cit., p. 20.
15 Princess Beatrice to 'Dear Archdeacon', 29 December 1926, private collection.
16 Grihangne, op. cit., p. 17.
17 Epton, op. cit., p. 205.
18 Erbach-Schönberg, op. cit., p. 277.
19 Lutyens, op. cit., p. 82.
20 Erbach-Schönberg, op. cit., p. 277.
21 Epton, op. cit., p. 176.
22 Hough, *Advice*, p. 118.
23 Vickers, op. cit., p. 34.
24 Hough, *Advice*, p. 118.
25 Vickers, op. cit., p. 34.
26 Pope-Hennessy, James, *Queen Mary* (Allen & Unwin, London, 1959), p. 134.
27 Vickers, op. cit., p. 34.
28 Hough, *Advice*, p. 118.
29 Epton, op. cit., p. 205.
30 Ibid., p. 206.

CHAPTER TWENTY: 'Blighted happiness'

1 Lutyens, op. cit., p. 157.
2 St-John Nevill, op. cit., p. 160.
3 Reid, op. cit., p. 167.
4 Princess Beatrice to Lady

Martin, 21 December 1896, private collection.

5 Langston, E. L., *Bishop Taylor Smith* (Marshall, Morgan & Scott, London, 1938), p. 73.

6 RA VIC Add X 8/32, Princess Beatrice to Canon Taylor Smith, 22 March 1898.

7 Erbach-Schönberg, op. cit., p. 274.

8 Duff, *Hessian Tapestry*, p. 243.

9 Mallet, op. cit., p. 71.

10 Weintraub, op. cit., p. 563.

11 Ernle, Lord, *Whippingham to Westminster: The Reminiscences of Lord Ernle (Rowland Prothero)* (John Murray, London, 1938), p. 181.

12 Lutyens, op. cit., p. 49.

13 Epton, op. cit., p. 207.

14 Weintraub, op. cit., p. 564.

15 Ibid., p. 565.

16 St-John Nevill, op. cit., p. 157.

17 Weintraub, op. cit., p. 565.

18 Ibid.

19 Princess Beatrice to Edith, Countess of Lytton, 6 February 1896, Knebworth Archive.

20 Buckle (ed.), *Letters of Queen Victoria 1886–1901*, third series, vol. iii (John Murray, London, 1932), p. 36.

21 Epton, op. cit., p. 207.

22 RA VIC Add X 8/2, Princess Beatrice to Canon Taylor Smith, 23 May 1896.

23 RA VIC Add X 8/8, Princess Beatrice to Canon Taylor Smith, 22 September 1896.

24 Princess Helena to Professor Story, 29 January 1896, Story Papers, Glasgow University

Archives, DC21/49.

25 Bishop Boyd-Carpenter to Queen Victoria, 18 March, 1896, Boyd-Carpenter Papers, British Library, Add 46720.

26 Lutyens, op. cit., p. 57.

27 RA VIC Add A 15/6078, Princess Beatrice to Prince Arthur, 15 April 1896.

28 RA VIC Add A 15/6082, Princess Beatrice to Prince Arthur, 29 April 1896.

29 Hough, *Advice,* p. 135.

30 Ramm (ed.), op. cit., p. 188.

31 Mallet, op. cit., p. 74.

32 Duff, *Shy Princess,* p. 178.

33 Lutyens, op. cit., p. 54.

34 RA VIC/Add X 8/22, Princess Beatrice to Canon Taylor Smith, 20 October 1897.

35 RA VIC/Add X 8/9, Princess Beatrice to Canon Taylor Smith, 26 November 1896.

36 Gelardi, op. cit., p. 74.

37 Princess Beatrice to Lady Martin, 21 December 1896, private collection.

38 Princess Beatrice to 'Dear Archdeacon', 29 December 1926, private collection.

CHAPTER TWENTY-ONE: 'I have taken up my life again'

1 Lutyens, op. cit., p. 157.

2 Wake, op. cit., p. 315.

3 Ibid., p. 316.

4 Lutyens, op. cit., p. 52.

5 Reid, op. cit., p. 103.

6 Ibid., p. 102.

7 Ibid., p. 208.

8 Lutyens, op. cit., p. 51.

9 Mallet, op. cit., p. 74.

10 Matson, op. cit., p. 113.
11 St-John Nevill, op. cit., p. 170.
12 RA/VIC Add X 8/21, Princess Beatrice to Canon Taylor Smith, 14 October 1897.
13 Princess Beatrice to Willingham Franklin Rawnsley, 26 December 1899, Dixon 19/4/3/30, Lincolnshire Archives.
14 Epton, op. cit., p. 209.
15 RA/VIC Add X 8/34, Princess Beatrice to Canon Taylor Smith, 15 July 1898.
16 St-John Nevill, op. cit., p. 170.
17 Hough, *Advice*, p. 143.
18 Reid, op. cit., p 84.
19 Ibid., p. 85.
20 Ramm (ed.), op. cit., p. 229.
21 Erickson, Carolly, *Her Little Majesty: the Life of Queen Victoria* (Robson Books, London, 1997), p. 237.
22 Epton, op. cit., p. 211.
23 Mallet, op. cit., p. 147.
24 Duff, *Shy Princess*, p. 193.
25 Wake, op. cit., p. 340.
26 Ponsonby, Frederick, op. cit., p. 71.

CHAPTER TWENTY-TWO: 'I ... can hardly realise ...'

1 Quigley, D. J., *The Isle of Wight Rifles*, privately printed, 1977.
2 Collection of Isle of Wight Record Office.
3 Ponsonby, Frederick, op. cit., p. 51.
4 St-John Nevill, op. cit., pp. 206–7.
5 Reid, op. cit., p. 190.
6 Princess Beatrice to Dr Story, 15 March 1901, Story Papers, Glasgow University Archives, 49.21 66.
7 Epton, op. cit., p. 234.
8 Princess Beatrice to Willingham Franklin Rawnsley, 31 October 1899, Dixon 19/4/3/29, Lincolnshire Archives.
9 Princess Beatrice to Willingham Franklin Rawnsley, 26 December 1899, Dixon 19/4/3/30, Lincolnshire Archives.
10 RA VIC/Add X 8/23, Princess Beatrice to Canon Taylor Smith, 26 October 1897.
11 RA VIC/Add X 8/23, Princess Beatrice to Canon Taylor Smith, 21 September 1897.
12 Reid, op. cit., p. 206.
13 Gelardi, op. cit., p. 29.
14 RA VIC/Add X 8/36, Princess Beatrice to Canon Taylor Smith, 9 February 1900.
15 Duff, *Shy Princess*, p. 195.
16 Longford, *Victoria RI*, p. 560.
17 Kuhn, William H., *Henry and Mary Ponsonby: Life at the Court of Queen Victoria* (Duckworth, London, 2002), p. 245.
18 Princess Beatrice to Dr Story, 15 March 1901, Story Papers, Glasgow University Archives, 49.21 66.
19 RA VIC/Add A 25/841, Princess Beatrice to Lady Elphinstone, 21 March 1901.
20 Epton, op. cit., p. 224.
21 RA VIC/Add X 8/22, Princess Beatrice to Canon Taylor Smith, 20 October 1897.

CHAPTER TWENTY-THREE: 'I have my dear Mother's... instructions'

1 Longford, Elizabeth (ed.), *Louisa, Lady-in-Waiting* (Jonathan Cape, London, 1979), p. 87.
2 Princess Beatrice to 'Dearest Violet, 25 June 1937, previously with Sophie Dupré.
3 Information from Royal Archives.
4 Howard McClintock, op. cit., p. 221.
5 Sir Sydney Cockerell to Sir Shane Leslie, 9 July 1945, Sir Shane Leslie Papers, Georgetown University Library, 3/35.
6 See ESHR 11/3, 13/12/1905, Esher Papers, Churchill Archive, Churchill College, Cambridge.
7 Ward, Yvonne M., *Editing Queen Victoria: How Men of Letters Constructed the Young Queen* (PhD thesis, La Trobe University, Australia, 2004), pp. 30–31.
8 Ibid, p. 143.
9 Brett, Maurice V. (ed.), *Journals & Letters of Reginald Viscount Esher* (Ivor Nicholson & Watson, London, 1934, 2 vols.), vol ii, p. 133.
10 Ward, op. cit., p. 17.
11 Brett (ed.), op. cit. (vol ii), p. 363.
12 Sir Sydney Cockerell to Sir Shane Leslie, 9 April 1945, Sir Shane Leslie Papers, Georgetown University Library, 3/35/1.
13 Ibid.
14 Fulford (ed.), *Darling Child*, p. 131.
15 Ibid., pp. 132/3.
16 Beatrice to Lord Esher, ESHR 11/3, 21/11/1904, Esher Papers, Churchill Archive.
17 Epton, op. cit., p. 224.

CHAPTER TWENTY-FOUR: 'Osborne ... is like the grave ...'

1 www.genogold.com/html/owen_charles_budd.html
2 Bessie Bulteel to Mrs Oglander, 17 May 1911, Isle of Wight Record Office, OG/07/218.
3 Epton, op. cit., p. 224.
4 Pope-Hennessy, *Queen Mary*, p. 356.
5 Brett (ed.), op. cit., vol i, p. 325.
6 Ibid.
7 Ibid.
8 Princess Beatrice to 'Evie' (Lady Mottistone), 2 July 1936, Mottistone Papers 5:115–6, Nuffield College Library.
9 Matson, op. cit., p. 131.
10 Unnamed to Mrs Oglander, 7 December 1903, Isle of Wight Record Office, OG/03/121.
11 RA VIC Add A7/227, Prince Maurice of Battenberg to Mr Theobold, 5 March 1904.
12 RA VIC Add A7/223, Princess Beatrice to Mr Theobold, 3 June 1903.

CHAPTER TWENTY-FIVE: 'Please God ...'

1 www.fbarnard.org.uk

2 Epton, op. cit., p. 224.
3 *The Sphere*, 2 June 1906.
4 Brett (ed.), op. cit., vol ii, p. 201.
5 Jullian, Philippe, *Edward and the Edwardians* (Sidgwick & Jackson, London, 1967), p. 291.
6 Duff, *Shy Princess*, p. 214.
7 Gelardi, op. cit., p. 131.
8 Princess Beatrice to Lady Bathurst, 8 May 1906, Special Collections, Brotherton Library, Leeds University, 1990/1/ 2778.
9 Archbishop of Canterbury to Princess Beatrice, 30 July 1905, Davidson Papers (vol. 21), Lambeth Palace Archives.
10 *The Sphere*, 9 June 1906.
11 RA VIC/W 48/31, Princess Beatrice to Edward VII, undated February 1906.
12 RA VIC/X 21/2, Princess Beatrice to Edward VII, 7 March 1906.
13 Pope-Hennessy, *Queen Mary*, p. 401.
14 Gelardi, op. cit., p. 131.
15 Pope-Hennessy, *Queen Mary*, p. 401.
16 Erbach-Schönberg, op. cit., p. 314.
17 Longford, *Louisa*, p. 125.
18 Erbach-Schönberg, op. cit., p. 313.
19 Gelardi, op. cit., p. 142.
20 Ibid., p. 151.
21 Prince Alexander of Battenberg to Onor, Grand Duchess of Hesse, 24 July 1908, Grand Ducal Family Archives, Hesse, D24 45/8.
22 Princess Beatrice to Colonel

Seely, 24 March 1913, Mottistone Papers MSM 20: 172–4, Nuffield College Library.

CHAPTER TWENTY-SIX: 'Days of overwhelming anxiety'

1 Letter from Princess Beatrice, 22 June 1911, Isle of Wight Record Office, CC/ED/A/ 10/1.
2 Epton, op. cit., p. 224.
3 Princess Beatrice to General Seely, 1 September 1924, Mottistone Papers MSM 3: 22– 26, Nuffield College Library.
4 Princess Beatrice to Lord Tennyson, 31 August 1914, Isle of Wight Record Office, TSN/2.
5 Prince Leopold of Battenberg to Colonel Seely, 16 March 1914, Mottistone Papers MSM 22:118, Nuffield College Library.
6 Duff, *Hessian Tapestry*, p. 305.
7 Epton, op. cit., p. 224.
8 Princess Beatrice to Ernest, Grand Duke of Hesse, 30 September 1909, Grand Ducal Family Archives, Hesse, D24/35/5.
9 Ibid.
10 Marie Louise, Princess, op. cit., p. 178.
11 Princess Beatrice to Sir Frederick Milner, 4 January 1915, private collection.
12 Lord Stamfordham to John Murray, 12 May 1917, John Murray Archive AN4.
13 Princess Beatrice to Colonel Seely, 13 December 1914,

Mottistone Papers MSSM
2:141–2, Nuffield College
Library.

14 The *Sketch*, 4 November 1914.

15 Gelardi, op. cit., p. 228.

16 RA VIC/Add A 25/877,
Princess Beatrice to Lady
Elphinstone, 13 November
1914.

17 RA VIC/Add A 21/234,
Princess Beatrice to Lord
Knutsford, 3 January 1915.

18 Marie Louise, Princess, op. cit.,
p. 179.

19 Princess Beatrice to Earl
Cadogan, 18 November 1914,
Cadogan Archives.

20 Princess Beatrice to Colonel
Seely, 13 December 1914,
Mottistone Papers, MSSM
2:141–2, Nuffield College
Library.

21 Princess Beatrice to Sir
Frederick Milner, 4 January
1915, private collection.

22 Rutter, Owen, *Portrait of a
Painter: The Life of Philip de
Laszlo* (Hodder & Stoughton,
London, 1939), p. 278.

23 Hough, *Louis and Victoria,*
p. 319.

24 Ibid., p. 320.

25 Vickers, op. cit., p. 126.

26 Princess Beatrice to 'Dear
Archdeacon', 29 December
1926, private collection.

CHAPTER TWENTY-SEVEN:
'The older one gets ...'

1 Longford, *Louisa*, p. 213.

2 Princess Beatrice to General
Seely, 1 September 1924,

Mottistone Papers, MSM 3:
22–26, Nuffield College
Library.

3 The *Tatler,* 8 December 1909.

4 Vickers, op. cit., p. 192.

5 Longford, *Darling Loosy*,
p. 297.

6 Princess Beatrice to Lady
Bathurst, 16 May 1920, Special
Collections, Brotherton Library,
Leeds University, 1990/1/
2780.

7 Duff, *Hessian Tapestry*, p. 325.

8 Frederick Ponsonby to Major
General Seely, 14 December
1931, Mottistone Papers,
MSSM 4:70, Nuffield College
Library.

9 Frederick Ponsonby to Major
General Seely, 14 December
1931, Mottistone Papers,
MSSM 4:67–8, Nuffield
College Library.

10 Van der Kiste, John, *Queen
Victoria's Children* (Sutton,
Stroud, 1986), p. 197.

11 Ponsonby, Frederick, op. cit.,
p. 112.

12 Princess Beatrice to Lady
Mottistone, 2 November 1934,
Mottistone Papers, MSSM
5:65–66, Nuffield College
Library.

13 Bessie Bulteel to Lady
Mottistone, 16 March 1936,
Mottistone Papers, MSSM
5:111, Nuffield College
Library.

14 Princess Beatrice to General
Seely, 13 February 1930,
Mottistone Papers, MSSM
25A:3, Nuffield College
Library.

15 Queen Sophie of Greece to Hon. Lady Corkran, 10 January 1931, previously with Sophie Dupré.

16 Bessie Bulteel to Lady Mottistone, 16 March 1936, Mottistone Papers, MSSM 5:111, Nuffield College Library.

17 *Isle of Wight County Press*, 9 October 1937.

18 Princess Beatrice to Lord Mottistone, 28 July 1940, Mottistone Papers, MSSM 6: 27–28, Nuffield College Library.

19 Mottistone Papers, MS25, 21 October 1944, Nuffield College Library.

CHAPTER TWENTY-EIGHT: 'She struggled so hard ...'

1 Longford, *Darling Loosy*, p. 319.

2 Ibid., p. 311.

3 Princess Beatrice to 'Evie' (Lady Mottistone), 2 July 1936, Mottistone Papers, MSSM 5:115–116, Nuffield College Library.

4 Surviving typescript, John Murray Archives.

5 John Murray to Princess Beatrice, 6 December 1940, John Murray Archives.

6 Longford, *Darling Loosy*, p. 311.

7 Minnie Cochrane to John Murray, 28 October 1940, John Murray Archives.

8 Princess Beatrice to Lord Mottistone, 28 July 1940, Mottistone Papers, MSSM 6: 27–28, Nuffield College Library.

9 Ibid.

10 Minnie Cochrane to John Murray, 1 November 1940, John Murray Archives, JMA 2.

11 Princess Beatrice to John Murray, 26 November 1940, John Murray Archives, JM3.

12 John Murray to Princess Beatrice, 6 December 1940, John Murray Archives.

13 John Murray to Owen Morshead, 15 January 1941, John Murray Archives.

14 John Murray to Princess Beatrice, 12 December 1940, John Murray Archives.

15 Norah Thomas to John Murray, 6 February 1941, John Murray Archives.

16 Princess Beatrice to John Murray, 24 January 1941, John Murray Archives.

17 Marchioness of Carisbrooke to Lady Mottistone, 7 November 1944, Mottistone Papers, MSSM 6:142, Nuffield College Library.

18 Princess Beatrice to Lord Mottistone, 11 November 1943, Mottistone Papers, MSSM 6:113, Nuffield College Library.

19 Vickers, op. cit., p. 314.

BIBLIOGRAPHY

PRIMARY SOURCES

The Royal Archives, Windsor Castle
Grand Ducal Family Archives, Darmstadt

Science Museum, London
Lady Waterpark's Diary, British Museum
Boyd-Carpenter Papers, British Museum
John Murray Archives, London
Knebworth Archive
Esher Papers, Churchill Archive Centre, Churchill College, Cambridge
Story Papers, Glasgow University Archives
Mottistone Papers, Nuffield College Library, Oxford
Cadogan Archives, London
Sir Shane Leslie Papers, Georgetown University Library, USA
Special Collections, Brotherton Library, University of Leeds
Oglander Papers, Isle of Wight Record Office
Tennyson Papers, Isle of Wight Record Office
File D4466/H/3/1, Staffordshire Record Office
Rochdale Metropolitan Borough Council
Dixon 19/4/3/30, Lincolnshire Archives

The *Illustrated London News*
The *Sketch*
The *Graphic*
The *Tatler*
The Times
Isle of Wight County Press

HRH The Princess Beatrice, *A Birthday Book* (Smith, Elder & Co. 1881)
HRH Princess Henry of Battenberg, *The Adventures of Count Georg Albert of Erbach* (John Murray, London, 1890)

HRH the Princess Beatrice, *In Napoleonic Days: Extracts from the private diary of Augusta, Duchess of Saxe-Coburg-Saalfeld, Queen Victoria's maternal grandmother, 1806 to 1821* (John Murray, London, 1941)

SECONDARY SOURCES

Arengo-Jones, Peter, *Queen Victoria in Switzerland* (Robert Hale, London, 1995)

Aronson, Theo, *Queen Victoria and the Bonapartes* (London, Cassell, 1972)

―――― *Grandmama of Europe* (John Murray paperback, London, 1984)

Auchincloss, Louis, *Persons of Consequence: Queen Victoria and her Circle* (Weidenfeld & Nicolson, London, 1979)

Battiscombe, Georgina, *Queen Alexandra* (Constable, London, 1969)

Bennett, Daphne, *Queen Victoria's Children* (Gollancz, London, 1980)

Benson, A. C. ed., *Letters of Queen Victoria* (John Murray, London, 1908)

Benson, E. F., *Daughters of Queen Victoria* (Cassell & Co., London, 1939)

Brett, Maurice V. (ed.), *Journals & Letters of Reginald Viscount Esher* (Ivor Nicholson & Watson, London, 1934, 2 vols.)

Brown, Ivor, *Balmoral: the history of a home* (Collins, London, 1955)

Buckle, (ed.), *Letters of Queen Victoria 1886–1901*, third series, vol. iii. (John Murray, London, 1932)

Bullock, Rev. Charles, *The Queen's Resolve: A Jubilee Memorial* (Home Words Publishing, London, 1887)

Cannizzo, Jeanne, *Our Highland Home: Victoria and Albert in Scotland* (National Galleries of Scotland, Edinburgh, 2005)

Caton, Donald, 'John Snow's Practice of Obstetric Anaesthesia' (*Anaestheology:* vol. 92 (1)), January 2000

Clark, Ronald W., *Balmoral: Queen Victoria's Highland Home* (Thames & Hudson, London, 1981)

Cook, Andrew, *Prince Eddy: The King Britain Never Had* (Tempus, Stroud, 2006)

Cullen, Tom, *The Empress Brown* (The Bodley Head, London, 1969)

De la Noy, Michael, *Queen Victoria at Home* (Constable, London, 2003)

Duff, David, *The Shy Princess* (Evans Brothers, London, 1958)

―――― *Hessian Tapestry* (Frederick Muller, London, 1967)

―――― *Victoria Travels: journeys of Queen Victoria between 1830 and 1900, with extracts from her journal* (Frederick Muller, London, 1970)

Dyson, Hope & Tennyson, Charles (ed.), *Dear & Honoured Lady: The Correspondence between Queen Victoria and Alfred Tennyson* (Macmillan, London, 1969)

Ednay, Peter, *Princess Beatrice: Island Governor* (Vectis, Isle of Wight, 1994)

Ellis, Richard (ed.), *The Case Books of Dr John Snow, Medical History Supplement No. 14* (Wellcome Institute for the History of Medicine, London, 1994)

Epton, Nina, *Victoria and her Daughters* (Weidenfeld & Nicolson, 1971)

Erbach-Schönberg, Princess Marie zu, Princess of Battenberg, *Reminiscences* (Royalty Digest reprint, Ticehurst, 1996)

Erickson, Carolly, *Her Little Majesty: the Life of Queen Victoria* (Robson Books, London, 1997)

Ernle, Lord, *Whippingham to Westminster: The Reminiscences of Lord Ernle (Rowland Prothero)* (John Murray, London, 1938)

Fraser, Flora, *Princesses: the Daughters of George III* (John Murray, London, 2004)

Fulford, Roger (ed.), *Dearest Child: letters from Queen Victoria and the Princess Royal, 1858–1861* (Evans Brothers, London, 1964)

―――― *Dearest Mama: letters between Queen Victoria and the Crown Princess of Prussia 1861–1864* (Evans Brothers, London, 1968)

―――― *Your Dear Letter: private correspondence of Queen Victoria and the Crown Princess of Prussia, 1865–1871* (Evans Brothers, London, 1971)

―――― *Darling Child: private correspondence of Queen Victoria and the Crown Princess of Prussia, 1871–1878* (Evans Brothers, London, 1976)

―――― *Beloved Mama: private correspondence of Queen Victoria and the German Crown Princess, 1878–1885* (Evans Brothers, London, 1981)

Gelardi, Julia, *Born to Rule* (St Martin's Press, New York, 2004)

Grihangne, Roger (trans. David Lockie), *Queen Victoria in Grasse* (Imprimerie Magenta, 1991)

Hibbert, Christopher, *Queen Victoria: A Personal History* (HarperCollins, London, 2000)

―――― , *Queen Victoria in her Letters & Journals* (Viking, London, 1985)

―――― , *George III: A Personal History* (Viking, London, 1998)

―――― , *Edward VII: A Portrait* (Allen Lane, London, 1976)

Hough, Richard, *Advice to a Grand-daughter: Letters from Queen Victoria to Princess Victoria of Hesse* (Heinemann, London, 1975)

―――― , *Louis and Victoria: The Family History of the Mountbattens* (Weidenfeld & Nicolson, London, 1974)

Howard McClintock, Mary, *The Queen Thanks Sir Howard* (John Murray, London, 1945)

Howarth, Patrick, *When the Riviera was Ours* (Routledge & Kegan Paul, London, 1977)

Impey, Edward, *Kensington Palace: The Official Illustrated History* (Merrell, London, 2003)

Jagow, Dr Kurt, *Letters of the Prince Consort 1831–1861* (John Murray, London, 1938)

Jullian, Philippe, *Edward and the Edwardians* (Sidgwick & Jackson, London, 1967)

Klein, Herman, *The Reign of Patti* (The Century Company, New York, 1920)

Kuhn, William H., *Henry and Mary Ponsonby: Life at the Court of Queen Victoria* (Duckworth, London, 2002)

Lamont-Brown, Raymond, *John Brown, Queen Victoria's Highland Servant* (Sutton, Stroud, 2000)

Lane, Marian (ed.), *Parish Churches of the Isle of Wight* (South Wight Borough Council, 1994)

Langston, E. L., *Bishop Taylor Smith* (Marshall Morgan & Scott, London, 1938)

Lant, Jeffrey L., *Insubstantial Pageant: Ceremony and Confusion at Queen Victoria's Court* (Hamish Hamilton, London, 1979)

Lee, Sidney, *King Edward VII*

Longford, Elizabeth, *Victoria RI* (Weidenfeld & Nicolson, London, 1964)

———, *Louisa, Lady-in-Waiting* (Jonathan Cape, London, 1979)

———, (ed.,), *Darling Loosy: Letters to Princess Louise 1856–1939* (Weidenfeld & Nicolson, London, 1991)

Lutyens, Mary (ed.), *Lady Lytton's Diary* (Rupert Hart-Davis, London, 1961)

Magnus, Philip, *King Edward VII* (John Murray, London, 1964)

Mallet, Victor (ed.), *Life with Queen Victoria: Marie Mallet's letters from court, 1887-1901* (John Murray, London, 1968)

Marie Louise, Princess, *My Memories of Six Reigns* (Evans Brothers, London, 1956)

Matson, John, *Dear Osborne* (Hamish Hamilton, London, 1978)

Meres, the Rev. H. J., 'A Sermon Preached in the Stowell Memorial Church, Salford, February 9, 1896, the Sunday after the Funeral of His Royal Highness Prince Henry Maurice of Battenberg'.

Meylan, Vincent, *Queens' Jewels* (Assouline, New York, 2002)

Millar, Oliver, *The Victorian Paintings in the Collection of Her Majesty the Queen* (Cambridge University Press, Cambridge, 1992)

Munn, Geoffrey, *Tiaras: A History of Splendour* (Antique Collectors' Club, Woodbridge, 2001)

———, *Castellani and Giulano: Revivalist Jewellers of the Nineteenth Century* (Trefoil Books, London, 1984)

Nelson, Michael, *Queen Victoria and the Discovery of the Riviera* (I. B. Tauris, London, 2001)

Noel, Gerard, *Ena: Spain's English Queen* (Constable, London, 1984)

——, *Princess Alice: Queen Victoria's Forgotten Daughter* (Constable, London, 1974)

Packard, Jerrold M., *Queen Victoria's Daughters* (St Martin's Press, New York, 1998)

——, *Farewell in Splendour: the Death of Queen Victoria and her Age* (Dutton, New York, 1995)

Pakula, Hannah, *An Uncommon Woman: The Empress Frederick* (Phoenix paperback, London, 1997)

Plunkett, John, *Queen Victoria First Media Monarch* (Oxford University Press, 2003)

Ponsonby, Frederick (ed.), *Letters of the Empress Frederick* (Macmillan, London, 1928)

——, *Recollections of Three Reigns* (Eyre & Spottiswoode, London, 1951)

Ponsonby, Magdalen (ed.), *Mary Ponsonby: A Memoir, Some Letters and a Journal* (John Murray, London, 1927)

Pope-Hennessy, James, *Queen Mary* (Allen & Unwin, London, 1959)

——, (ed.), *Queen Victoria at Windsor and Balmoral: Letters from her Granddaughter Princess Victoria of Prussia June 1889* (George Allen & Unwin, London, 1959)

Priestley, J. B., *The Edwardians* (Heinemann, London, 1970)

Quigley, D. J., *The Isle of Wight Rifles*, privately printed, 1977

Ramm, Agatha (ed.), *Beloved and Darling Child: last letters between Queen Victoria and her eldest daughter, 1886–1901* (Sutton, Stroud, 1990)

Reid, Michaela, *Ask Sir James* (Hodder & Stoughton, London, 1987)

Rennell, Tony, *Last Days of Glory* (Viking, London, 2000)

Roberts, Jane, *Royal Artists from Mary Queen of Scots to the Present Day* (Grafton Books, London, 1987)

Rowell, George, *Queen Victoria Goes to the Theatre* (Paul Elek, London, 1978)

Rutter, Owen, *Portrait of a Painter: The Life of Philip de Laszlo* (Hodder & Stoughton, London, 1939)

St Aubyn, Giles, *Edward VII Prince and King* (Collins, London, 1979)

St-John Nevill, Barry, *Life at the Court of Queen Victoria 1861–1901* (Webb & Bower, Exeter, 1984)

Sara, M. E., *The Life and Times of Her Royal Highness the Princess Beatrice* (Stanley Paul & Co., London, 1945)

Steuart Erskine, Mrs (ed.), *Twenty Years at Court: From the Cor-*

respondence of the Hon. Eleanor Stanley, 1842–62 (Nisbet & Co., London, 1916)

Stoney, Benita and Weltzein, Heinrich C., *My Mistress the Queen: the Letters of Frieda Arnold, Dresser to Queen Victoria, 1854–9*, trans. by Sheila de Bellaigue (Weidenfeld & Nicolson, London, 1994)

Stothard, Jane T., *The Life of the Empress Eugénie* (Hodder & Stoughton, London, 1906)

Stuart, D. M., *George III's Daughters* (John Murray, London, 1939)

Tisdall, E. E. P., *Queen Victoria's Private Life* (Jarrolds, London, 1961)

University of London Library, 'Friend & Foe: Anglo-German Affinities and Antipathies in the Long Nineteenth Century' (exhibition: 7 November 2003–2 April 2004)

Van der Kiste, John, *Childhood at Court 1819–1914* (Sutton, Stroud, 1995)

———, *Queen Victoria's Children* (Sutton, Stroud, 1986)

———, *Edward VII's Children* (Sutton, Stroud, 1989)

———, *George III's Children* (Sutton, Stroud, 1992)

Vickers, Hugo, *Alice, Princess Andrew of Greece* (Viking, London, 2000)

Victoria, Queen, *More Leaves from the Journal of a Life in the Highlands: from 1862 to 1882* (Smith, Elder & Co., London, 1884)

———, *Our Life in the Highlands* (Victorian & Modern History Book Club, Newton Abbot, 1972)

Wade, Alf, 'The Prince Imperial', *Military History Journal*, vol. 3 no. 2, The South African Military History Society, 1974

Wake, Jehanne, *Princess Louise: Queen Victoria's unconventional daughter* (London, Collins, 1988)

Ward, Yvonne M., *Editing Queen Victoria: How Men of Letters Constructed the Young Queen* (PhD thesis, La Trobe University, Australia, 2004)

Warner, Marina, *Queen Victoria's Sketchbook* (Macmillan, London, 1979)

Watson, Vera, *A Queen at Home: an intimate account of the social and domestic life of Queen Victoria's court* (W. H. Allen, London, 1952)

Weintraub, Stanley, *Victoria: Biography of a Queen* (Unwin, London, 1987)

Windsor, Dean of & Bolitho, Hector (eds.), *Letters of Lady Augusta Stanley* (Gerald Howe, London, 1927)

———, *Later Letters of Lady Augusta Stanley* (Jonathan Cape, London, 1929)

Zeepvat, Charlotte, *Prince Leopold: the untold story of Queen Victoria's youngest son* (Sutton, Stroud, 1988)

INDEX

the ROYAL OAK

VICTORIA REGINA 1837–1887.

A Jubilee Genealogical Tree, showing the Descendants of Her Majesty Queen Victoria.